A HANDBOOK OF
SCOTLAND'S
HISTORY

A HANDBOOK OF
SCOTLAND'S
HISTORY

Michael Kerrigan

Saraband

Published by Saraband
Suite 202, 98 Woodlands Road
Glasgow, G3 6HB, Scotland
www.saraband.net

Editor: Craig Hillsley

ISBN: 9781910192337

Printed in the UK on paper from sustainable sources.

The illustrations reproduced in this book are from the
author's collection or Saraband Image Library,
or else are sourced from shared-resource and public
domain collections. Colour images are credited with the
image, except those in the public domain.

*Title page: detail of "The Citie of Edinburgh from
the South" by Václav Hollar (etching, 1670).*

Publication of this book has been supported by Creative Scotland.

ALBA | CHRUTHACHAIL

10 9 8 7 6 5 4 3 2 1

CONTENTS

For Graham Whyte

*"Of course Scottish history has always mattered.
Without it Scotland would not exist."*
– EDWARD J COWAN,
Why Scottish History Still Matters, Saltire Society, 2012

*"Where is the coward that would not dare to fight
for such a land as Scotland?"*
– SIR WALTER SCOTT

*"The birth-place of Valour, the country of Worth;
Wherever I wander, wherever I rove,
The hills of the Highlands for ever I love."*
– ROBERT BURNS

INTRODUCTION

SEPTEMBER 2014 SAW the Scottish Independence Referendum. A noisy campaign led up to the fateful day. In the event, ironically, in the year that marked the 700th anniversary of Scotland's famous victory over the English at Bannockburn, a clear 'No' victory sent the Scottish Nationalist Party (SNP) leadership hamewart to think again. That the aftermath seems only to have brought SNP leader Nicola Sturgeon to the conclusion that one more heave might actually just do it (and that, within a few months of the Referendum, the SNP would sweep away a long-dominant Labour Party from Scotland in the 2015 General Election) just shows how quickly historical realities can change.

The whole Scottish story may arguably be read in the relation between 1314 and 2014, between one of Scotland's most heroic moments and one of the most extraordinary political dramas of recent times. The Battle of Bannockburn would certainly make an obvious starting point for a survey of Scotland's history – and of how that history has shaped today's Scotland.

History at Hand

Instead, however, let's consider another engagement, which took place 21 years later: the Battle of Boroughmuir, fought in 1335. It wasn't bigger than Bannockburn – quite the contrary, in fact. Nor was it to prove so pivotal historically. It was just one more glorified skirmish in the back-and-forth of the Wars of Scottish Independence. On that day, John Randolph, Earl of Moray, and his supporters, fought a small English force led by Guy II, Count of Namur (from Guelderland, in the Low Countries), a cousin of Queen Philippa of England. In the grand scheme of things, Moray's victory doesn't seem to have been an especially important one.

Introduction

In which case, what's so intriguing about Boroughmuir? On the one hand, it's because the only account we have – in Walter Bower's *Scotichronicon* (1447) – seems, like so much of Scotland's history, semi-mythic:

> *Here many were slain on either side, and a certain warrior maiden of Guelderland, arrayed in knightly armour, had a bout with a noble Scot of the name of Richard Schaw. On being killed by this Richard Schaw, she was found to be a woman, to the great astonishment of all.*

And, on the other hand, it's because Boroughmuir seems so 'real', evoking as it does what's still a recognisable topography for anyone who knows the Edinburgh of today. Though the Boroughmuir must have stretched across much of what are now the Scottish capital's southern suburbs, the concept of it still exists in Viewforth's Boroughmuir High School, and in Boroughmuirhead, at the crest of the hill in Bruntsfield Place. Tempting as it is to conjure up the picture of a valiant rearguard action outside Waitrose, or a clash of swords outside the fire station in Tollcross, Bower's narrative doesn't give us that sort of detail. It has its vivid moments, though:

> *Just as they of Guelderland were getting the upper hand, William Douglas and some nobles from Pentland came up and put them to flight as far as the town of Edinburgh and into the street which is called Mair Winde* [St Mary's Wynd – now St Mary's Street]; *and they fled as far as the hill of the Castle of Maidens, which was then in ruins …*

Edinburgh Castle was called the 'Castle of Maidens' for reasons that are basically unknown, though the 17th-century scholar Father Richard Augustin Hay put forth a colourful explanation involving a community of nuns who'd lived there once. At the castle, Bower's account goes on, the Count of Namur's men 'established and fortified themselves ... as best they could, making themselves, as some assert, an outer rampart out of the carcases of the horses killed'.

If the present work sets out to be a 'Handbook of Scottish History' in the sense that it brings the whole Scottish story together in a single text, it also tries to be a book about the Scottish history that's at hand. Whilst it does present a single, continuous and (it's hoped) coherent narrative, it attempts to show ways in which the historical record may be traced in the topography of today. It also, where possible, seeks to start out with concrete, local examples and work out towards more general historical trends, making Scotland itself a text we can try to read. Not just in the obvious things, like battlefields and bridges, castles and cathedrals, but more subtly, in the stuff of everyday.

There's a powerful romance in this perception that history's in our midst and we're amidst it. 'A city,' wrote G.K. Chesterton, is:

> more poetic even than a countryside, for while Nature is a chaos of unconscious forces, a city is a chaos of conscious ones. ... there is no stone in the street and no brick in the wall that is not actually a deliberate symbol – a message from some man, as much as if it were a telegram or a post-card. The narrowest street possesses, in every crook and twist of its intention, the soul of the man who built it, perhaps long in his grave. Every brick has as human a hieroglyph as if it were a graven brick of Babylon.

If there's a great deal of truth in this, there's also a point spectacularly missed: 'Nature', as posited here, barely exists in Scotland – or in Britain. The countryside itself is inscribed with human intentions, the 'wildest' bits of Scotland perhaps especially, given the impact of the Highland Clearances (see pages 180–81). But it's certainly true that every urban environment is completely constructed: someone in the past put every stone block, every brick in place in every building, laid every flagstone, set up every streetlight.

To sense and celebrate the complexity with which our human environment's been built is also to recognise that history is human. The years and centuries don't simply pass; they are experienced by men and women who live and act in them, modifying their world even as they're modified by it; they involve the accumulation of monuments, the accrual of significance. You don't have to live in Skara Brae or the Scott Monument to experience this. Much of our lives these days may, as anthropologist Marc Augé has said, be spent in impersonal 'non-places', but even malls and motorways have their history.

Past Perspectives

A millennium and a half ago, the kingdom of Dál Riata (see pages 35–37, below) spanned the strait between southwest Scotland and the northeast edge of Ireland. Such a state made sense during this period – in a way it really doesn't now. The sea was more a bridge than a barrier, more an open market square than a physical or figurative end-of-the-earth, in a period when land travel across such rugged terrain was so difficult.

The psychogeographical order has been pretty much reversed since then – though, again, much depends on exactly where one stands. The West Highland Line which, since 1901, has enabled most of us to get away from it all in some of Scotland's finest scenery, gave the people of the outlying settlements along the line at that time a much-needed connection with the world. George Heriot's School, on Edinburgh's Lauriston Place, occupies an impressive if not palatial pile. Strikingly, though, this faces the 'wrong' way – the school's main entrance is round the back. This is a consequence of the city's expansion since the 17th century. An institution that once stood at the edge of the city, looking inward, has over time found itself subtly reorientated relative to the shifting urban geography around it. The past is not only another country, but another point of view.

There are other unexpected angles: the Irish Republican hero James Connolly was born in Edinburgh's Cowgate; that other great Irish treasure, the *Book of Kells*, was probably made in Scotland (on Iona) too. John Paul Jones was not only the 'Father of the US Navy' but also a Son of Kirkcudbright. That one man's terrorist is another's freedom fighter is pretty much a modern cliché, but it could have no better illustration than Scotland's William Wallace. And, as Chapter One makes clear, Scottish history was well advanced (by some definitions getting on for halfway through) before there was even any such place as 'Scotland'.

Times Change

Time used to be looked at differently as well: the sun set the schedule for a working day that waxed and waned with the changing seasons (and the agricultural duties) of the year. Clocks may have allowed a new perspective, but it was the advent of industry, with its regimented shifts, that made the measurement of time more crucial, and the coming of the railways that set the nation synchronising watches. (Previously there'd been no particularly compelling reason for Glasgow to keep the same clock as Aberdeen.)

People's sense of space was different too. That the road journey to London could take several weeks (much longer than a sea-trip to Denmark or Danzig) had implications for Scots and the way they felt about themselves.

That said, people do seem to have been differently constituted somehow, with greater stamina and patience. They took lengthy journeys in their stride in a way it seems we can't. Different times, different conditions meant different expectations – and responses. Bonnie Prince Charlie's gone down in history as one of the great royal fops, a giant of effeteness, but the overland journey he made on foot (and largely in darkness) in the weeks and months after the Battle of Culloden (see pages 138–39) would have daunted the most determined outdoor enthusiast today.

If history is all about time and change, our sense of what it is has been transformed by time as well. Even over the decades of my lifetime. My elders' and betters' idea of history seems to have involved the recitation of the names and dates of kings and queens, with the odd battle thrown in to add analytical depth: certain luminaries would like to see this approach (characterised, hilariously, as a 'no-nonsense' one) restored. When not seeking to establish whether or not it was the case that the Bourbons had learned nothing and forgotten nothing, my own 'O' Level course might have been lifted directly from Hansard, so scrupulously did it record every change to every clause in every Victorian factory act. When my kids did history at school they seem to have spent the lion's share of their lessons under a table with their classmates, imagining they were in the hold of a slave ship, a coalmine, the trenches or an air-raid shelter. They did, however, come away with a real appreciation that historical truths depend on point of view – not a thought that ever troubled us much at school.

Looking at the Thistle

That view can of course be very different, depending whether you're standing in John o'Groats or Gretna; it's different in a different way if you're visiting from Canada or Japan. And in a different way again if you're in Edinburgh admiring Sir

Henry Raeburn's *The Skating Minister* or in Glasgow contemplating a celebrated Turner Prize–winning artwork – or an installation at the biennial Glasgow International festival.

As Brigadoon has given way to the Global Village, Scotland's mythic horizons have been expanding accordingly, to encompass the towers and battlements of Harry Potter's Hogwarts and the Hollywood hills of *Braveheart*. Today's imaginative traveller to Scotland has the choice of tak'-ing not just the high road or the low road but the thrillride streets of *Grand Theft Auto*, originally developed in Dundee – once better known for its marmalade than the cyber-traffic jam (see pages 208–9).

As this book will hope to show, however, the sense of a Scotland *sans frontières* has historically been more the rule than the exception. Think of shortbread, enjoyed around the world. Or think of the Lewis Chessmen, made somewhere in Scandinavia in the 12th century, yet deemed one of the most important 'Scottish' treasures of recent times. In this sense, the thorny but beautiful thistle – which occurs across several continents but is recognised worldwide as an emblem of Scotland – makes a fitting symbol for an extraordinary country and its uniquely compelling history of stoic resilience and unpretentious pride.

ONE

SCOTLAND
BEFORE
SCOTLAND

SCOTLAND STARTED OUT IN THE SAME WAY as it would carry on throughout the course of its history: in a process of coming together and conflict, with the establishment of boundaries that both divided and connected. But the country's human history at its most tumultuous can't begin to match the scale and violence of its geological formation. In the presence of such unimaginable forces, we do the best we can to comprehend them in human terms. Hence, perhaps, the story behind Fingal's Cave near the Isle of Mull.

Fingal was the name that the English-speaking 18th century gave to the Irish warrior-hero Fionn Mac Cumhaill or Finn McCool. He stood, it's said, more than 15m (50ft) tall. It was Fionn who, anxious to make the crossing between Ireland and Scotland without wetting his feet, built the Giant's Causeway off the Antrim coast. His final stepping stone, the story went, was the Isle of Staffa. And they do belong together: the basalt columns at Fingal's Cave are believed to have been formed by the same lava flow as the one that created the Giant's Causeway, crystallising into columns as it slowly cooled.

Orogenous Origins

By the time Fionn walked the Earth, Scotland was already extremely old news. Its origins lay in the time when the shifting of the world's tectonic plates was slowly shaping the surface of the modern globe. Something like 600 million years ago, an area of sea, the Iapetus Ocean, began to open up between what was eventually North America (Laurentia) and what would be the far northwest of Eurasia (Baltica). Subsequently – more like 400–350 million years ago – the Iapetus Ocean started to contract and these two continental plates began converging once again. Pushing up from southward, a third plate, the Avalonian – a small and separate block that included the landmass we now know as England and Wales

– was caught up in the collision, clashing with the other two in what geologists now refer to as the Caledonian Orogeny.

An orogeny is an episode of mountain-building: it takes place when masses of rock collide and buckle, creating clean-break faults or folds in the rocky strata. Very roughly, the convergence of Laurentia and Baltica brought into being the mountains of the Highlands as the Earth's crust buckled; where at one point it violently broke, a vast new fault formed the near-as-dammit-dead-straight line of the Great Glen.

A little further to the south and east, the Highland Boundary Fault marked out the line along which the rugged uplands would abruptly give way to a central rift valley and the much gentler contours of the Lowlands. Where this area abutted on the advancing Avalonian plate, further epic collisions of rock brought into being the Southern Uplands. The two plates met and melded along what geologists have come to call the Iapetus Suture, which runs between the Solway Firth and northern Northumberland – really quite close, in other words, to the Scottish border.

Does this scientific record underline the separateness of Scotland – or was it, on the contrary, this act of geological union that gave it form? Does Scotland stand alone in splendid 'Wha's like us?' isolation, or can it only make sense in an equilibrium of relationship with and opposition to its southern neighbour? It's a question that has kept on recurring over the millions of years since the Caledonian Orogeny – most recently in the Independence Referendum of 2014.

A Wall of Ice

The volcano whose lava created Staffa and the Giant's Causeway subsided and disappeared long ago. It was scoured away by successive glaciations in the Pleistocene period (2.5 million–12,000 years ago), leaving just these splendid formations in splendid isolation. All in all, the Pleistocene can be seen as having left Scotland as a blank slate: when we look for a Year Zero in the Scottish story, we find we hit a wall of ice.

And this was long after human communities were flourishing further south. So deep and far-reaching was the grip of the Ice Age this far north that it seems to have held back human settlement in Scotland by a great many millennia. Whilst in southern England the earliest traces of occupation unearthed by archaeologists date back some 500,000 years, the first to be found in Scotland are only about 14,000 years old.

A Melancholy Cycle?

That said, even in the Scottish context, talk of the Ice Age as something singular and straightforward is liable to create confusion. Really the Pleistocene saw a succession of temperature and climatic conditions. Even simplifying things, it makes much more sense to see the period as a cycle of 'stadial' freezes several millennia in their duration, with much milder 'interstadials' between. At such times, the retreat of the ice sheet would have left behind a razed and more or less levelled landscape, punctuated by lakes and crisscrossed by running streams. This bare wasteland, as it opened up, would have been slowly colonised from southward – first by scabby grasses and low bushes, then by scrubby little stands of birch and pine. So it would go for several centuries, bare tundra becoming gradually greener, before the mercury dropped and the glaciers returned to sweep it all away.

All that growth, and for nothing? To find this cycle melancholy is to import inappropriately anthropocentric values: the Goddess Gaia won't have been troubled by such an ebb and flow. But we *are* human and it's understandable that we should see things from this standpoint. And there were indeed human implications. For the last interstadial thaw, some 14,000 years ago, appears to have been the window for the first human settlement in Scotland. Stone arrowheads and other tools found at Howburn Farm, beside the A721 near Biggar in southern Lanarkshire, date from around this time. Though not much more than flakes of flint, these points have plainly been sharpened by human agency – and, as important, left with blunt projecting 'tangs' to be inserted into wooden shafts or handles.

Here Today...

Flint tools: not much to show for humankind's first appearance on the Scottish stage, you might argue. Neither was it to be an enduring presence, because around 11,000 years ago, at the start of what geologists refer to as the Younger Dryas phase, temperatures once more plunged, and the ice again advanced across northern Britain. So, scarcely had the first Scots appeared than they vanished from the record... although that doesn't necessarily mean they weren't around.

In what's known to archaeologists as the Palaeolithic, or Old Stone Age, period, humans lived in small, extended-family communities, following a hunter-gatherer lifestyle. We can make an educated guess as to what life was like for them, on the basis of those comparable cultures that – in the Earth's remotest reaches – have pursued this pattern into recent times.

Briefly: the men go out to hunt or fish, whilst the women and children gather nuts, fruits, herbs, shellfish and other foods. The group is necessarily nomadic: it goes where the food is to be found at different times of year, according to the patterns of seasonal growth and animal breeding and migration. The basic unit of Palaeolithic society seems to have been a group of 25 to 30 people – including a dozen or so adults and their children. Each group would have had intermittent social and ceremonial contacts with a larger community, with perhaps 500 members in all – just enough to allow marriage ties to be made beyond the immediate family but within the tribe. There would have been no chief: leadership was dispersed among the group; possessions were minimal. This appears to be why such societies have often been looked back on as utopian – though they have, of course, been utopias of barely getting by.

That said, there's obviously an upside. The hunter-gatherer diet has in most known cases been intrinsically varied, meat and fish being complemented by nuts, berries and greenery. 'Hunting' and 'gathering' vary in their relative importance. While hunting may be profitable in terms of protein-yield, it involves a high expenditure of energy and can be dangerous; gathering birds' eggs, berries or shellfish in season might give a greater nutritional return on efforts made. On the other hand, the size of the 'package' the food comes in also has its implications: nuts might be a rich source of protein, for instance, but the time and effort involved in extracting them might be considerable. A deer might be hard to hunt and kill, but a large one could feed the community for days on end.

It's no particular mark of primitiveness, then, that such communities have tended to travel light, living in caves, or in hastily assembled shelters here and there. That we've found so little evidence of their existence in Scotland is, in part, very likely a consequence of the slightness of their 'footprint', then, but it's likely too that the overall population was very small. Before the advent of agriculture, populations pretty much had to be: it takes an extensive territory to support the smallest numbers in a hunter-gatherer lifestyle. On the other hand, it's a lifestyle that is readily responsive to climatic and environmental changes, so we've no real reason to imagine some kind of glacial holocaust wiping these communities out once the ice returned. The big freeze that followed the interstadial thaw would have descended only very slowly in human-lifetime terms – allowing plenty of time for nomadic communities to adapt and, when necessary, move.

Useful Tips

Evidence of a human presence in Scotland starts stacking up during the Mesolithic period – that is, the Middle Stone Age: after the retreat of the ice but before the coming of farming. Communities from this time still lived as nomadic hunter-gatherers, however, so by definition they travelled light and left few traces. Those they did leave were for the most part middens – basically waste-heaps, piles of discarded shells, bones and other rubbish. One such tip discovered at Cramond, northwestern Edinburgh, has been dated to around 10,500 years ago; another, at South Queensferry, to around 10,000 years ago.

The midden found at Warren Field, near Banchory, Aberdeenshire, is also believed to be 10,000 years old: this one stands out in not being closer to the coast. As we've seen, nomadic hunter-gatherers expected to range far and wide in search for their subsistence, but coastal sites would obviously have afforded additional resources. Along with anything that the woods and grasslands, rivers, lakes or streams might have to offer, the sea would have yielded other products, from fish and shellfish to seaweed and birds' eggs. Most of the other middens excavated up to now have been on or near coasts: the one at Sand, near Applecross, Wester Ross, appears to have been in use some 9,500 years ago, before being abandoned for a period of 2,000 years. Then, around 7,500 years ago, a new generation of human settlers seem to have started adding new layers of refuse to the pile. Mesolithic middens have also been unearthed in the Western Isles, for example, at Staosnaig on eastern Colonsay (around 8,700 years old) and along the southern coast of Oronsay (around 7,000 years old).

For the most part these Mesolithic middens are made up of food waste, but there are also king scallop shells, which appear to have been used as dishes. The shell midden at Sand, Applecross, meanwhile, includes limpet shells that have been perforated, perhaps for use in jewellery, as well as decorated cowrie shells. Cowries were prized by many ancient cultures, because with their crinkled openings they were considered to resemble the vulva (or, in some cases, alternately, the eye!) and were often strung together to make ceremonial necklaces or amulets.

A late-Mesolithic midden on Risga, an island in Loch Sunart, Argyll, was found to contain – along with large quantities of discarded shells and animal bones – fragments of a bone harpoon-point, as well as fishhooks made from bone. There were also bone digging tools, an antler mattock (a tool similar to a pickaxe) and a range of other items like limpet-hammers and flint knives. The discovery in several middens of the bones of fish species typically caught by line is also testimony to the use of fishhooks, though by this time nets were also very likely being used. Fishing nets were made in the Middle East some 12,000 years ago, and there's no particular reason to doubt that they would have been used in Scotland too. A great many carved stone spheres have also been found at Scottish sites. Too big and too plain for beads, it's believed that these may have been made as weights for fishing nets, though it's impossible to say this with certainty, of course. The point of a (sharpened antler) harpoon or multi-pronged fish-spear has been found at Shewalton Sands, Ayrshire.

We're getting ahead of ourselves chronologically here, but the dugout canoe from the Bronze Age, discovered in tidal waters in the Tay near Perth in 2001, may quite easily have been the latest in a long line extending back into Mesolithic times. At 7.6m (25ft) long, it's a craft of some size, but there's no obvious reason why similar vessels couldn't have been fashioned from charred-out tree-trunks with Stone-Age tools.

Settling Down

In the meantime, though, the Neolithic, or New Stone Age, Revolution had begun taking place: hunter-gatherers were settling down and devoting themselves to agriculture. It's known as a revolution because there was a lot more to it than the domestication of livestock, the digging of the ground and the planting of seeds, as important as these innovations doubtless were. The cultivation of crops necessitates a wholesale switch to a sedentary lifestyle, in which the construction of permanent homes, and the establishment of larger village communities, starts making sense.

It also allows the production of surpluses, with all that this entails: the accumulation of wealth, and consequently the emergence of social rank or caste; the construction of prestige homes and tombs; the freeing up of a specialised force of craft-workers with the skills to create precious objects; or traders to go out and barter for luxuries.

All this was to take time, though: the great cities of Mesopotamia, the Middle East and Egypt were still several millennia away, and in Scotland, as in Sumeria, development was slow. The people who, around 5,500 years ago, conducted rituals atop Cairnpapple Hill, West Lothian, building a circular henge, or ceremonial enclosure, for the purpose, were later to occupy the site themselves. The existence of this sort of ceremonial site suggests a degree of civilisation on the part of a people who had a cultural and ritual regime, which extended beyond simply getting by. Several stone hearths have been found, the centres for a rich domestic life: tools and ceramics had been imported from as far away as the Lake District and North Wales.

Dignity in Death

Dating from about 5,000 years ago, Maeshowe, on Orkney's Mainland, is a mound some 7.3m (24ft) high and 35m (115ft) across. The heaped-up earth conceals a chambered cairn, whose central tomb is reached by a lengthy passage lined with stone. The whole construction, it has been calculated, involved 100,000 man-hours' labour – work that, again, had to be spared from the daily effort to secure subsistence. The Neolithic was as much an economic as a scientific and cultural revolution: the men who raised this tomb must have enjoyed considerable wealth and status. It's a similar story at Camster, north of Lybster, in Caithness, where two great burial cairns were built, one long and thin; the other simply round. 'Camster Long' is actually a double tomb itself – quite possibly two circular mounds which were subsequently run together. Narrow, tapered 'horns' project on each side at either end.

On a hilltop high above the A75 a few miles to the west of Gatehouse of Fleet, Dumfries & Galloway, are the pair of chambered tombs now known together as Cairnholy. Both were long, as opposed to circular, in construction. That said, the Upper Cairn – much wider and more curved in plan – would have seemed stubby in profile by comparison with the Lower Cairn, which was over 40m (140ft) in length.

Neolithic Living

So much for the sorts of places in which chieftains of the Scottish Neolithic were laid in death. What about where they spent their lives? At the Knap of Howar, on Papa Westray, Orkney, are the remains of what's believed to be a Neolithic homestead: a larger and smaller house sit side by side. Built of stone but seemingly covered over with earth, they would have appeared to form a natural part of the grassy hillside; though linked by a low passage, they are otherwise self-contained. What seems to have been the kitchen in the larger house comes complete with quern, or grinding-stone; in its other room there's apparently storage space and a stone hearth. The natural assumption might have been that the smaller hut was intended as stabling for livestock, except that this too has a stone hearth. Both buildings would have

Scotland Before Scotland

offered compact but comfortable living quarters, their thick stone walls well proofed against Atlantic gales. Dating back to approximately 3500 BCE, these are believed to be the oldest preserved stone houses in northern Europe. Wheat and barley were both grown there, while cattle, pigs and sheep were all kept, on the evidence of bones unearthed – deer and seabirds were hunted too, and fish caught from the sea.

Even so, they can hardly compare in sheer impressiveness with Skara Brae, just a few miles away as the seagull flies, beside the Bay of Skaill on the western coast of Orkney's Mainland. Excavated in the 1920s, this late-Neolithic settlement built around 3000 BCE is quite astonishingly well-preserved – and, quite frankly, one of the wonders of the prehistoric world. Famously, it lay forgotten for many centuries, only to be exposed virtually at a stroke by the waves from a storm of 1850, which tore the topsoil from what had been just a grassy slope above the sea. Digging down into pre-existing Palaeolithic middens, the Neolithic builders had set stone walls into the hillside to create huts which were then covered over with soil and turf; hearths, beds and dressers were created inside with slabs of stone. There too, the evidence suggests, barley and wheat were systematically cultivated and livestock kept, supplemented by fish and hunted game. Elsewhere in Orkney, research on soils at the site of a Neolithic homestead at Tofts Ness, on Sanday, has shown that they were deliberately treated with manure.

Sacred Sites?

The first of the standing stones at Callanish, on the Isle of Lewis, seem to have been erected at around the same time, around 3000 BCE, though there's evidence that the henge was regularly added to, growing in size and complexity over generations. Quite why the stones are there is uncertain (a cairn within the central circle seems to date from a few centuries later). It's generally assumed, though, that they must have served some ceremonial purpose of immense importance, and it's clear that they're to some extent lined up with both the surrounding topography and the stars. It's a similar story at Balnuaran of Clava, east of Inverness, where we find, up on a bank above the River Nairn, a row of three Neolithic cairns – all beautifully preserved, and each surrounded by a small stone circle of its own.

As imposing in their way (though much reduced now, with only four of an original 12 standing stones still remaining) are the Stones of Stenness, northeast of Stromness on Orkney's Mainland. And, just across the causeway between the Lochs of Stromness and Harray, the awe-inspiring Ring of Brodgar. On the Scottish mainland, meanwhile, there's the Loanhead of Daviot stone circle in Aberdeenshire. This is striking in the prominence given to the gigantic recumbent (literally, lying down) stone on one side of the circle, the ring-cairn within, and what remains of a little cremation cemetery off to one side. Again, while its mystic purpose may remain obscure, its monumental scale is impressive in itself. If it tells us nothing else, it testifies to the ability of this society to mobilise labour on a massive scale: the recumbent stone at Loanhead of Daviot weighs over 60 tonnes.

Technological Advance

The breathtaking beauty of the polished-stone axehead found on Angus' Hill of Bolshan in 1995, and since displayed at the Montrose Museum, testifies to the technical accomplishment (and, surely, the aesthetic sense) of the Neolithic worker. (If the suggestion that it was imported and of Danish manufacture seems a slight to 'Scottish' skills, it still says much for the sophistication of an economic system that had such far-reaching commercial contacts.) Artefacts found at Skara Brae and other such sites only underline the miraculous flair of so much ancient work in stone. However astonishing their skills, though, humans could only go so far with Stone Age technology: the introduction of metal-working brought about another revolution in life at large. Hence the importance of Christian Jürgensen Thomsen's schema – proposed as long ago as the middle of the 19th century – of archaeological ages: of stone, of bronze and iron.

The first smelting, of copper, believed to have taken place in the Middle East some 8,500 years ago, may be seen as the backward step from which a great leap forward could be made. So soft is copper on its own that, its incontestable beauty apart, it's of limited use in making the kind of tools on which Neolithic communities relied in order to survive. Alloyed with tin and other metals, however, it made bronze – a much stronger and more durable metal, capable of sharpening to make viable tools and weapons. No one flicked a switch, of course: there was considerable overlap between the old Stone Age technology and the use of bronze, which seems to have begun towards the end of the third millennium BCE.

At Tonderghie, near Whithorn, Dumfries & Galloway, prehistoric mine workings have been identified from the discovery not just of copper ingots but of digging tools and spoil heaps around an open vein. This was surely only one of many such sources in the Scotland of the time.

Overlapping Ages

The late-Neolithic shades over into the Bronze Age at sites like Machrie Moor, north of Blackwaterfoot, on the western coast of Arran: bronze and flint tools have been unearthed there, along with Neolithic tombs and cairns and hut-remains of a later date. Earth ramparts at the top of Eildon Hill, near

Melrose in the Borders, meanwhile, point to the presence of a prehistoric hillfort, which archaeologists have dated to about 1000 BCE – the middle of the Bronze Age. The monoliths that give Caithness' Hill O' Many Stanes its name (and they weren't exaggerating: there are getting on for 200) are also believed to have been set up during the Bronze Age.

Just as the Neolithic and Bronze Ages overlapped on the ground in Scotland, so too did the Bronze and Iron Age – though the introduction of iron was even more transformative than that of bronze had been. Again, the relevant skills seem to have emerged in the Middle East. Whilst evidence from Anatolia (present-day Turkey) suggests a start-date for ironworking of about 1200 BCE, the skills spread only very slowly over generations. At Kilmartin Glen, Argyll, we see evidence of occupation not only from the Neolithic and Bronze Age but also from the Iron Age. This area – in the middle of nowhere now – seems to have been a bustling centre of activity in prehistoric times: Kilmartin Museum is full of fascinating treasures from the district's past.

Further Iron Age sites are to be seen at Gurness, Shetland, where the remains of a settlement cluster about the ruins of a round, defensive drystone tower or 'broch'. Evidence suggests that their first settlement of around 500 BCE was subsequently demolished and built over anew in later, Pictish times.

Fortress Mentality

The Iron Age hillforts atop the Brown and White Caterthun, near Edzell in Strathmore, Angus, appear to have been inhabited over several centuries, starting from the middle of the first millennium BCE. The Brown Caterthun fort is smaller, and its ramparts are all earthen; the White Caterthun includes drystone fortifications and seems more substantial and permanent generally: there was a spring for water there and a central building made of stone.

FROM BROCH TO BARRACKS

The broch is among the most characteristic buildings of the Scottish Iron Age: examples abound, albeit for the most part they're in ruins. When not actually sacked by attackers, they seem simply to have been pulled apart for building stone in medieval and early-modern times. The best-preserved example is the one on the island of Mousa, Shetland, which stands over 13m (40ft) high, and has a spiral staircase round the walls inside. Clickimin Broch, southwest of Lerwick, is impressive too. The finest surviving example on the Scottish mainland is perhaps Dun Telve, outside Glenelg, in Highland.

Nearby Dun Troddan was said to have been intact as recently as the 1720s when it was largely demolished for stone for the construction of Bernera Barracks – a historic monument in its own right, built in response to the Jacobite rising of 1715 (see Chapter Five). A sad story of vandalism, or a fascinating example of history at work, each generation turning over and reinventing a past it then adapts to its own perspectives?

But the Brown and White Caterthuns are only among the most strikingly well-preserved of a great many such strongholds that appeared in the Iron Age: traces of over 1,000 hillforts have been found in the southern part of Scotland. There was one on the summit of Arthur's Seat in Edinburgh. Crop terraces, carved out of the slopes below over generations, are quite clearly visible from the suburbs to the southeast.

The growing interest in security is confirmed by the increasing resort to constructing crannogs – artificial islands in lakes or slow-moving rivers, generally on platforms held up on timber pilings, reached by little footbridges that could easily be cut off. One example was found in 1898 at Dumbuck, off the northern shore of the Firth of Clyde near Dumbarton Rock. Although opportunistic fortune-hunters

also 'found' a great many fake tools and weapons, the crannog itself seems to have been genuine. Others have been discovered since: the reconstructed example to be seen at the
Scottish Crannog Centre at Kenmore, Perthshire, is based
on the nearby Oakbank Crannog – one of 17 found around
the shores of Loch Tay.

Of all the various inferences we can make, perhaps the
most obvious is that the overall population in Scotland seems
to have been soaring; the second is that this was a nation
under arms. The two things aren't unconnected, of course:
the advent of agriculture had not only allowed the same
amount of land to support a much larger population, it had
also permitted the production of surpluses such as earlier
hunter-gatherer populations could never conceivably have
envisaged, and the establishment of a comparatively rich and
leisured warrior-class. We think of agriculture as a peaceable
activity, and for the ordinary 'peasantry' (for want of a better
word) it very likely was, but it also allowed the emergence of
a new and powerful elite with no trade other than warfare.
Wealth could be accumulated. Not only that, but it could be
transported: flocks and herds could be driven away; crops
could be destroyed or carried off.

Hail Caledonia!

Julius Caesar's 'invasions' of Britannia (Britain) in 55 and 54
BCE didn't get much beyond the area around the Thames
Estuary. Not for almost a century was what we now call
England invaded in earnest. In 43 CE, the Emperor Claudius
sent a serious force under his general, Aulus Plautius. Again,
his conquest started in the southeast. In fact, it was to take
a couple of decades for England and Wales to be brought
under the Roman *Imperium* and for Governor Gnaeus Julius
Agricola to find the leisure to look north, to where the for-
merly-Romanised Brigantes were now rising up against his

rule. At that time, the Scottish border as we know it was straddled by the Brigantes' territory: what we think of as Agricola's 'invasion of Scotland' was first and foremost an attack on them.

Far from being unconquerable, Scotland's tribes seem not to have posed Agricola too many problems. Partly thanks to an effective policy of diplomatic divide and rule. Partly too, though, by force of arms: according to his son-in-law and biographer (or hagiographer) the historian Tacitus, he set off in the summer of 81 CE with an impressive army to 'ravage the territory of tribes as far north as the estuary they call the Tay'. He then set about securing his presence in southern Scotland with a network of roads and forts, like the ones at Birrens, Dumfries & Galloway, and Trimontium (Newstead), Borders. Not far from Newstead, just off the A68 north of Lauder at Soutra Aisle, a stretch of 'Dere Street' can be seen running across open country, now grassed over, but very clearly a thoroughfare. Dere Street was the arterial north–south route running between Eboracum (York) and Cramond. Another section (with associated camps and earthworks) can be seen at Pennymuir, southeast of Jedburgh, and another still a little further north at Whitton Edge (you can also see the roadside pits from which the soldiers quarried stone). Further west, near Motherwell, there's a Roman bridge to be seen in Strathclyde Country Park.

Altogether, Agricola and his armies took this part of Caledonia firmly in hand. As Tacitus put it:

> The Clyde and the Forth, carried inland to a great depth on the tides of opposing seas, are divided only by a narrow neck of land. This isthmus was now securely held by our garrisons, the whole area to the south now unequivocally in Roman hands. The enemy had been confined in what amounted to another island.

Not that Agricola stopped there. The following year he carried his war of conquest onward to the north. At this point, though, the picture becomes confused. Whilst Tacitus doesn't leave much doubt as to his father-in-law's further progress – or, indeed, his famous victory over the Caledonian tribes of Calgacus at 'Mons Graupius' – we have no clear idea where this epic engagement was actually fought. The whereabouts of the battlefield seem to have been lost in the mists of time as comprehensively as Rome's Ninth Legion was lost in the mists of the Highlands three decades later. (That is, if the Ninth was lost at all, rather than simply misplaced, as recent scholarship has suggested, conjured out of existence by some bureaucratic decision back in Rome.) Among the possible locations for the battle advanced by historians have been the Bennachie, Kempstone and Megray Hills in Aberdeenshire.

Good Fences...

Another mooted Mons Graupius location has been somewhere or other along the Gask Ridge in Perthshire's Highland foothills – where Roman fortifications from the 70s CE have indeed been found. Whether or not the battle was fought there, the Gask Ridge is obviously significant as the first 'fixed frontier' to be established by the Romans at a time when it was coming to be felt that the Empire as a whole had reached an extent beyond which it was going to start becoming unmanageable – however strong the legions were. Traces of these fortifications are still to be seen at a number of locations, including Strathacro, Angus, Inchtuthill, near Perth, Doune, near Stirling, and Camelon, not far from Falkirk.

Built from about 122, Hadrian's Wall was to represent a falling-back, a retrenchment. (And none of it, of course, lies in what we would now – or have for centuries – seen as Scotland.) The construction of the Antonine Wall (between 138 and 140) marked a renewed expansionism on the part of the Emperor Antoninus. This too, however, we're told by the anonymous author of the *Lives of the Later Caesars* (late-4th century), was prompted by incursions by barbarians: Antoninus' governor, Quintus Lollius Urbicus, had to 'drive them back' and keep them at bay by building another wall. Running for 58 km (36 miles) between the eastern edge of Bo'ness on the Firth of Forth and Old Kilpatrick on the River Clyde, the Antonine Wall took advantage of the natural 'narrow neck of land' Tacitus had mentioned. Fronted by a deep and open ditch (which may even have been flooded with water), its sturdy stone foundation was built up to a height of over 3m (10ft) with piled-up turf by the men of the Sixth and Twentieth Legions and associated auxiliaries.

Traces of the Antonine Wall may be seen to this day at, for example, Callendar Park, Rough Castle, Seabegs Wood, Bonnybridge, or at the Bar Hill or Croy Hill forts. You can see it all by following a long-distance footpath, the Antonine Way. As we've seen, already under Hadrian, the Romans had fallen back to a frontier south of what we now call Scotland. For some time, the tide of occupation ebbed and flowed. Under Antonine's successors, Rome withdrew from Scotland. Not until Septimius Severus' campaign of 209–10 did the Romans attempt to enforce their hold on southern Caledonia once again. The Roman historian Cassius Dio reported:

> *As he advanced through the country he experienced countless hardships in cutting down the forests, levelling the heights, filling up the swamps, and bridging the rivers; but he fought no battle and beheld no enemy in battle array. The enemy purposely put sheep and cattle in front of the soldiers for them to seize, in order that they might be lured on still further until they were worn out; for in fact the water caused great suffering to the Romans, and when they became scattered, they would be*

> *attacked. Then, unable to walk, they would be slain by*
> *their own men, in order to avoid capture, so that a full*
> *fifty thousand died.*

Faced with so determined a guerrilla action, Severus decided – as commanders so often have in similar circumstances ever since – that a reaction verging on the genocidal was required. Fortunately, the erudite emperor was able to find a fitting quotation in Homer's *Iliad*, in which an angry Agamemnon upbraids a Menelaus who shows signs of pitying the defeated Trojans (VI, 51):

> *Let no one escape sheer destruction,*
> *No one our hands, not even the babe in the womb of the*
> * mother,*
> *If it be male; let it nevertheless not escape sheer destruction.*

Severus' campaign, costly as it was in lives on both sides, did eventually succeed in re-establishing Roman rule as far north as the Antonine Wall. And indeed beyond: the abandoned Agricolan camp at Kintore, Aberdeenshire, seems to have been put back into commission at this time. Hardly had he returned to his headquarters in Eboracum (York), however, than Severus fell sick and died. The territories he'd secured in Scotland were more or less abandoned.

As Pictish as They're Painted?

The Romans' enemies in Caledonia were, as everybody knows, the Picts. Who were they, though? Was there ever even any such people? Did they ever actually exist, except in opposition, in their capacity as Scottish enemies of Rome? The Latin word *picti* just means 'painted', of course: the name seems to have been used for all the native north-Britons because of their ceremonial body-art. How far the Picts ever

saw themselves as a single, identity-sharing people, we can only speculate. And even if they did,
would it ever have occurred to them to do so
had they not been forced to come together to
defend against the external threat the Roman
legions posed?

In fact, the indications are that, even as a
name, the word was largely applied in retrospect. Its first recorded usage in Latin literature was not to occur till 297 – only a century or
so before the Roman legions were to withdraw from Britain
altogether. And if they were conjured into existence by the
use of a single word, were the Picts to be abolished in the
same way too when – in the chronicles of the 9th century
– that word was abandoned in favour of others, such as
'Alba'? The reality is that the Picts were in Scotland well
before the Romans arrived and were there not only long after
they had left, but long after their name for this people – or
these peoples – had been discarded. Who they were, though,
is more difficult to say.

All we know for (something like) sure is that they were
a collection of Celtic tribes that formed some sort of alliance in opposition to the Romans. Even to say that they were
'Celtic' may mislead, however: the label means a lot less than
we may think, being far more a matter of language and culture than what we might see as 'race'. The original Celts,
a warrior elite from central Europe, had fanned out across
the continent in the course of the Iron Age, taking charge in
territories from Scotland and Ireland to Asia Minor. But the
widespread adoption of their lifestyle, language and artistic
style across this area was perhaps more comparable to the
reach of modern American fast-food and cartoon culture in
the wider world than to the direct conquest and occupation
of an imperial power like Rome.

Culture and Christianity

And it is indeed in the area of culture that the Pictish legacy has most obviously survived, though all the archaeological evidence we have seems to date from the centuries after the Roman departure. The sort of brooches, pins and jewellery to be seen in the National Museum of Scotland are very obviously close kin to artefacts unearthed at burial mounds and other sites the length and breadth of Celtic Europe. Likewise, the sort of symbol stones on show at the Meigle Sculptured Stone Museum, Strathmore, show all the decorative dynamism we're accustomed to in Celtic art: the rich elaboration, the looping, foliate forms, the curvilinear swirls. So too with examples like the Brandsbutt Stone, outside Inverurie, and the Barochan Cross (in Paisley Abbey now) – evidence of the Christianisation of the Picts some time towards the end of the first millennium.

How far Christianity could be said to have 'tamed' the Picts is by no means clear. The stone unmemorably known as Aberlemno II, in the kirkyard of Aberlemno, Angus – a village rich in Pictish sculptures – has pagan symbols on one face and a Celtic cross upon the other. Whilst the stone was fashioned fairly late – towards the 10th century – it shows undiminished pride in the warlike achievements of the past: the 'pagan' side depicts a scene from the Battle of Nechtansmere, fought at Dunnichen Moss in Angus (or, just possibly, by Loch Insh at Dunachton, Badenoch and Strathspey), at which King Bridei III's Picts routed Ecgfrith's Northumbrian forces. And whilst the designs on the Dupplin Cross (in St Serf's Church, Dunning, Perthshire) clearly compare the Pictish King Constantine with the Biblical King David, we see him not as a shepherd-boy or psalmist-poet, but as a warlord.

Nation Formation

This early history of Scotland in the centuries after the Roman withdrawal (traditionally dated 410) is one we see only in passing glimpses in later (and quite possibly unreliable) monastic texts like the 12th-century Irish *Annals of Tigernach* or the 8th-century writings of the Venerable Bede. What results is a fairly confusing picture – if, indeed, it can even be called a 'picture' rather than a historiographical kaleidoscope of partial, tangential and sometimes conflicting views.

It makes no sense from our modern standpoint that for information on the history of southeastern Scotland at this time we should have to go to a chronicle written in Welsh to read about the Goddodin and their victory over the Angles at the Battle of Catraeth (perhaps Catterick, Yorkshire), in around 600. But then neither does it seem sensible that further to the west there should have been a Gaelic kingdom, Dál Riata, which spanned the North Channel to take in the glens of Antrim on the Irish shore. Dál Riata was named for its people's mythic progenitor, Eochu Riata. What's believed to have been its capital at Dunadd hillfort, Argyll (you can still see the stone slab with the 'footprint' depression into which the new king stepped at his inauguration), is mentioned in the *Annals of Ulster* (683). By that time, though, Dál Riata was already history – of a sketchy sort.

Holy Grounds

The complex relationship between the Irish Gaelic culture of Dál Riata and that of Celtic Christianity is by no means fully understood, but certainly the two went together both geographically and chronologically. Iona – famous to this day as a place of retreat (its religious role reinvigorated by the Church of Scotland Moderator George MacLeod in the 1930s) – was settled by monks in early-medieval times.

St Columba is said to have founded his abbey on the island in 563, and to have carried out a mission on the mainland. Traditionally, his travels took him up the Great Glen, where (according to Adamnan's *Life* of 565) he had to quell the Loch Ness Monster. What's supposed to be 'Columba's Chapel' on Iona isn't really old enough to have fulfilled this role: it's believed to have been built in the 9th century.

But Columba isn't generally considered to have introduced Christianity to Scotland. That honour falls to St Ninian over a century before. Having been born (by tradition in Galloway) in the mid-4th century, Ninian left to travel Europe, where he converted to the faith of Christ. He then returned – via Northumbria, according to the ancient chronicles – landing at Whithorn, south of Wigtown, to start his mission to his homeland. The present parish church, atmospherically sited on the windswept hillside above the harbour, was only built in the 1860s, but it's believed to occupy the site of the Candida Casa ('Shining White House') established by the saint almost a millennium and a half before. A little way round the coast, on the west coast of the Machars Peninsula near Port William, is St Ninian's Cave – a cleft in the rocks where the holy man is traditionally supposed to have established his hermitage. Whether he actually did or not is impossible to know, but the belief that he did is of ancient standing: crosses were carved into the wall there as long ago as the 8th century.

Going Native

Here, on Europe's outer edge, the power of the papacy must have seemed remote: home rule wasn't really Rome rule, as far as Celtic Christians were concerned. The special status of Celtic Christianity can quite easily be overstated – very often has been, indeed, by those who'd like to imagine an old-world New-Age and female-friendly spirituality flourishing along the Celtic fringe. It remains the case, however, that to some extent the Celtic Church did go its own way with regard to everything from the sacred calendar (the dating of Easter) to the styling of the tonsure (the shaved area of hair on the monk's head). In its views on marriage too the Church here attended more to Celtic tradition than to the decrees of Rome: divorce was allowed freely for both men and women, as was marriage well within what the continental Church regarded as the forbidden degrees of kinship. On the other hand, the practice of private (and confidential) confession seems to have been an innovation of the Celtic Church brought back to continental Europe in the 7th century – till then, worshippers had just made a collective declaration of repentance and act of penance.

The insistence of the Irish that their country was at this time the 'Land of Saints and Scholars' overlooks the competing claims of Hebridean havens of learning, such as Iona. One of Ireland's greatest treasures, the *Book of Kells*, is believed to have been created by scribes at Columba's Scottish monastery. It was taken to the Abbey of Kells (in County Meath) for safe-keeping sometime after the start of the Viking raids. The monasteries of the High Middle Ages were famously to become important centres of literature and culture. In this early-medieval stage, however, with much of Europe up in flames between barbarian invasions, internecine wars and Viking raids, it's arguably thanks to the monks in far-flung communities like this that Western civilisation survived at all.

Cross References

Not that Christianity was ever just Celtic, of course: by the late-7th century, the Anglo-Saxons were converting too. The Ruthwell Cross is now housed inside the local church outside which it stood for centuries in this little village southeast of Dumfries, once part of the kingdom of Northumbria.

SCRIPT AND CIVILISATION

Now in the National Museum of Scotland, the Hunterston Brooch was made around 700, a stunning example of Celtic craftsmanship. Sumptuously rich and colourful, cast in silver, gilded and exquisitely ornamented with amber and gold filigree, it's rich in Christian symbolism, scholars say. But it also speaks more directly: scratched into the back are a series of thin and spindly signs – all verticals and angled strokes, no curves, serifs or fussy features of any other kind. Runes, as they are called, were an old Germanic type of characters, specifically designed (some time in the 2nd century CE) to be easily cut into stone. The brooch's inscription is in Old Norse ('Melbrigda owns this brooch', it says), but Anglo-Saxon stonemasons used them too.

Ornately carved in stone, in stereotypically Celtic style, with swirling animal and vegetal figures and decorative effects, it also features panels with pictorial representations of Mary Magdalen washing Jesus' feet, the Visitation of the Virgin Mary, the Holy Family's Flight into Egypt and other biblical scenes. In addition, it's inscribed with snatches of scripture in Latin characters as well as runic verses from the 7th-century Anglo-Saxon poem, *The Dream of the Rood*. In this extraordinary work, Christ's cross itself describes to the dreamer-narrator what it felt like to be 'embraced' by Jesus, a 'warrior' eager to give up his life for the redemption of mankind. The cross goes on to reveal how it felt to experience the wrenching pain of having the nails driven through from the dying hero's hands and feet, and to feel its timbers running wet with the Saviour's blood.

In another of those curious collisions in which Scottish history abounds, this monument was deliberately broken up in iconoclastic zeal by Covenanters in 1642 (see pages 101–9). Not until the 1880s did Ruthwell's minister, Henry

Duncan, reassemble the pieces he could find and restore the rest – some of the interpretative judgements he made in doing so seem questionable now, but overall he did Scottish history an important service.

If it seems odd to see runes in this Celtic context, it's perhaps not so surprising when we recall that in pagan times the Celts had maintained a prohibition on any form of writing. Hence the fact that the old Irish epics have been transmitted to us by monastic scribes using Latin characters, and the resort elsewhere to runic script.

Ogham, a perhaps related form, primarily carved into stone, seems like little more than a row of notches to the uninitiated, though there's a pattern to the way the cross-strokes are clustered and angled that gives them meaning. Whilst it was mainly used in Ireland, Ogham script crops up in Scotland too. For reasons which are far from clear, though, inscriptions in Ogham have for the most part not been found where expected – in the west, in what was once Dál Riata – but in the old Pictish heartlands further east. Of the two Pictish cross-slabs in the ruined church of St Fergus, Dyce, north of Aberdeen, for instance, one has an Ogham inscription running across its horizontal arm. As so often, though, whilst the letters can be deciphered, the language it is written in isn't known, so we're really none the wiser as to what it means. It's the same story with the cross-slab from outside the Old Parish Church at Aboyne, on Deeside, now displayed inside the nearby Victory Hall.

Dál Riata Defeated

The defeat of Domnall Brecc by the High King Domnall II at Mag Rath, County Down, in 639 saw the collapse of Dál Riata on its Irish shores. In Scotland, Dál Riata's adversity represented an opportunity for Fortriu, the Pictish kingdom of east and central Scotland whose boundaries are disputed but which seems to have centred around Strathearn in Perthshire. By the end of the 7th century, encroachments on that kingdom from the south by Anglo-Saxon Northumbria saw the Picts again eclipsed and Dál Riata given a second chance. But when both Dál Riata and Fortriu were defeated in a great battle (at an unknown location) with the Vikings in 839, a leadership vacuum was left in Scotland into which Kenneth MacAlpin was able to step. A man of myth more than history, King Kenneth I supposedly conquered the Picts and founded the kingdom of Alba – and earned himself a place in legend as the first king of Scots.

The 9th-century Forteviot Arch in Strathearn is believed to be among the only surviving traces of MacAlpin's palace; the so-called Sueno Stone, outside Forres, may well commemorate his reign. His grandson, King Constantine II of Scotland, created an alliance of Strathclyde and Pictish Scots and Vikings based in Dublin to check expansion by the King of Wessex, Aethelstan. Striking southward through Northumbria in 937, this combined force met the English at Brunanburh (perhaps Bromborough, in the Wirral), but Aethelstan's army won a crushing victory. 'The Scotsmen and ship-raiders,' asserted the Anglo-Saxon bard, as translated by the modern American poet Robert Hass, 'fell as if fated.' Left on the ground were 'bodies of Norsemen sprawled on their scutcheons, and the Scotsmen as well.' Never before had there been 'so many cut down by the sword's edge'.

Out of the North

The involvement of the Norsemen in such a large-scale action as King Constantine's invasion of England suggests that they'd moved on to some extent from their original status as 'ship-raiders'. It's in this role that their image has endured, of course: the longship looming out of the mist; the surprise-attack on an isolated settlement; the shouts, the fire, the rape-and-pillage; the 'fury of the Northmen' from which Christians prayed to the Lord to be delivered ... The stereotype isn't untrue, as such – even though it may indeed be 'mythic' – but these smash-and-grab raids were just a phase in the Viking story.

It was a nasty phase while it lasted. On 8 June 793, according to the *Anglo-Saxon Chronicle*, 'the ravages of heathen men miserably destroyed God's church on Lindisfarne, with plunder and slaughter.' The next year the Norsemen struck a few miles down England's eastern coast at Bede's alma mater monastery of Jarrow, but in 795 it was Iona's turn. This was only the first of several raids, in the course of which many people were killed and priceless treasures taken: in one attack of 806, 68 monks were slain. (Ironically, brethren from Iona had just established the monastery at Kells, in Ireland's County Meath, intended as a safe haven, well inland.)

It was a long phase too, and one which in some ways institutionalised the sudden raid as a routine, a way of life. However, warbands quickly tired of the commute across the sea from Scandinavia and started wintering at sites in Ireland and in France along the Loire. In the late 840s, a Viking force was heavily defeated by a Muslim army in al-Andalus, Islamic southern Spain – but not before the raiders had sacked Lisbon, Cádiz and Seville. In 860 Viking longships mounted raids in northwestern Italy. There were even attacks on Morocco in North Africa. Swedish Vikings pushed their way up the Russian river system from the Baltic: in 860 they attacked Constantinople from the Black Sea. Back in Scotland, Dumbarton Castle had remained an important centre (despite Dál Riata's downfall), commanding as it did the trade routes in and out of the Firth of Clyde. When, in 870, however, it was sacked by Vikings, this only underlined the sad decline of fortunes of the Scottish kingdoms at this time.

Homes from Home

The raiding lifestyle was dangerous – even for the Vikings themselves – and its results were unpredictable: if they could find good land in a safe situation, Vikings would often settle down. They may have arrived as raiders but, increasingly, the Vikings stayed as settlers. Certainly on Scotland's northern isles. The biggest and best-known settlement site was at Jarlshof, near the southernmost end of Shetland's Mainland. What seems to have been a favoured spot shows signs of occupation all the way through from the Neolithic to the Viking periods. The remains of a communal longhouse and associated outbuildings from the 9th century have been found there. At the Udal, on North Uist, the Vikings also overbuilt a site of earlier settlement: there, in addition to a range of dwellings, they constructed what appears to have been a fort.

A less obvious legacy was left at Rubha an Dùnain, on the western coast of Skye, where what remains of a Viking-built canal has been discovered. This allowed boats to be moved from the sea to the more sheltered waters of Loch na h-Airde, where they could lie sheltered from the worst of the winter storms.

The Vikings' indissoluble connection with the sea was obviously underlined by the practice of boat-burial. Examples have been found at Scar, on Sanday, Orkney, and on the Scottish mainland at Port an Eilean Mhòir, Ardnamurchan. These weren't generally the full-scale dragon-prowed longships of popular modern myth but smaller, four-oared *faerings*. In later (and, perhaps, less prestigious) burials, the boat might be more notional – little more than shaped stone slabs to represent a bow and stern. Viking burial sites have been found in several places around the coasts of the northern and western islands, from the Cnip headland of Bhaltos, Lewis, to King's Cross Point on Arran. At Westness, on the Orkney island of Rousay, in addition to a couple of Viking longhouses, a number of boat burials have been found. In one of these a warrior lay buried with his shield. A woman and some animals seem to have been killed in sacrifice upon his grave.

The Westness cemetery also includes several earlier, Pictish graves. The Vikings would appear to have respected these. On the other hand, graffiti left by Viking looters on the Maeshowe tomb in Orkney suggests that the historical overlap at such sites could be brutally violent as well as peaceful. Or, perhaps, a bit of both – as at the Brough of Birsay, northwest of Orkney's Mainland. The Picts living there between the 7th and 8th centuries seem to have been replaced – or forcibly *dis*placed? – by Vikings during the 9th century. So complete was the 'Scandinavianisation' of Orkney at this time, so rich the islands' Nordic heritage now, that it almost doesn't occur to us to ask what became of the population that had previously inhabited the place.

Christian Advent

The Viking Age lasted a long time in the far north, though its nature changed over generations as former raiders became farmers and (in the course of the 10th century) converted to Christianity. At Orphir, on Orkney's Mainland, Earl Paul gave a great Yule feast in 1136 and, according to the *Orkneyinga Saga*, he had a *bu* or 'drinking-hall' there, with 'many large ale vessels', and next door a 'magnificent church', whose circular foundations may still be seen. St Nicholas' Church had been built by the Earl's father, Haakon Paulsson: its unusual shape was very likely inspired by that of the Church of the Holy Sepulchre in Jerusalem, to which he'd made a penitential pilgrimage after murdering a rival earl in 1116.

Should we be more struck by his piety or by the barbaric violence that prompted it? In so far as Christianity was a civilising influence in the north, progress was evidently slow. These northern islands were, if not actually lawless, then at least a law unto themselves. Whilst, well into the 13th century, Orkney and Shetland would look to Norway rather than to the Scottish mainland for leadership, they were by no means necessarily obedient to the authority of the Norwegian crown. Even so, Christianity continued to consolidate its hold. St Mary's Chapel, on the Orkney island of Wyre, was built sometime around 1150 – as was Cubbie Row's Castle, nearby.

Meanwhile, on the Scottish mainland, the kingdom of Alba had slowly grown in strength. During the 950s, it had taken Dun Edin – Edinburgh – and the Lothians under its control from the Anglian Northumbrians. Malcolm I's victory over Moray (what remained of the old Pictish kingdom of Fortriu) shifted the balance of power in Alba's favour. Malcolm II's triumph at Carham, outside Coldstream (1018), secured the Scottish border to the south, the situation being ratified in negotiation with King Cnut (or Canute) of Denmark and England, in 1030. Macbeth of Moray, 'the renowned', according to the contemporaneous poem the *Duan Albanach*, became High King of Alba in 1040 after defeating Duncan II, who'd launched an attack on the northern kingdom. After years of fighting, Macbeth was eventually – in 1057 – defeated, deposed and executed by Duncan's son, Malcolm III.

Malcolm's marriage to Margaret of Wessex took place in 1070 or thereabouts – she'd arrived in Scotland with her mother, Agatha, a refugee from England's Norman Conquest. Later canonised as St Margaret of Scotland, she's remembered mostly for her extraordinary piety, for founding the pilgrims' ferries across the Forth to Fife for the onward journey to St Andrews – and, more prosaically, for her efforts to reconcile the rituals of the Celtic Church with those of Rome. 'Her' chapel, in Edinburgh Castle, probably wasn't built till several decades after her death in 1090, but it's still the oldest construction in the capital.

Scotland Before Scotland

THE SCOTTISH PLAY

*The historical Macbeth, while he definitely did exist, showed
only passing similarities to the Machiavellian anti-hero of
Shakespeare's play. Apart, that is, from the fact of his violent rise
and fall. Having lost his crown in battle, Macbeth was executed
on the orders of his longtime rival's son, the future Malcolm III,
who had defeated him at Lumphanan, Aberdeenshire, in 1057.
A stone marks the spot where he was supposedly beheaded.*

Shakespeare's narrative follows Raphael Holinshed's
Chronicles, *a popular history first published in 1577. As far as
the rivalry between Macbeth and Duncan is concerned, it freely
conflates the characters of Macbeth and of the earlier Donwalde,
a courtier of King Duffe who, having dispatched his lord, then
killed some of his servants, framing them for the king's murder.*

*From Holinshed too we get the story of the prophecy – albeit
from 'a certaine [singular] witch' – that Macbeth needn't
fear defeat before he sees Birnam Wood coming to the castle at
Dunsinane. This fort was Macbeth's own construction in the*
Chronicles:

> To the end he might the more cruellie oppresse
> his subiects with all tyrantlike wrongs, he builded
> a strong castell on the top of an hie hill called

Dunsinane, situate in Gowrie, ten miles from Perth, on such a proud height, that standing there aloft, a man might behold well neere all the countries of Angus, Fife, Stermond and Ernedale, as it were lieng underneath him.

Dunsinane still survives – or at least its elevated site and associated earthworks do. So too does nearby Birnam Wood, though it's quite stationary these days.

Shakespeare's Macbeth *may well also make reference to important events in the playwright's own time – and in the life of England's James I, for whom it was written. As James VI of Scotland, still a teenager, Shakespeare's royal patron had himself been abducted by the Earl of Ruthven and his men, who'd hoped to replace him in a coup (see page 84). There was also the drama of Guy Fawkes' Gunpowder Plot, 1605.*

TWO

FOR
FREEDOM

THE NARRATIVE OF SCOTTISH HISTORY in the High Middle Ages has popularly been seen as one of a struggle for independence, and that's all right, as far as the analysis goes. Some Scots were always going to be more 'independent' than others, though: the emergence of a ruling elite had, as we've already seen, been among the earliest consequences of the transition to agriculture in the Neolithic period and the economic consolidation of the Bronze and Iron Ages.

Even so, there had been an anarchic aspect to what was not so much a society as a collection of disparate communities, each one ruled by its own local warlord, backed by his men. His prestige underpinned the strength of the band of warriors he had around him; this in turn underwrote his wider authority. For the chief was more than a paterfamilias – though he was that too. What we call the 'clan' went beyond the kinship-tribe. Whilst the chieftain's biological family got to share in – and ultimately inherit – his reflected glamour and his wealth, the actual basis of their power lay in the security they were able to offer the ordinary populace that gathered round them for protection.

By the 9th century, as we've seen, larger-scale kingdoms had slowly been taking shape – most notably Alba. Malcolm's victory at Lumphanan in 1057 had left him unchallenged ruler of something like what we would call 'Scotland' – just in time for the fall of Saxon England to the south.

1066 Not All That

The Norman Conquest may have been pivotal to English history, but its implications for Scotland aren't so easily identified. That the Conquest didn't immediately put Norman 'boots on the ground' up here obviously doesn't mean that it had no impact at all, but it didn't bring about anything like the same seismic political, cultural and social change.

For Freedom

At first, indeed, Malcolm III was able to play the situation to his own advantage – and that of Scotland as his kingdom. William the Conqueror's struggles to subdue the region north of the Humber weren't his problem. Nor, for that matter, were the sufferings of the English during the angry William's 'Harrying of the North' (1069–70). For several years, indeed, Malcolm was able to take advantage of the confusion beyond his border to carry out a succession of slave-raids in the English north. William had little alternative but to put up with these incursions whilst his conquest of England as a whole remained incomplete. By 1072, however, he was in a position to get tough with Malcolm, marching north with his army, defeating him in battle and forcing him into an accommodation at the Treaty of Abernethy.

One of Scotland's two Irish-style 'round towers' (the other's at Brechin) is now just about the only clue we have to Abernethy's importance in Pictish times, when this little township southeast of Perth appears to have been a major administrative and ecclesiastical centre. The treaty signed there did bring the Scottish king some important guarantees. Malcolm secured the Norman conqueror's acknowledgement of his kingship in Scotland itself, along with titles in Cumbria and the north of England. Altogether, though, it represented a clear and significant climb-down on Malcolm's part, involving the handing over of important English exiles, including Edgar the Aetheling, Malcolm's brother-in-law, and the main Saxon claimant to the English throne.

Still smarting at his humiliation two decades later, Malcolm invaded northern England again in 1091, by which time the Conqueror's son, William Rufus, was on the throne. Malcolm was once again repulsed and, making a renewed assault two years later, badly beaten by the Anglo-Normans at Alnwick, in Northumberland. He himself was killed – a cross outside Alnwick Castle shows the spot on which he is said to have died.

Succession Struggles

Malcolm's greatest innovation, perhaps, had been his introduction of a system of primogeniture – the idea that the king should be succeeded by his eldest son. Previously, Alba had followed the ancient Celtic system of tanistry, in which a tanist, or heir apparent, was elected from among the monarch's sons while he was still alive – a recipe, if not for disaster, then for division at the very least. The first Scottish king to benefit from this new dispensation should have been Malcolm's eldest son. In the event, though, Edward was killed alongside his father at Alnwick in 1093. A tanist-type succession took place, accordingly, with the late king's brother, Donald III, ascending the throne – only to have to fight off a series of challenges from rivals backed by England's William Rufus (rivals who fought every bit as fiercely among themselves).

King Duncan II managed to topple Donald in the summer of 1094 and was crowned in his place, though by 12 November he'd been murdered, and Donald was back on the throne. Duncan's half-brother, Edgar, succeeded when Donald died in 1097; he was followed in turn by his younger brother, Alexander I. *His* younger brother, David, came after him in 1124, despite the claims of Alexander's son, Malcolm – and of the principle of primogeniture.

The backing of Henry I of England helped. What's often called the Davidian Revolution – and, under that title, it sounds extremely daring and dynamic – can alternatively be seen as a wholesale capitulation to Anglo-Norman ways. (That view would, admittedly, be every bit as tendentious: the nation state of Scotland scarcely existed; the idea that it was possible to be unpatriotic towards it is obviously anachronistic.) The 'Scoto-Norman' nobles who came north to help King David hang on to the throne in the face of bitter opposition from Malcolm and his supporters reorganised the country along Anglo-Norman, feudal lines.

A Country of Castles

That meant, in the first place, a country under arms – under occupation, even. Castles were built – for conquest, then for administrative order. As the Normans had done previously wherever they went on campaign, they threw up what amounted to 'instant castles', all made by the same standard motte-and-bailey method. First, a 'motte' or mound of earth was thrown up (or an existing rise or outcrop might be used) and a wooden stronghold or 'keep' constructed on top. A 'curtain wall' was then placed around the motte, enclosing an open area or 'bailey' in which arms and equipment could be stored and horses grazed. A temporary fortification could be made ready almost overnight. If required, the whole thing could later be rebuilt in stone.

The sites of getting on for 60 motte-and-bailey castles have been identified in Dumfries & Galloway alone, testimony to the determination both of the Normans and the Scottish resistance. The Motte of Urr, outside Dalbeattie, is impressive enough as a mighty earthwork, even without the timber superstructure which once stood there. It's the same with Druchtag Motte, at Mochrum, southwest of Wigtown, and the motte at Doune of Inverlochty, Aberdeenshire – which also had a moat. Duffus Castle, outside Elgin, Moray, is a relatively modern construction, last significantly modified in the 18th century, but it stands atop the motte of a timber-built fortress from Norman times.

Some of Scotland's most celebrated castles pre-date this period but were rebuilt and seriously strengthened now. Those at Stirling and Edinburgh both occupy natural outcrops whose defensive qualities had been recognised way back into prehistoric times; so too did Urquhart Castle, beside Loch Ness. Other castles built as part of a more widespread process of pacification and rationalisation included Caerlaverock Castle, Dumfries & Galloway, with its distinctive triangular plan and its impressive moat (though this castle was radically refurbished and to some extent modernised in the early 17th century). Rothesay Castle, Bute, and Dunstaffnage Castle, north of Oban, are also products of this period. So is Duart Castle on the Isle of Mull, and the original Eilean Donan Castle would have been also – though what we see now is an imaginative confection of more modern times. Hermitage Castle, in the Borders, was built at this time too – though again what we see now are later redevelopments, albeit in this case dating only from the 14th century. The castles at Dirleton, East Lothian, Kildrummy, Aberdeenshire and Bothwell, South Lanarkshire, belong to the second half of the Norman period, having been built at various points during the 13th century.

Burgh Necessities

The serf working his lord's estate whilst scratching a living for his family from the little acre or so his lord allowed him; the lord himself in 'fiefdom' to a baron who held his lands directly from the king ... Feudalism may ultimately have been a system of social organisation but it had its basis in the management of land. As a reward for his services in the field of war, and in expectation of further support, the aristocrat was granted real fields for farming: the feudal world was envisaged as essentially rural, in other words.

Such an arrangement might make for social stability, but it was inherently conservative – even static – and so it didn't allow much scope for economic progress of any sort. Hence the decision of the Anglo-Norman kings to allow the licensing of 'burghs'. These little urban centres weren't tied to particular manors or estates; their tradesmen and craftsmen were absolved from the normal feudal bonds. The burghs occupied a place outside the normal feudal order in all day-to-day concerns, though they paid for this autonomy in regular taxes to the Crown.

One important aspect of the Davidian Revolution was the establishment of a collection of royal burghs. David I was barely on his throne before he chartered Berwick and Roxburgh in 1124. These two border towns were almost in England anyway, it might be argued: over the next few years, though, the burghs of Edinburgh, Stirling, Dunfermline, Perth and Scone would quickly follow, after which came others, like Elgin and Aberdeen. Burgh status brought with it a certain established set of political and economic privileges, such as toll- and tax-levying powers. A set sort of urban geography also emerged, which consisted of a walled town, dominated by its castle, with a main street and a market, complete with 'mercat cross', of the sort that's still to be seen in the centre of Forres (founded 1140) to this day. It also had certain set officials and interest groups: a provost (or mayor), baillies (senior councillors or magistrates) and burgesses (free townsmen). As in the English town of the time, craftsmen and merchants formed themselves into trade-guilds – part professional association, part trades union, part charity.

The chartering of burghs was to be an important engine of economic development in Scotland over the next few centuries. The last foundation (Ardrossan's) wasn't to be till 1846. By that time, historian George Smith Pryde calculates, there were no fewer than 482 burghs. Of these, 141 had been burghs since the medieval period. Long before the era of *No Mean City* and *Trainspotting*, Scottish society had been predominantly urban.

Monastic Scotland

As important as the burghs were in driving economic development in medieval Scotland, they had a rival in the religious houses of the time. As strange as this may sound in modern terms, in the Middle Ages it made perfect sense. As long ago as the 6th century, St Benedict had established his first

THE KINGDOM AND THE CLAN

'Wild' Scotland still existed. Out there in the 'land of the mountain and the flood', the agrarian economy on which feudalism had always been based couldn't really work; nor had the Norman ways in general been able to take hold to any great extent. Clan chieftains still held sway across the Highlands; there was a different way of doing things there, which would remain more or less in place till 1745.

Through that time, it would evolve, of course. It already was doing, the old Celtic sense of dùthchas (the idea of the people's loyalty to the local chief and his to them as their protector) gradually giving way to that of oighreachd, a license from the Crown that gave the chief a quasi-feudal title not just as leader but as landowner in his territories.

The association of lord with land, rather than with family, is key to the feudal system as classically imagined: so, for example, today's Aeneas Simon Mackay is Lord Reay (a place in Caithness) but Chief of the Mackays. The traditional clan chief allocated lands to his tacksmen, who, under the 'run rig' system, divided it up into strips, which were allocated in turn to be farmed a year at a time by junior members of the clan. This meant that everyone had their share of the best lands and had to take their turn with the worst. Widely idealised as egalitarian in spirit, run rig was also a way of weakening the identification between any individual and the land he farmed, and maintaining the personal authority of the clan chief.

monastery at Mount Cassino, south of Rome, a community of monks dedicated to a life of hard work, collective worship and private prayer. The 'Benedictine Rule' he'd drawn up then had no fewer than 73 clauses, covering everything from management hierarchies to clothing and prescribing fixed regimes for collective worship, private prayer and study.

But it also allowed time for daily stints of manual labour, which Benedict saw as an important way of suppressing personal pride and of giving praise to God. Spiritual contemplation wasn't just about meditation: the monks offered up their work to God, from consummate calligraphy to hard labour in the fields and creative time in workshops. The typical medieval monastery was as much an economic complex as a place of prayer. As consumers of foodstuffs and raw materials, and as producers of luxury goods, from mead and beer to books and metalwork, the monasteries grew crucial to the development of extensive hinterlands. As educators and employers too they had their impact on ways of life that had previously gone unchanged for centuries.

Such monasteries were rapidly becoming important centres of industry and trade; their abbots had influence with local rulers. Founded towards the end of the 11th century, Dunfermline Abbey was formally re-endowed in 1128 by David I as part of a larger complex, which included a royal palace for the king himself. Inchcolm Abbey, on an island in the Firth of Forth, also started out as a priory in the 11th century before its re-establishment by David in 1128. Another of his foundations, Holyrood Abbey, is now tucked away behind Holyrood Palace (which started out as a 15th-century development of the abbey's guesthouse). The tendency in modern times has been to feel that the institutions of church and state should be kept separate, but no such scruple seems to have been felt by medieval monarchs (or, for that matter, medieval prelates). Beside St Magnus' Cathedral in Kirkwall, Orkney (1137), stands the Bishop's Palace – indistinguishable from a noble's castle (the nearby Earl's Palace wasn't built till the 17th century). So grand were the archbishops of St Andrews that they built themselves a castle. Dunblane and Elgin Cathedrals also testify to the wealth of the Church in the 13th century.

Inevitably, some began to ask whether too high a spiritual price was being paid for the worldly wealth and political influence the Church had been accruing. A succession of reformist movements sought to take the monastic movement 'back to basics'. William the Pious' monastery at Cluny in France was the first of these, in the 9th century. Paisley Abbey was founded by followers of his in 1163, as was Crossraguel, in Ayrshire (1244). By that time, the Cistercian order had been founded (in 1098): again, its intention was to return to first Benedictine principles. In 1106, St Bernard of Thiron founded his Tironensians, the 'Grey Monks'. These reforming orders had been created just in time for the establishment of the great monasteries in the Scottish Borders. Kelso Abbey (1128) was a Tironensian foundation (as was Arbroath Abbey, created 50 years later by monks from Kelso). Melrose (1136), Newbattle (1140), Dundrennan (1142) and Glenluce (1190) were all Cistercian, as, later, were Culross (1217) and Sweetheart (1275) Abbeys. Walking the Borders Abbeys Way gives an impressive sense of the power of these old foundations and their influence upon the development of an entire region. Just over 100km (64 miles) around, it links Kelso, Jedburgh (1147), Melrose and Dryburgh (1150) Abbeys.

The economic impact of these monasteries was immediate. Richly endowed by benefactors (who hoped to benefit from the prayers of their monks as they embarked upon their afterlives), and straddling the spiritual and the material spheres, they didn't have to scrabble to survive, but could afford to experiment, pursue 'progressive' projects. The monks of Newbattle mined for lead and coal; the other Borders abbeys became important as centres for stockbreeding, especially sheep and horses. The monks were modernising landlords, helping their non-religious tenants to farm their own plots better and develop skills in blacksmithing, leather, textiles and other trades. Eventually, the power of the Church over trades and crafts would alienate the urban public: for now, though, the monasteries were seen as a force not just for good, but even for prosperity.

Monastic houses were important in other ways too: at Soutra Aisle, in Midlothian, are the remains of the House of the Holy Trinity, an Augustinian-run medieval hospital. In addition to the remains of masonry, traces of medicinal herbs and plants have been found, including hemlock, black henbane and (imported) opium poppies. This hospice is known to have continued functioning until the 17th century – some time after the Reformation, in other words.

Fish on Friday

The Catholic tradition of the Friday Fast, and the abstention from meat that this involved, was interpreted (in pre-vegetarian medieval times) as a Fish-on-Friday rule. This obviously made monasteries important consumers of fish (hence what's thought to have been a fishpond in the grounds of Sweetheart Abbey). More than this, though, it seemed only 'natural' for the Church to have a role in overseeing the fishing trade in general. So it was that the monks of Balmerino Abbey controlled fishing from the Fife port of Anstruther, whilst Arbroath harbour was developed and maintained by monks from the nearby abbey.

On the western shore of Loch Broom, northwestern Ross and Cromarty, an old *yair*, or fish trap, was built by medieval monks (though it was maintained and remained in use into the early 20th century). Basically, it was an underwater wall: fish swam in at high tide, then, just as the waters started to retreat, the narrow exit was sealed with a wattle barrier and fish speared or netted, perhaps from the skin-covered coracle boats that remained in use for fishing until early-modern times. Similar traps were made for salmon. Often natural inlets had only to be slightly modified, with a simple wickerwork barrier or *cruive*, as used by Augustinian monks from Cambuskenneth Abbey (founded 1140) on the Forth, downstream from Stirling. Another such *cruive* near Thurso caught 6,250 salmon at a single tide. Not that all fishing necessarily happened under the direct auspices of the Church. There's no obvious connection between any religious foundation and the medieval fishing village whose traces were discovered in 2012 on the shores of Loch Euport, North Uist. Over time, what had been a supplementary activity became a specialised industry in its own right: by the 14th century, boats with drift nets would have built a significant herring fishery in the Firths of Forth and Clyde.

Blessed Bones

Historic St Andrews as we see it today was a creation of the 12th century, though it's believed that by then there'd already been a monastery there for quite some time. It may have been as early as the 4th century that this little settlement became home to important relics of the apostle: to wit, three fingers of the right hand, an upper armbone, a kneecap and a tooth.

Protestants never would buy the Church's traditional insistence that objects like this weren't idolatrously worshipped but were, rather, venerated for the sake of the love and faith they represented. In Scotland such relics – which had till this point abounded the length and breadth of Christian Europe – were frequently destroyed or lost after the Reformation.

For an Enlightenment that struggled to see the rational sense in religious belief of any sort, beyond the acknowledged difficulty of imagining a universe without some supreme being as creator, these talismans seemed somehow primitive and grotesque. As, indeed, they do to most people – even to most religious people, perhaps – in our present time, which makes it hard to imagine the importance St Andrews had in the High Middle Ages.

For Freedom

THE SAINT AND THE SALMON

'Fishers of Men', Christ had called his proselytising apostles; and the ichthys, or 'Jesus Fish', is a centuries-old symbol of Christian faith. But the fish of fertility, the 'salmon of knowledge' – and, of course, the image of the stream of life – were important to Celtic paganism too. The story of St Mungo (6th century) and the Queen of Cadzow's Ring derives its resonance from all these different associations.

The unhappy queen, so the story goes, was asked for her ring and accused by her husband of infidelity when she could not produce it – even though he himself had stolen it and thrown it into the River Clyde. Frantic with distress, she came to see the saint and begged for help. He sent a servant to the river and told him to catch the first fish he could and bring it back to him. When they cut the salmon open, they found the missing ring inside.

The chroniclers of medieval times could obviously be slack by modern academic standards. Where hagiography (the writing of saints' lives) was concerned, the spiritual ends justified practically any historiographical means. Yet if this gave such stories the unreliability of myth, it also gave them the resonance, powerful and lasting: the cult of St Mungo was to go on till the Reformation and was to be an important factor in drawing pilgrims (and consequently trade) to Glasgow throughout that time.

Nonsense or not, then, the story of the salmon and the ring was to be quite significant enough to warrant a prominent role in the city's coat of arms. Glasgow's Gothic cathedral is dedicated to St Mungo: it was built from the 12th century onwards, on the site of the church the saint had founded in the 6th century, and beneath which his remains were reputed to have been buried.

Profitable Purgatory

The idea of Purgatory, an intermediate state or place to which the good but not-quite-saintly would be consigned to have their sins burned away to make them fit for final salvation, had taken hold in the course of the 5th century. Pope Gregory the Great had taken the idea further in the 6th century, arguing that prayerful observance or good deeds in this life could bring 'indulgence' – a remission of punishment in Purgatory. What had started out as an inspirational idea was soon a fully articulated system, with set periods of indulgence appointed for particular observances or acts: so many years off for a series of masses; so many for a donation to the poor; so many for a pilgrimage to Rome, to Jerusalem – or to St Andrews, whither thousands were soon coming from the farthest corners of Christian Europe.

It was a radical step (if, as the Protestant reformers were later to point out, completely unscriptural) and it re-energised Christianity, giving good but less-than-perfect men and women new grounds for hope. Few could hope to attain perfection, but all could strive to do better in their daily lives, to throw themselves into their regimes of prayer and charitable works. The other great thing about the system was that, since people could earn indulgence not just for themselves but for their departed loved ones, it fostered a sense of solidarity between the living and the dead.

Carl Watkins' *The Undiscovered Country – Journeys Among the Dead* (Vintage, 2013) paints a vivid picture of a medieval way of life in which this 'Church Suffering' (as the souls in Purgatory were called) formed part of an economic community that straddled the realms of this life and the next. The endowment of monasteries, churches, almshouses, donations of land and sums of money: these were gifts bequeathed by the dying to those who followed after. Golden chalices, jewelled reliquaries, stained-glass windows, wood-carvings – all the splendour of the medieval Church was underwritten by the dead, with wider consequences for the economy as a whole in St Andrews and Scotland.

The Prayer Factory

Built in the 1450s, so towards the end of Scotland's Catholic history, Rosslyn Chapel in Midlothian was inspired and shaped by the fondness for indulgences. The First Earl of Caithness, William Sinclair, wanted a place in which religious services could be offered in continuous succession round the clock in perpetuity, and he left the funds to allow this to take place. Rosslyn Chapel was, accordingly, intended as a sort of prayer-factory for the benefit of the souls of the devout dead in general and of the Sinclair family in particular.

By comparison with that original intention – to be confounded, of course, by the Reformation – the other 'mysteries' of Rosslyn, perpetuated by its starring role in *The Da Vinci Code*, don't actually seem all that strange. Not that this isn't an amazing place: indeed, it seems a bit of a pity to waste time with Knights Templar, the Holy Grail, Mary Magdalen, Freemasonry and all the other paraphernalia when there's such sumptuous stone statuary to be enjoyed.

Such peculiar stonework, at that – though it isn't necessarily all as strange as it may appear in isolation. The distinctive 'green man' heads – grotesque faces with vegetal stems and leaves growing out of their mouths – which so abound around the chapel were actually anything but unusual in the medieval scheme. Researcher Mike Harding estimated that there were five times as many green men in Exeter Cathedral as there were faces of Christ. Again, though, this is a case of the scholarly facts being stranger and more mysterious than the pop fiction.

Much work has been done on the study of the 'green man' – and the 'wild man' or *wodewose* – who preceded him in medieval art. It's still not clear quite what these figures represented. Nature, and humanity's relation to it, for sure – but from what perspective? It seems unlikely that Christian Europe would actually have looked back with nostalgia to some imagined primal, wild state; but the sense that civilisation had its discontents was well-recognised.

The sculpted 'maize cobs' (if that's what they really are) in Rosslyn Chapel are undoubtedly intriguing – even if they don't realistically amount to conclusive proof of pre-Columbian visits to the Americas, as has been suggested. The Apprentice Pillar is awe-inspiring in its elaboration, whatever its origins. The various bits of natural and scriptural imagery around the chapel are all beautifully done. The real 'masonic mysteries' to be found there, are, first, that of how the iconography is to be interpreted in conventional Christian terms and, second, how these craftsmen did such stunning work.

Pilgrims and Progress

It's in this wider context that we have to see the otherwise inexplicable grandeur of the medieval Church – even such limited remains as are still to be seen in what has for centuries now been an assertively post-Reformation Scotland. It's against this background too that we have to try to understand the 'point' of a place like St Andrews – an impressive ecclesiastical centre in the middle of nowhere. (OK, it has its university too, though historically this was very much secondary to the shrine...) It was, however, a major place of pilgrimage in the Middle Ages, a time when (as we see in Chaucer's *The Canterbury Tales*) this sort of spiritual tourism was an important industry, catering to men and women from every walk and rank of life.

And St Andrews was just the end-point of a pilgrimage route that ran all the way up through England and southern Scotland. North and South Queensferry (for the last century or so the termini for the two Forth Bridges) were traditionally established by Queen Margaret for the use of pilgrims. Another 'pilgrim ferry' plied regularly between North Berwick and Earlsferry, in Fife.

St Ninian's shrine, at Whithorn, was also a place of pilgrimage. Robert the Bruce came in 1329, during his final illness, stopping off at several sacred (and supposedly healing) wells en route through Galloway – it's believed he may have been suffering from leprosy. So too, at the end of the 15th century, did King James IV – to a town that had by now grown prosperous on the proceeds of pilgrimage. As Catriona McMillan points out in a fascinating report for the Whithorn Trust, however, by the late-16th century, pilgrimage had been made 'a punishable offence'.*

Even for a great many Catholics today it's hard to understand the simple piety that drove these pilgrims, but it's vital that we try to, if we're going to appreciate the historic implications of their quest. It wasn't just in its economic implications that this 'industry' mattered: feudal society was inherently static; people stayed put, both geographically and mentally. Pilgrimage put medieval society on the march.

Great Alexanders?

The 13th century saw Scotland slotting into something like its present-day form: the death of Alan of Galloway in 1234 (he was buried at Dundrennan Abbey) brought that region's independent existence to an end. It also helped to crystallise the situation in what had been the Kingdom of the Isles,

---

* www.gla.ac.uk/media/media_335306_en.pdf

founded by the Norse-Gaelic warlord Somerled some time in the mid-12th century, which still controlled the Inner and Outer Hebrides, plus Kintyre, parts of Argyll and the Isle of Man. Alan had been involved in a bitter dynastic struggle over this curiously-constituted offshore state.

The Treaty of York (1237) brought agreement between Alexander II and England's Henry III that, whilst Scotland's kings could keep feudal overlordship in certain lands in Cumbria and Northumberland, they would no longer claim royal rule over these northern English territories.

Alexander's son and successor, Alexander III, made it pretty much the point of his reign to establish Scottish sovereignty over the Kingdom of the Isles. At first, things seemed to be going in the other direction, with Norwegian forces harrying his shipping and raiding Scotland's western coast at will. But these attacks were curtailed by Scotland's victory at Largs, in 1263, when Alexander III's troops defeated a Norwegian force on the Ayrshire coast. Three years later, Norway's Magnus I signed over the Kingdom of the Isles to Alexander in the Treaty of Perth – though local lords were to retain a remarkable degree of autonomy.

Great Cause – and Effects

In 1286, Alexander III died suddenly. Riding out from Edinburgh Castle to visit Queen Margaret at Kinghorn, on the southern coast of Fife, on a wild and stormy night, he seems to have got separated from his attendants in the dark and ridden his horse over a cliff. His body was found on the rocks below when morning came, and his death is commemorated by a Victorian monument, which was erected on the site to mark its 600th anniversary. His death wasn't just a shock: it precipitated a dynastic crisis. Both his sons had died already and his nominated heiress – his granddaughter, Margaret, Maid of Norway – was only three years old. So the succession lay wide open, with 14 different claimants, including Robert Bruce 'the Competitor' (*the* Robert Bruce's grandfather). King Edward I of England was asked to referee the contest for the succession and demanded the right of overlordship – a 'right' that was angrily rejected by the Scots.

John Balliol's coronation in 1292 was an uneasy compromise. (Balliol's claim to the throne was as a descendant of King David I, 1124–53.) Far from respecting Balliol's rule, Edward I continued to insist on his overlordship. Under attack from his own side too, Balliol was quickly sidelined in favour of a 'Council of Twelve' who looked to France for support: the result, in 1295, was the (as yet brand new) 'Auld Alliance'. Edward reacted furiously, invading Scotland. He sacked Berwick-upon-Tweed, with great atrocities (anything up to 20,000 men, women and children are said to have been put to the sword) before defeating the Scots at Dunbar.

This engagement was probably fought on open ground some way to the southwest of the town by two forces of mounted knights, on the northern slopes of Brunt Hill, on either side of the Spott Burn. Catching up with John Balliol at Strathacro, near Montrose, Edward forced him to abdicate his throne. (By odd chance, in 2012, archaeologists investigating the Roman fortifications at this site along the Gask Ridge found medieval foundations, which may have belonged to the church where Balliol made his surrender to the English king.) Edward carried off the Stone of Scone, on which the kings of Scotland had traditionally been crowned, and had it placed in Westminster Abbey.

Wallace's Rising

The following year, William Wallace led a rebellion of minor nobles. On 11 September 1297, they met the Earl of Surrey's army at Stirling Bridge. Some 300 Scottish knights were matched against 10 times that many English cavalry, whilst

Wallace's 10,000 infantry faced up to 50,000 English foot-soldiers. We say 'Scottish' and 'English' here, and as a matter of geographical and genealogical fact the labels are no doubt fair enough, but this was arguably no more than a dispute between aristocratic groupings. The patriotic mantles were placed on both William Wallace and Robert Bruce in retrospect.

The heroism of Wallace's victory has justly been acclaimed, but this was a triumph too for tactical cunning and discipline. The medieval Stirling Bridge, which was built of wood, lay a little way upriver from the stone bridge we see today. The Scots waited on higher ground to the north, above the River Forth, on the slopes of the outcrop on which the Wallace Monument was later built. Not until the English vanguard had crossed the narrow bridge did they surge downhill and seize the bridge, cutting up the English advance-party while Surrey and his main army watched helplessly from the other side. Psychology did the rest: Wallace's victory had hardly been significant, let alone complete, but a demoralised Surrey ordered the retreat.

Enraged, Edward led a second invasion, with 2,000 knights and 10,000 infantry. On 22 July 1298, he met Wallace at Falkirk. Overwhelmingly outnumbered, the Scottish knights fled. Formed up in defensive *schiltroms* (a compact body of troops making a circular shield wall), however, the spearmen held firm, exacting heavy casualties from Edward's knights and infantry. Then the English king brought up his longbowmen: now the Scots in their static *schiltroms* were sitting ducks. The arrows opened up gaping holes in their formations, through which Edward's knights could charge. Hundreds were cut down as Wallace's revolt met its bloody end. The site of the battle isn't known for sure: one possibility, south of Callendar Wood, has at least the virtue of being visitable; the other, further to the north, centring on the area between the railway and the canal, is more or less completely built-over nowadays. (Neither is known to have yielded any archaeological finds.)

The Road to Bannockburn

As for William Wallace, he escaped to France and didn't return to Scotland till 1303. But he was caught and taken down to London for execution two years later. Born in 1274, meanwhile, the grandson of John Balliol's great rival 'the Competitor' had been more interested in furthering his family's ambitions than his nation's (if, again, he'd even have understood that word). Having sworn fealty to Edward I in 1296, Robert Bruce promptly joined a Scottish revolt; he switched his allegiances several times thereafter. Not until 1306 did he commit himself irrevocably to the Scottish cause after killing John Comyn, his main rival for the throne of Scotland, in a fight. He was quickly crowned King Robert I, but now had enemies both in England and in Comyn's family, who, with Edward I's support, surprised Robert at Methven, near Perth, in 1306. (The site can be reached along the little track that continues on along the valley of the burn when College Road, off Main Street, crooks off at right angles to the left.)

Bruce's army was almost entirely wiped out, and Robert was forced to flee. He's thought to have lain low on Rathlin Island, off Ulster's Antrim coast, though it's not certain. It was at this time that the episode (or story) of 'Bruce and the Spider' would have taken place. Not until early the following year did he feel confident enough to risk returning to Scotland. Even then, he landed in what was still the semi-detached earldom of Carrick and Galloway – coming ashore by a supporter's castle at Turnberry, on the Ayrshire coast.

In the months that followed, he relaunched his campaign. Short of knightly forces, though, he was reduced to waging a guerrilla war. In April 1307, his men rolled giant boulders down a steep hillside on to an unsuspecting English army in Glen Trool, deep in what is now the Galloway Forest Park. A monument – fittingly enough, a great granite stone – marks the site of this engagement. It can barely be called a battle, but Bruce took his triumphs where he could find them.

Gradually, he rebuilt his strength and his supporters' spirits. Events south of the border contributed to the more upbeat mood. Edward I had only too obviously warranted his historic nickname, the 'Hammer of the Scots', but he died in the summer of 1307. His son, Edward II, was weak and indecisive. The stories of his homosexuality may or may not have been true – we've no way of knowing – but they do suggest that he wasn't held in high regard by those who should have been his strongest supporters. He was eventually deposed by his wife and her lover, of course. At this time, however, England's king could still call upon a big and powerful army. Over 2,000 knights and 14,000 infantrymen came north with him in 1314. They met Robert's forces south of Stirling, in open country beside a stream – the Bannock Burn.

A Famous Victory

On 23 June, during preliminary manoeuvring, an English knight noticed Bruce on his horse out in open ground some distance from his own front line. Unarmoured, he was carrying only a battleaxe. The knight charged, lance lowered for the kill. Refusing to flinch in sight of his watching soldiers, Scotland's king calmly sidestepped and swung his axe, splitting the Englishman's helmet and skull wide open. An impressive display of aplomb – and an omen for the next day's battle.

Again, the Scots infantry formed *schiltroms*, bristling with long spears; the English cavalry had to retreat with heavy losses. In the years since Falkirk, however, the Scots had learned to press forward without losing shape: the *schiltrom* was no longer a purely defensive formation. As the Scots advanced, their enemy were forced back. The English turned and fled, losing hundreds more lives in their chaotic stampede across the Bannock Burn. (Some have felt that the elaborate graphics in the NTS visitor centre at the site make a

THE DECLARATION OF ARBROATH

Bannockburn left Bruce a hero. Even now, though, he was apparently on probation. What is widely seen as Scotland's founding document, the Declaration of Arbroath, ostensibly a letter to Pope John XXII in Avignon signed by the Scottish lords at a meeting at Arbroath Abbey in 1320, was as much and as explicitly a warning to Robert Bruce. If he did sell Scotland out to England, they warned, then:

> we should exert ourselves at once to drive him out
> as our enemy and a subverter of his own rights and
> ours, and make some other man who was well able
> to defend us our King; for, as long as but a hundred
> of us remain alive, never will we on any conditions
> be brought under English rule.

Till now we've taken care to make – if not to labour – the point that 'patriotism' as we might understand it had no real place in 'Scotland's' struggle. Now that it was starting to, it was very clearly in opposition to an English 'Other'.

computer-game out of Scotland's freedom struggle, but they do help make more sense of what can be a confusing scene.)

Robert Bruce died in 1329, upon which his body was buried at Dunfermline Abbey – all except his heart, which, at his own express wish, was cut out, embalmed and taken on crusade. Bruce's friend, Sir James Douglas, did the honours, taking his late friend's heart with him to Granada, southern Spain, to smite the Saracen, before bringing it back for formal interment in Melrose Abbey.

Defeat ... and Beyond

This was Scotland's finest hour: the Treaty of Edinburgh–Northampton, 1328 (which was approved by Robert Bruce in the former city and by representatives of England in the latter), acknowledged Scotland's right to exist as an independent nation. But Edward II's son and successor, Edward III, was cast in his grandfather's mould. He made common cause with the disgruntled 'Disinherited' faction (the Balliols and their supporters) against Robert the Bruce's young son, King David II. In 1332, John Balliol's son, Edward, defeated the Scottish army at Dupplin Moor, on the northern bank of the River Earn, a few kilometres southwest of Perth. He had his knights fight on foot, while his archers rained in arrows from either flank. He was unable to build on that victory, but a year later Edward III came to his assistance.

By July 1333, Berwick was under siege, and when Sir Archibald Douglas' Scottish army came to its relief, the English king inflicted a crushing defeat on it at Halidon Hill, just north of the city. Berwick itself surrendered the next day. The capture of Berwick had broken down the door. Full-scale English occupation appeared inevitable: it was merely a matter of how long it took. The Scots offered some small-scale resistance, with hit-and-run attacks and skirmishes, but they avoided the head-on confrontation they knew they could not win.

In the event, though, time was to come to their assistance. Their strategy of harrying and hoping may have been born of abject despair, but it was ultimately to succeed beyond their wildest dreams. England's momentum ebbed away as the 1330s went on: in 1338, a Dunbar garrison led for the occasion by 'Black Agnes' Randolph (her husband, Patrick, having been caught away from home) held out successfully against a six-month siege by William Montagu, the Earl of Salisbury, and his army.

Through the 1340s, Edward III became more and more preoccupied by his hostilities with France (during the first phase of the Hundred Years' War). At the highest levels, England might be in the ascendant: in 1357, David II signed the Treaty of Berwick with Edward, agreeing that the English king should succeed him in Scotland on his death. But the Scots nobles never accepted this and appointed their own king, Robert II, when David died in 1371. And, in the event, England was powerless to prevent them.

BLACK-ISH DEATH

The Black Death wasn't quite so black as it's been painted, at least in Scotland. Indeed, the kingdom might have entirely escaped what was complacently referred to as 'the foul death of the English' had not its army mounted an opportunistic raid across the border into an afflicted England, in 1349. The troops got as far as Selkirk Forest before being struck down by plague, which they promptly carried  *straight back with them to Edinburgh. By 1350, the plague had arrived in Glasgow. Rather than the bubonic plague, however, it may have been the pneumonic version of the disease, which spreads the* Yersinia pestis *bacterium on the breath, for no archaeological evidence of rats at the Scottish sites of the period has been found.*

Scotland didn't just succumb comparatively late to the infection: it's thought to have got off fairly lightly – its population was small and relatively scattered, hindering the disease's spread.

The Clach a' Phlàigh or 'Plague Stone' at Fortingall, Perthshire, is said to mark the grave (in what had originally been a Bronze-Age burial mound) in which victims were interred during the Black Death. The corpses, says the stone's inscription, were 'taken here on a sledge drawn by a white horse led by an old woman'.

THREE

BOUNDARY
ISSUES

SCOTLAND WAS INDEPENDENT BY DEFAULT as the 14th century approached its end, but its autonomy was anything but secure. Nor, for that matter, was its domestic situation, the precariousness of the kingdom's position creating uncertainty and suspicion. A new wave of castle-building bears testimony to continuing instability. During this period, both Tantallon (East Lothian) and Threave (Dumfries & Galloway) Castles were built by the Douglas family – aristocratic rivals to the early Jameses – for example. Doune Castle, near Stirling, was built (or at least substantially reinforced) around this time too, as a stronghold for the Duke of Albany, Robert II's son. Meanwhile, that king's son-in-law and supporter, John Lyon, was building Glamis Castle (1376). Robert II himself built Ayrshire's Dundonald Castle in the 1370s.

English-style barons were now dominating Scotland – nominally, at least, under the king, though it's interesting that the Scots invasion that ended with a notable victory over the English at Otterburn, in August 1388, seems to have been a more or less unilateral action on the Earl of Douglas' part. The Preston family built an imposing headquarters at Craigmillar Castle, south of Edinburgh, in the 14th century. Castle Campbell, outside Dollar, Clackmannanshire, was built in the 1430s, whilst Sir George Crichton's Blackness Castle, on a headland on the southern shore of the Firth of Forth outside Linlithgow, followed a decade later.

Subject to Debate

There were actual Debatable Lands – their title disputed between England and Scotland – for a couple of hundred years, though these were just a small pocket, stretching some 10 miles or so inland from the Solway Firth through southern Dumfriesshire, divided between the two countries in an agreement of 1552. But less orderly 'debate' existed along the whole line of the frontier, and wide areas on either side were subject to raiding, or 'reiving', back-and-forth for centuries. Raiders from the Scottish side pushed as far south as Richmond, Yorkshire; English attackers struck as far north as Biggar.

As with earlier wars, though, it's anachronistic to see this conflict as a war of nations as we might understand it now: the reivers' first loyalties seem to have been to their families and their supporters, and they didn't necessarily spare their own compatriots where there were spoils to be won. Things weren't really to settle down along this wild frontier till the Union of the Crowns in 1603 – and even then it took concerted action on King James' part.

As a result, the Borders were well stocked with fortified homes of one sort or another – the castle's transition from fortress to status symbol was yet to happen there. These included tower houses. Orchardton Tower, south of Dalbeattie, would look very ordinary elsewhere, with its rounded, cylindrical shape, but this very fact makes it unique in Scotland. Scottish tower houses – like most Scottish castles from the late-medieval period on – are boxlike with angled corners: if they aren't actually square, they're L- or T-shaped.

The 15th-century Cardoness Castle, outside Gatehouse of Fleet, Dumfries & Galloway, has a square plan, for example, whilst Darnick Tower, outside Melrose (1425) is T-shaped. Smailholm Tower, west of Kelso (15th–16th centuries) and Horsburgh Tower, east of Peebles on the A72, both have straightforward, square ground-plans; the 16th-century Greenknowe Tower, northeast of Earlston, is L-shaped. The demarcation between the full-sized 'tower house' and the shorter, stubbier 'pele', or 'peel', tower isn't definitive. Most experts, though, would argue that constructions like Fatlips Castle, on the Minto Crags northwest of Denholm, and Slack's and Mervinslaw Towers, south of Jedburgh (both 16th century) are 'peles'.

'Bastle' houses aren't much to look at. The name is supposedly a Scots rendering of *bastille*, the French word for 'fortress', though thoughts of the Paris mob attacking a mighty castle aren't especially helpful here. Really, these redoubts are just fortified farmhouses with super-thick stone walls. But it must have been good to have those to rely on when the reivers came. There are remains at Windgate, in Lanarkshire, but not much beyond the foundations and the outline of the walls. Whisper it, but the best bastles today are to be seen on the Northumberland side – at Rebellion House, High Callerton, or Black Middens, near Bellingham (both from the 16th century), or Woodhouses, west of Hepple (1602). Unspectacular they may be, but these squat civilian blockhouses underline how dangerous life in the Borders could be for the most ordinary farming family.

Local Patriotisms

There's an old medieval English tradition – recently revived in several places – of 'beating the bounds'. Parents and parish priest went in procession with the youth of the village around all its boundary stones and lashed them (the boundary stones mostly, but sometimes the youths as well) with rods or branches. This instilled a rigorous understanding of where their home community ended and the next began. Which was important from a fiscal, administrative, legal and land-management point of view in an agrarian society in an age before sophisticated mapping – or even much literacy. The presence of the priest – who blessed both the boundaries and the land of the village – gave this ritual a religious dimension, if not necessarily a solemn one.

The Common Ridings that sprang up in the 14th century in towns like Lauder, Langholm, Selkirk and Hawick clearly shared some features of the English tradition: again, they centred on a ceremonial marking-out of the communities' boundaries. Here, though, there's the additional sense (understandable, given the region's history) that the boundaries were being reaffirmed in a spirit of defensiveness, defiance. Today, it's all good festive fun, albeit with a distinct air of militarism (however tongue-in-cheek): at Selkirk, for instance, a flag is carried to commemorate a banner captured by a local man in 1513 – very much against the run of play, at Flodden. A similar flag at Hawick recalls one captured the following year in an otherwise-forgotten fight in which local men sent a raiding party packing back to England.

Some Common Ridings are of much more recent introduction. They're 'invented traditions', in E.J. Hobsbawm and T.O. Ranger's term. But (as those authors would themselves have realised) that doesn't necessarily invalidate the annual rideouts at Musselburgh (1935) and Jedburgh (1947): they're much newer, sure, but are they in any sense less 'historic'? If, in some communities, the realities of Border living fostered a fierce local patriotism, the 20th century brought new challenges of its own. These didn't have to be so high-flown as the modern existential concerns that caused the poet Hugh MacDiarmid, in *A Drunk Man Looks at the Thistle* (1926), to hark back so longingly to boyhood fun in Langholm ('Drums in the Walligate, pipes in the air,/Come and hear the cryin' o' the Fair./A' as it used to be, when I was a loon/On Common Ridin' day in the Muckle Toon.') But they clearly answer to some need for community connection, nonetheless.

The Lordship of the Isles

Even more 'debatable' than the Borders in some respects, the Western Isles had remained largely autonomous throughout this period. The founder of the Kingdom of the Isles, Somerled, had been so ambitious for his state that he'd actually launched an invasion of the mainland, in the course of which, in around 1164, he'd died. His fall, at the Battle of Renfrew (the site's supposed to be in the area around Teucheen Wood, Inchinnan – just a javelin's throw from the A8, behind what is now Balmoral Crescent), didn't bring down his kingdom, but it was clearly a serious setback.

Whilst the lords of the Western Isles essentially remained in power, they were increasingly overshadowed by a Stuart Crown, which finally and formally established actual control in 1493, during the reign of James IV. The ruins of Finlaggan Castle, Loch Finlaggan, Islay, where the lords convened their councils between the 13th and 15th centuries, are fairly scanty now but can still be seen.

Commerce and Culture

It wasn't all war and raiding: Scotland by now was a significant trading nation, with a busy commerce with its northern European neighbours. The exchange of raw wool, not only for finished textiles but for a wide variety of other products, was governed by various agreements. One of William Wallace's first actions after pulling off his famous victory at Stirling Bridge in 1297 had been to dash off the Lübeck Letter, informing that city's burghers that a Scotland 'recovered by war from the power of the English' was back in business. What is known as the 'Staple' trade with the Low Countries had been established as early as the 1320s: Scottish trade with Flanders went first through Bruges, then later through Middleburg and Veere.

There had been brisk business between Scotland and France as well since the treaty of 1295: this would only grow as the Auld Alliance was strengthened. There was contact, too, with the Hanseatic League – which, since 1358, had brought together the major Baltic ports into a single trading entity – though Scotland's links with Danzig seem to have been particularly close. (The merchant William Forbes was to build

Craigievar Castle (1626), one of Scotland's most spectacular piles, outside Alford, Aberdeenshire, with the profits he had made in the Danzig trade.) And, of course, except in times of war, there was an important maritime trade with England, at a time when land transport was still difficult and slow.

The trade by sea, at least to begin with, was very local in its character, with a great many little ports sending small vessels out in all directions. That didn't mean that it wasn't profitable. The Pier House Museum at Symbister, on Whalsay in the Shetlands, gives a sense of the prosperity that could be enjoyed by a truly tiny port. Another Hanseatic *böd*, or 'booth', was built at Hillswick, on the western coast of Shetland's Mainland. Gradually, though, bigger ships were being built and economies being found in scale: from the 15th century, bigger ports like Leith grew in importance. Timber, iron, wine and other luxuries were all imported, while, along with the raw materials (wool, linen, coal and salt), a stream of Scottish entrepreneurs and agents flowed in the other direction.

Not all Poles were too impressed by the Caledonian immigrants they now found in their midst: one, the noble Lukasz Opalinksi, commented: 'This nation, ashamed of its miserable and barren fatherland, flees over the seas and seeks its fortune in Poland.' For the most part, though, the contacts between Scotland and the Baltic were more positive; they were certainly enduring. They were also to occasion alarm in London. In the 17th century, King Christian IV (of Denmark and Norway) was suspected of giving support for Covenanters (devotees of the Presbyterian doctrine, and bitter opponents of England's King Charles I – see Chapter Four, Covenant and Crown). Not that the 'other side' didn't have connections too: the Swedish city of Gothenburg's support for the former Covenanter, now-Royalist James Graham, Montrose, in 1649, was vital, though it was to be withdrawn when he seemed to have fallen out of favour with Charles I.

Going Dutch

The traffic was not just to be in commodities but in ideas, difficult as this may be to pin down in retrospect. They are to be found in concrete form, though, in the Dutch-influenced architecture to be seen in Crail, southeastern Fife, whose tollbooth wouldn't be out of place in an old city square in the Netherlands; or Culross, which boasts a beautiful and characterful Townhouse; or Anstruther Wester, whose White House (on the Harbour Esplanade) has several distinctively Dutch features. The red rooftiles on so many buildings in Anstruther, Culross, and other Fife ports are said to have been brought over as ballast in ships returning from the Low Countries. Similar tiles can be seen on some of the roofs in Dunbar, East Lothian.

Built in the 1640s, Edinburgh's Tron Kirk had a number of Dutch features, but the most striking one – its steeple – was lost in a fire of 1824 and never fittingly replaced. The 'corbie-stepped' gables to be seen on so many old buildings on the east coast – not just the Culross Townhouse but the Stonehaven Tollbooth, Muchalls Castle, Aberdeenshire, and Monboddo House, Kincardine – could equally well be Dutch or Hanseatic in origin. Lamb's House, on the Shore in Leith, which was built in 1610, has spacious storage on its lower floors and a dwelling-area above and is essentially a Hanseatic merchant's house in Scotland.

Auld and Past It?

Scotland's invasion of England in 1513 was mounted in support of the French and of the 'Auld Alliance'. England's Henry VIII was away in France campaigning and had left Queen Catherine (of Aragon) minding the shop. An optimistic army mustered south of Edinburgh on the Borough Muir – by the so-called Burgh Stane, now set into a wall on the eastern side of Morningside Road, south of Church Hill.

FLOWERS OF THE FOREST

This famous lament commemorating Scotland's losses at Flodden has come to serve as a commemorative lament for all those lost in war. Various lyrics have been written for what seems to have been a much earlier folk tune. The best known are those by Jean Elliot, 1756:

> I've heard the lilting, at the yowe-milking,
> Lassies a-lilting before dawn o' day;
> But now they are moaning on ilka green loaning;
> The Flowers of the Forest are a' wede away...

Jean Elliot died at Monteviot House, near Jedburgh, in 1805. The fact that she wrote her famous lament over two centuries after the battle it memorialises is a reminder of the semi-mythic status the defeat at Flodden was to have.

Catherine, however, was proving a more effective war-leader than might have been imagined: she'd lost no time in giving the order for an army to be raised and in sending Thomas Howard, Earl of Surrey, marching northward at its head.

Fought on 9 September 1513, near Branxton, Northumberland (there's a visitor centre of sorts there), the Battle of Flodden resulted in a crushing defeat for the Scots; a crippling blow to Scottish self-esteem. But pride wasn't the only casualty, by any means: 17,000 Scots are believed to have been killed in the engagement, which was unusually bloody for a battle of its time. Along with the 'flowers' of the nation's nobility, these included King James IV himself. In the panic-stricken aftermath, the people of Edinburgh threw up the Flodden Wall around their city to protect their homes.

It was scant consolation to Scotland that a group of patriots disguised as Frenchmen soon after succeeded in hijacking Henry VIII's entire wine fleet and diverted it to Aberdeen. (However, an agent for John Dudley, the future Duke of Northumberland, bought it on his behalf and forwarded it to the English king as an ingratiating favour.)

Between 1636 and 1638, the Flodden Wall was extended to enclose new land bought by the city beyond Greyfriars' Kirk. This extension now largely forms the boundary of George Heriot's School, which subsequently bought the land, but the section known as the Telfer Wall (after the master mason working on it, John Taillefer) can still clearly be seen from outside the school on Lauriston Place.

Rough Treatment

The 1540s brought the 'Rough Wooing', so called because it stemmed from Scotland's refusal to accept Henry VIII's insistent urging that his son Edward VI and James V's daughter, Mary (the future Queen of Scots), should one day wed. The quarrel was in many ways academic as Edward (born 1537) was still some years off adulthood, whilst his putative bride (born 1542) was a tiny child being brought up in France.

The 'roughness' was real enough, though, Edinburgh and Dundee both being sacked in what was really a series of conflicts. In November 1542, James V was killed at Solway Moss (the battlefield lies north of the A6021, midway between Gretna and Longtown). Hawthornden Castle, near Eskdale's Rosslyn Chapel, was sacked in 1544, though the tables seemed to be turning when the Scots won the Battle of Ancrum Moor (the site's a couple of miles north of Ancrum, east of the A68 to St Boswell's).

The Battle of Pinkie (1547) proved climactic, though –
and historically significant, not only as the last full-on fight
between Scottish and English armies but as an early example
of what we'd now call 'combined operations'. English ships,
at anchor, bombarded a massive phalanx of Scottish pike-
men as they surged across the Esk just yards upstream of its
estuary outside Musselburgh, while the Duke of Somerset's
cavalry countered, and his infantry pretty much stood by on
the eastern bank. Anything up to 10,000 Scots were killed,
to approximately 250 English casualties. The English occupied the southeast of Scotland, setting up a separate base at
Dundee, with a headquarters in Broughty Castle.

The Dissolution of the Monasteries of 1536 hadn't
affected the Scottish religious foundations directly, but what
we might now call 'sectarian' attacks by English soldiers in
the course of the Rough Wooing caused untold damage to
the abbeys at Melrose, Kelso, Dryburgh and Jedburgh, for
example. (In this sense, much of the iconoclasm carried out
in Scotland – the breaking of stained-glass and statues and
the whitewashing over of religious images – predated the
actual Reformation in the country.)

Popery Prolonged

Henry VIII may have roughed up Scotland, but he'd never
actually reigned here. So, for a long time, Scotland sat out
the Reformation … officially, at least. Patrick Hamilton
became Scotland's first martyr for (Lutheran) Protestantism
in 1528 – he was burned at the stake in front of St Salvator's,
St Andrews. George Wishart followed him in 1546. You can
see monuments where these executions took place. There
was widespread anger at this ruthlessness, and conspiracies
against Cardinal David Beaton – who was seen as something
of a figurehead for religious reaction. A couple of months
after Wishart's death, a group of local lairds blagged their

way into St Andrews Castle and assassinated the Cardinal before displaying his mutilated corpse outside.

A great many of the minor aristocracy were sympathetic to reforming ends, in fact. In the course of the Middle Ages, as we've seen, the Church had become thoroughly knitted, not just into the institutions of Scottish life but into its economic structures. This had been fine up to a point, but had eventually caused friction at local level, bringing important clergy into conflict with both the burghs and the lairds. James V's brinkmanship can't have helped: whilst essentially loyal in his religious allegiances, he'd flirted with the Lutheran powers of northern Europe to wind up the Pope and win concessions, but this had arguably given his people implicit 'permission' to take things further.

Blasts and Bombardments

James V's death in 1542 left a near-vacuum, his newborn daughter Mary having to 'rule' under the regency of her mother, Mary of Guise. That the Regent reacted to Protestant and English pressure by seeking support from the (Catholic) French government didn't help the situation. The passing of Henry VIII in 1547 didn't bring the relief the Regent and her supporters had been hoping for. Only nine when he came to the throne, Edward VI of England was easily underestimated in his own day. (Subsequently, too: Henry's successor died aged just 15 after a short and sickly reign, so it's been tempting for history to write him off as a 'lame duck' king.) He was bright and educated, though, deeply curious about all things theological and seriously committed to the cause of Protestantism. In this particular sphere, then, he had much more impact than is generally assumed.

Mary of Guise's initial reaction to young Edward's accession was to up the stakes in her dispute with England, in 1548 bringing in French troops to garrison her capital city of Edinburgh. But if such a show of defiance made it clear to England that its northern neighbour wasn't to be bullied, it sent out a message to the Regent's Scottish Protestant subjects too. So did the accession of the Catholic 'Bloody' Mary I after Edward's death in 1553: Protestantism, it seemed, was seriously under threat. Hence the role of the 'Lords of the Congregation' (or, as they called themselves, the 'Faithful Congregation of Christ Jesus in Scotland') from 1557. The group first crystallised around opposition to the marriage of the young Princess Mary to the Dauphin, François II, which they felt threatened to set the Auld Alliance in stone and make Scotland a French satellite. But the group became an influential voice for the reform movement in general. John Knox's *The First Blast of the Trumpet Against the Monstrous Regiment of Women* (1558) may have been as misogynistic as has always been assumed, but his main objection to the 'regiment' (or rule) of Mary of Guise and Mary I of England was their shared commitment to the Catholic cause.

England was, of course, no happier with the idea of a French-dominated Scotland than the Scottish lords were, so was only too ready to come to their aid with discreet support – and, in April 1560, with direct military assistance. The French were sent packing from Edinburgh after a naval bombardment of the port of Leith so intense that, one eyewitness wrote, 'the stones in the street, the tiles, and slates of the houses flew about.'

Religious conflict may have masked more political rivalries: it generally does. But real theological issues were very definitely at stake. In 1560, Walter Adie described the sacrament of the Eucharist as 'The Devil's dirt'. That same year, after a meeting of Kirk and aristocratic leaders at Holyroodhouse, a reformist 'Scots Confession' of Faith was issued.

NOT AT HOME

John Knox's House, on Edinburgh's High Street, is well worth a visit as one of the Scottish capital's oldest buildings, dating from 1470. The preacher only stayed there a few weeks, though – if he ever even visited at all. The real John Knox's House was a little

way up the hill in Warriston Close, joining High Street to Cockburn Street to the north, though there's no more than a plaque where his residence used to be. After his death in 1572 he was buried not far away in what's now the little car park behind the High Kirk of St Giles.

Mary in the Mix

Mary Queen of Scots didn't actually come back to her home country until after François' death in 1561 – just in time for the Reformation, in other words. Which was unfortunate for a devout, if naïve, Catholic who arrived in an Edinburgh from which her French protectors had just been unceremoniously dislodged. She found Scotland's Catholic supporters demoralised, its Protestant leaders cock-a-hoop.

Romanticised in retrospect, Mary was undoubtedly an appealing figure in some respects: intelligent and accomplished, she brought a bit of French fashion and civilisation with her when she came (one of her pages was the future poet Pierre de Ronsard). But she had a huge culture clash with the macho, Protestant Scottish lords and their patriarchal clergy. James V's daughter pretty much personified the Auld Alliance, and her presence polarised things in what was already a divided country.

Boundary Issues

This is perhaps the first period in Scottish history from which a fairly dense concentration of real-life (as opposed to later, simply memorialising) monuments survive. Mary had been born in Linlithgow Palace (which, though built in the 14th century, had burned down and been rebuilt in the 15th). As Queen she was to give birth to her son, James, in Edinburgh Castle and to live in Holyroodhouse – where, in 1566, her secretary and alleged lover, David Rizzio, was murdered. Her then-husband Henry Stuart, Lord Darnley, who'd had the Italian killed, was murdered himself the following year in the Provost's Lodgings in the central court of the Kirk o' Fields (which was where Edinburgh's Chambers Street is now, near the National Museum) by James Hepburn, Earl of Bothwell, who went on to marry her – albeit quite possibly by coercion. And whilst there's nothing to see at 'Little France', outside the city, where her courtiers set up their own little Gallic exclave on arriving in Scotland, the name lives on as the location of the new Edinburgh Royal Infirmary.

In fact, you can pretty much do the Mary Queen of Scots Trail, taking in some of the long list of Scottish castles and palaces she at one point or another lived in, visited, or took refuge in as she fled the various factions who pursued her during her 'reign'. Linlithgow, Edinburgh, Holyroodhouse, Dumbarton, Stirling, Craigmillar, Tantallon, Hailes, Crichton, Borthwick, Dunbar, Loch Leven ... the list goes on. She suffered her final defeat in Scotland in 1568 (one year after she had actually abdicated in favour of her son, James VI) at Langside – now a southern suburb of Glasgow: there's a Battle Place there, with a commemorative monument. Losing there, she was left no option but to throw herself on the mercies (none too tender, as it turned out) of her relation, England's Elizabeth I. Queen Bess saw Mary as, at best, a destabilising influence among her own country's Catholic-sympathisers and, at worst, an active conspirator against her, and so kept Mary prisoner and had her executed in 1587.

Troubled Times

These were violent, slightly anarchic times: Linlithgow High Street became the scene (on 23 January 1570) of the assassination of the infant James VI's Regent, James Stuart, the Earl of Moray. Riding through the town in cavalcade, he was shot at from a window above, JFK-style, by James Hamilton, a supporter of the exiled Mary. Suspicion was rife, with many Protestants convinced that their Reformation was being stolen from them, its advances clawed back by the Catholic party in the country. Or, as John Knox's friend John Craig put it in the 'Negative' or 'King's Confession' he drafted in 1581:

> *many are stirred up by Satan, and that Roman Antichrist, to promise, swear, subscribe, and for a time use the holy sacraments in the kirk deceitfully, against their own conscience; minding hereby, first, under the external cloak of religion, to corrupt and subvert secretly God's true religion within the kirk; and afterward, when time may serve, to become open enemies and persecutors of the same, under vain hope of the Pope's dispensation, devised against the word of God, to his greater confusion, and their double condemnation in the day of the Lord Jesus.*

Essentially, this new confession was just a reiteration of the 'Scots Confession' of 1560: the fact that it didn't seem redundant is remarkable. In hindsight it's hard to imagine Scotland being in any serious danger from the 'Roman Antichrist', but that was certainly the fear that haunted powerful Protestants in the country.

Hence the Ruthven Raid of 1582 – in practical terms, a coup. Now 16 years old, King James VI was abducted while out hunting near Ruthven (now Huntingtower) Castle, outside Perth, and taken first to that city (to the Provost's House) and thence to Stirling Castle. Where Hamilton had resented James' effective usurpation of his Catholic mother, these conspirators questioned his Protestant loyalty. James managed to escape after being held for 10 months and took refuge in St Andrews Castle. He regained his throne, but in the meantime his conspirators had passed legislation that effectively licensed their earlier actions. But when they made a second attempt to oust their king, encouraged – it's widely believed – by England's Elizabeth I, their plot was foiled and they themselves were executed. There are earlier influences, of course (see page 41) but it's been suggested that, at least in part, this plot may have inspired Shakespeare's *Macbeth*.

A Church for Scotland

Protestantism Scottish-style, or Presbyterianism, is rooted in Calvinist thinking, whereas Anglicanism, as it developed, looked to Lutheranism for its inspiration. For most of us in modern times, Calvinism has been associated with a certain sort of wild religious rhetoric – about hell and its fires, damnation and salvation. But arguably of more importance were some of the wider attitudes that sprang from the theology. Calvin's view was that the individual soul was to be saved only by God's predestined will. That being so, ecclesiastical institutions – any human institutions, indeed – could do no more than offer administrative structures for what remained essentially a personal relationship between the individual soul and God.

The Church of Scotland governed itself through a series of courts, councils of elders. Kirk Sessions were held at grass-roots level – one for each church; then there were local Presbyteries, above which were regional Synods and, at the very top, the General Assembly, with its own imposing hall at the top of the Mound in Edinburgh. But these organisational levels didn't represent a hierarchy of authority and power as they might in other denominations, such as Roman Catholicism and, to some extent, Anglicanism and

Episcopalianism (which, crucially, recognised the authority of the king and his appointed bishops).

The fact that, in charismatic preachers like John Knox and others, Presbyterianism tended to involve a more fiery rhetoric and uncompromising puritanism than Episcopalianism was not in itself the problem in the eyes of the Scottish and English Crowns. But the intense emphasis on individual piety, and the view that the individual soul was to be saved only by God's predestined will, meant that Presbyterianism and Calvinism had an in-built contempt for the earthly authorities of Church and state. To the absolutist Stuarts, then, Presbyterianism was a rebellion waiting to happen. As we shall see, the Stuart kings would take steps – such as insisting on the need for bishops – to try and keep the Presbyterians in their place.

Witching Hour

If Protestantism in Scotland arguably opened the door to a certain democratisation of attitudes, it opened the door to some less appealing things as well. One of these was witch-phobia, at which the Roman Church had scoffed for centuries, refusing to grant that the Devil and his spirits could have the sort of powers that were attributed to them in popular belief. (Catholicism had, it's true, been turning this way too to some extent, with the publication of *Malleus Maleficarum*, 1487, though it seems to have been much more interested in the interface between supposed 'magic' and religious heresy.) In 1080, Pope Gregory VII had written to Denmark's King Harold explicitly forbidding him from executing 'witches' accused of causing crop failures or storms. It was, ironically, from Denmark that King James VI was returning, after going to fetch his bride, Queen Anne, when he was very nearly shipwrecked and became convinced that he'd been the object of witches' spells.

James, notoriously, became an enthusiast for this new Protestant crusade, even publishing a pamphlet on the subject, *Daemonologie* (1597). In his Preface he explained his motivation:

> *The fearefull aboundinge at this time in this countrie, of these detestable slaues of the Deuill, the Witches or enchaunters, hath moved me (beloued reader) to dispatch in post, this following treatise of mine, not in any wise (as I protest) to serue for a shew of my learning & ingine, but onely (mooued of conscience) to preasse thereby, so farre as I can, to resolue the doubting harts of many; both that such assaultes of Sathan are most certainly practised, & that the instrumentes thereof, merits most severly to be punished.*

And 'most severly' were they punished indeed. Over a hundred people ultimately came under suspicion of having raised the storm. First, Gillis Duncan, a maidservant working in Tranent, was denounced by her employer as a witch. Subjected to torture, she implicated scores of others – men as well as women (this was an equal-opportunity witch hunt) – including Agnes Sampson of Humble, southwest of Haddington, and John Fian, schoolmaster of Prestonpans. They too were tortured and implicated others in their turn, Agnes Sampson admitting to have brewed up the magic potion that had whipped up the winds against King James' ship, whilst another defendant, Agnes Thompson, lent colour with her account, as recorded in *A true discourse, of the apprehension of sundrye Witches lately taken in Scotland, some are executed, and some are yet imprisoned*:

> *the saide* Agnis Tompson *was after brought againe before the Kings Maiestie and his Counsell, and being examined of the meetings and detestable dealings of those witches,*

she confessed that vpon the night of Allhollon *Euen last,
she was accompanied aswell with the persons aforesaide,
as also with a great many other witches, to the number
of two hundreth: and that all they together went by Sea
each one in a Riddle or Ciue, and went in the same very
substantially with Flaggons of wine making merrie and
drinking by the waye in the same Riddles or Ciues, to the
Kerke of North Barrick in Lowthian, and that after they
had landed, tooke handes on the land and daunced this
reill or short daunce, singing all with one voice.*

Commer goe ye before, commer goe ye,
If ye will not goe before, commer let me.

At which time she confessed, that this Geilles Duncane
*did goe before them playing this reill or daunce vpon a
small Trump, called a Iewes Trump, vntill they entred
into the Kerk of north Barrick.*

It is difficult now to imagine the seriousness with which
such cases were taken, or the kind of testimony that was
wheeled out in the course of trials – sometimes in James'
presence. North Berwick's Auld Kirk, outside which the
coven is supposed to have gathered, is gone; even its site
has been partly washed away by erosion (the burgh's ruined
Parish Kirk wasn't built till the middle of the 17th century).
But the Auld Kirk Green on which the witches danced their
reel, remains, as the Anchor Green beside the harbour.

Anything up to 4,000 people (mainly, but by no means
solely, women) were killed in witch hunts in Scotland over
the decades that followed. A plaque above a wall-fountain
indicates the place on Edinburgh's Castle Esplanade where
over 300 witches were burned, after being strangled, during this time. The last nationwide witch hunt (which once
again started out in the Lothians before spreading out across

the whole of Scotland) came in 1661–2, but 'witches' were being hanged at Corbiehall, Bo'ness, as late as 1679. Over 20 years after that, indeed, 1697 saw seven women being tried in Paisley, after being accused by an 11-year-old girl. (Only five were executed: of the other two defendants, one 'escaped' by hanging herself, the other died mysteriously in gaol.) In the garden outside a cottage at the eastern end of Little Town in Dornoch stands a small stone that marks the spot to which, in 1727 (the stone mistakenly says 1722), an elderly woman, Janet Horne, was paraded through the town, her naked body daubed with tar. Made to stand in an open barrel of oil, she was then burned alive, becoming the last alleged 'witch' to be executed in Scotland – and in Britain as a whole.

Awa' wi' the Fairies

History seldom obliges us by conforming to the sort of neat schemas of centuries or 'ages' we find it helpful to work with. This is certainly brought home to us if we try to draw a definitive chronological cut-off between the times of old-world benightedness and those of new-look Enlightenment. The Age of Reason and the apparently unreasonable age that went before it actually overlapped enormously in time. Things were further complicated by such factors as class, education, culture and politics. Not to mention the sheer inertia of old ideas.

Consider, for example, Robert Kirk's book, *The Secret Commonwealth* (1691). 'Every age hath some secret left for its discovery,' said Kirk. For his own, he suggested, it was 'the nature and actions of the subterranean (and for the most part) invisible people, heretofore going under the name of elves, fauns and fairies.' *The Secret Commonwealth* was a sober and in some ways admirably rigorous study of what we would now see as an utterly nonsensical subject. It is intriguing to find that Kirk's researches were supported by Robert Boyle (1627–91), the Anglo-Irish philosopher, chemist and

HELLFIRE, HUMANISM, HOGMANAY

A great many of Scotland's problems, real and imagined, have been laid at the door of Calvinism, encompassing everything from licensing laws to sexual self-disgust. The Scots have been stereotypically dour, their religious culture saturated in a profound spiritual pessimism that's given a general joylessness to just about every aspect of life. Like most such stereotypes, along with an immense amount of nonsense, this view does contain a grain of truth. There isn't much doubt that the Scottish Reformation ended up being more Calvinistic in doctrine and in tone than Henry VIII's transformation of the English Church (though that of course got 'lower' and more Lutheran as time went on).

John Calvin (1509–64) was a French theologian forced to flee to Switzerland in the 1530s. For him, the corruption of the Catholic Church was not so much an argument for ecclesiastical reform as a demonstration that no hope of salvation could be found in human institutions of any kind. Adam and Eve's Original Sin, Calvin believed, so thoroughly damns us in advance of our existence that we can't hope to gain salvation by our own efforts. It doesn't matter how hard we strive, however much our Church may help us, our eternal fate is the predestined will of God. Most of us, then, come into the world and start out our moral lives with no chance of attaining anything but an eternity in Hell. God knows this in advance – He's all-knowing – but lets us be born for everlasting suffering anyway. That's fine, said Calvin: God is not just omniscient and omnipotent but the sum of all goodness too, and if this is how He has it, that's how it should be.

The Catholic Church has always condemned this doctrine as cruel and pernicious, and it's easy to see why. Even if its own view of the problem – that God knows we're going to screw up, allows us to exist anyway, watches us stumbling into damnation (as He knew we were going to) but can't be held responsible for

making us mess up because we have something called 'free will'
– is, for many, more ingenious than it is convincing… And even
if Calvin's thinking follows in a more or less direct line from that
of St Augustine of Hippo (354–430), one of the acknowledged
Fathers of the Roman Church.

The reputation of John Knox in particular has tended to
create a sense of Scotland's as a ranting-Reformation. But one
of its greatest luminaries, George Buchanan (1506–82), had
been a leading Humanist in his day. He had taught the young
French essayist Michel de Montaigne in France and argued with
divines at Portugal's University of Coimbra before settling in
France again. In the end, he'd almost dead-heated with Mary
Queen of Scots in his return from France to Scotland in about
1560 (though in his case he was fleeing persecution as a heretic).
George Buchanan became the young queen's tutor, but was
to end up as the avowedly Protestant tutor to her son, James.
Appointed Principal of St Leonard's College (now St Leonard's
School), St Andrews, 1566, he was to be an important influence
on King James VI.

Protestant puritanism did bring about a decline in the fortunes
of Christmas in Scotland's festive calendar. But there was
still some space for fun
amidst all the solemnity
and prayer. New Year
was deemed a more
appropriate moment for
celebration, though, than
the 'mass' of Christ – even
though it was arguably
just as much a hangover
of the pagan Yule/
Samhain as Christmas
had ever been.

physicist who, not content with formulating the famous law on the relation of volume to pressure in gas, is also widely credited with having helped bring about the proper pursuit of scientific method. Kirk (1644–92) was a native of Aberfoyle, whose minister he eventually became. He died there in strange circumstances on Doon Hill – though his spirit may live on in David Semphill, the Church of Scotland Minister who's the protagonist in John Buchan's novel, *Witch Wood* (1927).

It had been long before that, in the 13th century, that Thomas the Rhymer had written his famous account of his seduction by the 'Queen of Elfland' and his sojourn with her beneath the Eildon Hills. His poem was later adapted in various different forms. Like so much other Borders lore, his story was revived by Sir Walter Scott: in making the transition to literature, though, as a work of fantasy, it left behind the realm of popular belief.

For there does indeed seem to have been some real belief in fairies on the people's part. Certainly, such stories keep recurring. In the 17th century, the 10-year-old 'Fairy Boy of Leith' assured questioners that, every Thursday night, he went down deep into the heart of Edinburgh's Calton Hill through an imposing set of gates (which were, however, invisible to other people) to play his drum while fairies danced and made merry. At around the same time, one Johnny Williamson, the 'Boy of Borgue' descended into a bank of earth outside this Dumfries & Galloway village where he'd remain with the fairies – in his case, staying with them for days on end. As arresting as these stories are, their reception is still more striking: if they weren't implicitly believed, they don't seem to have been axiomatically *dis*-believed.

Nor did people quickly dispense with what had traditionally been seen as wise precautions. In the early 19th century, for example, one farmer, Alexander Simpson of Winchburgh, West Lothian, was keeping a corner of every field unculti-vated as the Devil's share or 'Guidman's Croft'. Within a few decades, his grandson, James Young Simpson, would be pioneering the anaesthetic use of chloroform. Even in the 20th century, by which time Scotland would arguably be leading the world in the scientific study of medicine, folkloric remedies would have their place. Especially, of course, in the countryside: the writer John McNeillie reports a cat being killed and lashed to the neck of an injured horse in the rural Galloway of the 1930s.

Better Together?

Royal successions can move in mysterious ways: England's Virgin Queen may have held his mother prisoner and had her executed, but on Elizabeth I's death on 24 March 1603, James VI of Scotland – her cousin twice removed – was her nearest heir. This meant that, though Scotland and England were, in terms of law and sovereignty, separate kingdoms, there was nevertheless a Union of the Crowns.

James' arrival in England for his coronation as James I that May was marred by controversy when, during a stop at Newark, Nottinghamshire, he ordered that a thief who'd just been caught should be summarily hanged. The idea that the new Stuart Crown was going to be dispensing 'justice' without putting itself to the inconvenience of trials was taken as a warning by wary courtiers in England, who were also alarmed by the number of supporters the new king knighted on his journey down.

James' Protestant piety might be unimpeachable, but there was no sign that he'd taken on any of the democratising instincts of his Presbyterian countrymen. At the Hampton Court Conference of 1604, he warned that English Puritans would have to conform. He also boasted of the power he had in his home country: 'I sit and govern it with my pen; I write and it is done,' he said. The Stuarts' besetting sin was to be their insistence on what came to be called the 'divine right of kings'. That doctrine had been most famously articulated in James' pamphlet of 1597, *Basilikon Doron* ('Royal Gift'). For the moment, it was England that seemed to be getting the worst of it with the arrival of James and the Union of the Crowns, but things were going to start getting worse for Scotland soon.

THE BLOO TOON

'Bloo', it's said, because of the colour its fishermen wore about their work, Peterhead was specifically founded for the herring fishery. Chartered as a burgh by James VI in 1587, it was built around the protected channel between Keith Inch (then an island) and the mainland. Its founder was George Keith, the 5th Earl Marischal (a hereditary title denoting charge of the royal bodyguard), and it was open for business by 1593. This makes it an early example of the sort of 'planned settlement' that was to characterise Scottish urban development in the industrial age that followed.

A causeway connecting the Inch to the shore was built in the 1730s; the South Harbour built at the end of the 18th century. Thomas Telford (see pages 172–73) designed the North Harbour, which opened in the 1820s to service what was becoming Britain's most important whaling centre. By the end of the 19th century, that trade was in decline, but its place had been taken by a modernised and much-expanded herring fishery.

In the early 19th century, Peterhead juggled its development as a fishing port with its new status as a fashionable health spa. 'Many elegant houses for the accommodation of strangers have been erected,' enthused Robert Forsyth in 1806. Strangers were to be accommodated in rather less style after Peterhead Prison opened in 1888. Increasing controversy surrounded conditions in the prison, which was the scene of serious rioting in 1987. It finally closed its doors in 2013.

FOUR

COVENANT
AND CROWN

IN 1615 – SO 87 YEARS AFTER the martyrdom of the Lutheran preacher Patrick Hamilton in St Andrews – the Jesuit priest John Ogilvie was hanged at Glasgow Cross. The more things change, the more they stay the same. One thing really was different, though: that Anglo-Scottish rivalry that had so often flared up into war in the previous centuries had been more or less settled by the Union of the Crowns.

Not that there weren't still tensions, though the initial sense of ignominy the English elite felt at being ruled by Scots soon passed as James VI became more obviously at home in his role as James I of England. No one was asking ordinary Scots how they felt, of course; for their betters, any feeling that face was being lost must have at least been palliated to some extent by the promise of enhanced possibilities for personal advancement, and of improving opportunities for trade.

Good Chear

Some Scots certainly thrived: their prosperity and stability bred a certain sense of contentment, and this led in turn to a certain charitable impulse. 'I Distribute Chearfullie' was the motto of George Heriot's Hospital, which King James' jeweller (and, effectively, banker) founded in 1628 as a home for Edinburgh's orphaned boys. Later adapted to serve as a guildhall, Cowane's Hospital in Stirling's Old Town was built as an almshouse by the local merchant John Cowane, opening its doors in 1637. Glasgow's Hutchesons' Grammar School started not long after, being established by George and Thomas Hutcheson in the Trongate in 1641. Again, the idea was to offer a home and education to some of the city's orphans. 'Hutchie' was to move about over the ensuing centuries, ending up on its present site in Crossmylouf, in the south of the city, in 1960. But Heriot's sat tight and remains in its original building just outside

Edinburgh's city walls, though it is now, of course, a fee-paying school. Its 'Wark' or 'Old Building' is a magnificent Renaissance-style palace and an imposing monument to the distributive spirit of the 17th century – even if its charitable status may be more contested now.

Crowning Glory

The Union of the Crowns is not of course to be confused with the sort of full union which was to follow a century later, but James VI/I himself seems to have had trouble with the distinction. Or, rather, perhaps, he saw his kingship as being so important in itself as to render insignificant any differences between the realms. James was certainly in control as king: he was something of a control-freak, indeed, perhaps taking his monarchical authority more seriously – and certainly articulating it more explicitly, in works like *Basilikon Doron* – than any English ruler had before.

James VI/I doesn't seem to have had any problems with the Protestant doctrines of the Scottish Church in which he'd been brought up, but their uneasiness with the idea of a clerical hierarchy bothered him. 'No bishops, no King', he reasoned, logically enough for one who'd convinced himself that his own kingly status came straight from God. James' Stuart successors, Charles I and II and James VII/II, were to take an absolutist view of this 'divine right' of kings – and to be similarly authoritarian in their approaches to religion. The new parliament building constructed off the Royal Mile in 1632 was festooned in Stuart iconography, underlining the importance of the monarchy – and this specific dynasty – in what might have been expected to be a more democratic forum within the state. (Now it's known as Parliament Hall, though only its interior exists in anything like its original state; the outside was given a neoclassical makeover from 1810.)

Real differences in religious attitudes made conflict between what was now effectively an English Crown and Scotland inevitable. Doctrinal questions seem to have mattered less to the Stuart kings than issues of institutional control, but, even so, in 1637, Charles I imposed a new Anglican liturgy on the Scottish Church. In Edinburgh's High Kirk (so, at least, tradition has it), a street-trader by the name of Jenny Geddes threw a three-legged stool at Dean James Hanna's head as he preached from the offending prayerbook. Her heroic insubordination sparked serious rioting – within St Giles, outside in the streets of Edinburgh, and beyond.

'No King but Christ!'

This sort of public disturbance, shocking as it may be, blows over quickly enough. But a more serious groundswell was quietly building all this time. On 28 February 1638, Scots crowded into the kirkyard of Edinburgh's Greyfriars under the cover of darkness to sign a National Covenant, which bound them to uphold what was, in its essentials, the Negative Confession of 1581 (see page 84). 'No king but Christ!' was the slogan as, in the weeks that followed, copies of the National Covenant were carried up and down the country, and committed Presbyterians flocked to register their defiance. The Covenanters would continue to influence events throughout the 17th century.

'Ulster Scots'

Other Protestants flocked to Ulster, hoping to find a freer climate for their own forms of worship in a new country further away from the metropolitan centre. The 'Pilgrim Fathers'-like idealism of these settlers shouldn't be over-emphasised, perhaps. Even so, their presence lent a radical religious edge to the policy of 'plantation' – the organised colonisation of

Ulster by settlers from Britain – first introduced by James VI/I and continued by Charles I to pacify what had been Ireland's most ungovernable province.

Lands in western Ulster, from County Cavan to Donegal, were parcelled out into 'proportions' of 2,000, 1,000 and 500 acres (approximately 800, 400 and 200 hectares) and handed out to 'undertakers' from England and Scotland. The Scots contingent came predominantly from Galloway and Ayrshire – just a short hop away across the North Channel. Responsibilities came with these land-rights: the new rulers were to undertake their territories' fortification and defence, and ensure that the majority of their tenants were English and Scottish. An overall cap was set on the number of native Irish, who were additionally required to conform to British farming practices, thus ensuring the extensive demographic and cultural re-creation of much of Ulster.

The idea that the purpose of the plantation was to impose Protestantism on Ulster has, to some extent, taken shape in retrospect. Whilst the need to get this part of Ireland out of the hands of its Gaelic chieftains was obviously of primary importance, this seems to have been closely followed by the opportunity it gave the king to do a favour for his friends on the one hand and, on the other, profit from a little speculative boom. The livery companies of London, descendants of the old crafts guilds, saw their settlements as an economic investment; aristocratic recipients often as not saw their grants as a windfall to be cashed in.

Donegal, for example, was divided into seven 'precincts': those of Portlough and Boylagh were granted to Scottish undertakers. Those settlers who were awarded lands in Boylagh, western Donegal, for instance, all immediately sold their interests on to another Scot, Sir Robert Gordon of Lochinvar, Kirkcudbrightshire. He in turn sold shares to several friends – most of them fellow Gallowegians, like George Murray of Broughton, Wigtown, an Episcopalian. (Murray's interest in cattle-farming, developed at this time on a Donegal estate whose lands were largely unsuitable for arable farming, was to be taken further by his descendants after their move to an estate at Cally, near Gatehouse of Fleet.)

Portlough stayed in the hands of the original undertakers: mostly Stewarts from Stirlingshire, or Cunninghams from Ayrshire. These were only an elite, of course: the land was actively managed by their Scottish tenants, whilst it was worked by those same Irish 'churls' who'd always worked it in the past. As Marianne Elliott, chronicler of *The Catholics of Ulster* (Allen Lane, 2000), observes, they 'may well have fared a good deal better under the new dispensation than under the Gaelic land system. But the elite did not, and it is their voice we hear'. The Protestant 'Ulster Scots' of stereotype were the descendants of that middle rank of farmers, strong from the first in their Presbyterian principles, but increasingly beleaguered, embittered – and consequently strident – over time.

Battling the Bishops

Those radical Protestants who stayed in Scotland were ready to fight for their religious way of life. In 1639 and 1640, Charles I lost successive Bishops'Wars over his right to impose his religious will on the Scots. Turriff, in Aberdeenshire, was the epicentre for the first – the scene of not one but two epic episcopal confrontations. The Raid of Turriff on 14 February 1639, when the Earl of Huntly descended on the town with 2,000 men to prevent a Covenanters' meeting from taking place but was forced into an ignominious retreat; and the Trot of Turriff, when, on 14 May, Sir George Ogilvy took the town on the king's behalf and forced its populace to sign a pledge of loyalty to Crown and Church. Would that all military conflicts could be as comparatively innocuous as the First Bishops' War, which seems to have claimed only a single casualty.

The Pacification of Berwick (signed on 18 June, in Charles' camp outside that city) followed the form of a peace treaty, but was really a massive climbdown on the king's part. He tried to redress the balance in the Second Bishops' War of 1640, but the English army commanded by Edward, Lord Conway, was defeated on 28 August at Newburn – an important ford across the River Tyne, just west of Newcastle. Alexander Leslie's Scottish victory there, and his subsequent occupation of Newcastle (with the hold it gave him over the supply of coal to London) forced Charles to agree substantial compensation to the Scots.

Civil War

The Bishops' Wars also presented much bigger problems for the king when, that November, he summoned his Westminster parliament to try to bully its members into raising tax revenues to continue with the conflict. Parliament's dogged refusal to roll over; its moves to impeach the king's highest officials; and Charles I's high-handed reactions precipitated the crisis which, in 1642, was to pitch England into Civil War.

Given their Presbyterian theology, as well as the anti-hierarchical ideology which arguably flowed from that, it's hardly surprising that the Scots should by and large have felt more sympathy for the Parliamentarian than the Royalist side. But some certainly believed that, in refusing bishops, the National Covenant had gone far enough: they didn't want to usher in a Presbyterian state. James Graham, 1st Earl of Montrose (1612–50), an important Covenanting leader during the Bishops' Wars, refused to put his name to the 'Solemn League and Covenant' that so many of his former comrades now signed with the English Parliamentarians. Montrose now indeed became the leader of Scotland's Royalists.

A Handbook of Scotland's History

But any about-face on Montrose's part (he would, of course, have argued that it was the Covenanting cause which had changed) pales into insignificance beside that made by both the Scots Presbyterians and Charles I (in 1647) and then three years later by Charles II, his son, when they made alliances with one another. Montrose's capture and execution (his head was exhibited on a spike atop Edinburgh's Old Tolbooth for more than a decade) was so much collateral damage as far as the would-be English king was concerned. In return for Scottish acknowledgement of his status as King Charles II, he was (he pledged) prepared to agree to their terms of their Solemn League and Covenant for the establishment of Presbyterianism in Scotland and of a reformed Church, along Scots Presbyterian lines, in England.

So it was that a sometime Covenanter commander, General David Leslie, led a Scottish army into England, only to be beaten back by Oliver Cromwell, and defeated at Dunbar. It was a needless loss. Leslie had the English completely pinned down, but his paymasters the Kirk Elders, who begrudged the continuing costs, insisted that he attacked, and his triumph was left in tatters.

While in Edinburgh, Cromwell lodged at Moray House (174 Canongate), now home to the University's School of Education. Cromwell also – rather pointedly – stabled his horses inside Greyfriars, showing his contempt for a Kirk that had thrown in its lot with a Stuart king. His own iconoclastic instincts seem, R. Scott Spurlock suggests in *Cromwell and Scotland* (John Donald, 2007), to have extended only to undermining the political power of the Church in Scotland, but many of Cromwell's rank-and-file soldiers felt much more strongly. However violent, though, Spurlock continues, the shake-up of these times did help to create a more 'open market' in religious views, busting what had become a quite restrictive and stifling Presbyterian orthodoxy.

Pestilential Times

Scotland is believed to have got off lightly during the Black Death of the 1340s. Further visitations had followed: Robert Henryson wrote his heartfelt lament – and plea to God for mercy on his people – 'Ane Prayer for the Pest' in response to an outbreak towards the very end of the 15th century.

When the plague returned in the 17th century, however, things were vastly worse. The higher population densities in this (rapidly urbanising) society facilitated the disease's spread, whilst improved communications made people – and, consequently, rats and accompanying microbes – much more mobile. According to David Aldinstone, Session Clerk to South Leith Parish Church at the time, the pestilence that erupted in Edinburgh in 1645 had been 'brought into Scotland by John Downie's ship, called the William, of Leith, from Dantzick'. Aldinstone kept a careful record, finding that half the population of Leith died.

Elsewhere, Dundee lost 20 per cent of its population, whilst in Aberdeen a ghostly silence reigned: 'The grass was in the streets,' one witness wrote, 'and not a smoake in both towns' (that is, in the two burghs – Old and New – comprising the city). Edinburgh's dead were flung into communal plague pits outside the town on Leith Links and on the Buroughmuir (across that extensive sweep to the south of the city where Polwarth, Merchiston, Bruntsfield, Morningside, Grange and Newington are now). Indeed, the 'burgh muirs' of all the main towns were pressed into use for this purpose.

And for quarantining the living-but-exposed. Generally, there'd be a 'clean' end for people who'd had contact with the sick but shown no symptoms; and a 'foull' end for those who were actually ill. One curious relic of this period is the tomb of John Livingstone, apothecary, set back from the pavement on the northern side of Chamberlain Road, near Holy Corner, Edinburgh. The plague ebbed away in 1647, never (really) to return.

'WAGEIT MEN OF WEARE'

'Gallowglass' (mercenary) soldiers from Scotland's Highlands and Islands served the Gaelic chiefs and Norman lords of Ireland from the 13th to the 17th century. Mercenary soldiering became a tradition, indeed: of all Scottish males born in the 17th century, it has been calculated, one-fifth went soldiering on the Continent at some point in their lives. Many went to Germany to serve in the Thirty Years' War (1618–48), which was fought almost entirely by foreign mercenaries. Such experiences equipped both what would become the Covenanter armies and loyal Lowland regiments like the Royal Scots, who (as the Royal Regiment of Foot) were founded in 1633. The Cameronians bridged that divide, becoming the only regiment of the British Army to have been originally a Covenanting sect, who joined up en masse with James, Earl of Angus, in 1689. The Highland regiments came later, the Black Watch in response to the Jacobite rising of 1715 (see pages 130–32). The National War Museum of Scotland is in Edinburgh Castle, but it's also worth visiting the individual regimental museums. The Cameronians have one at Low Parks, Hamilton, Lanarkshire; the Black Watch at Balhousie Castle, Perth; the Coldstream Guards have a gallery in the town museum in (where else?) Coldstream.

The Scots – especially the Islanders – also often worked as seafarers for hire. They were involved from very early on in the history of the Hudson's Bay Company, which was founded in 1670. Stromness was an important centre for the Company from 1702: by the late 18th century, three-quarters of those working for the HBC in Canada were Orcadians. (And this brawn-drain was causing

considerable concern in the Scottish Islands generally.) The
connection continued into the early 20th century. Lots of whaling
crews were picked up there too. Herman Melville mentions this in
Moby-Dick *(1851):*

> The Greenland whalers sailing out of Hull or
> London, put in at the Shetland Islands, to receive
> the full complement of their crew. Upon the passage
> homewards, they drop them there again. How it is,
> there is no telling, but Islanders seem to make the
> best whalemen.

Hostilities Restored

In 1660, King Charles II was invited back from exile to take
up his father's throne. The Restoration appears to have been
greeted with great relief in England. In Scotland, however,
the accession of the Merry Monarch prompted a good deal
of gloom, because he also reintroduced the episcopacy (rule
of the Church by bishops). Whilst many ministers bowed to
what they saw as the inevitable, others stood up for their
Presbyterian principles and the Covenanting conflict flared
up once again.

The so-called 'Pentland Rising' of 1666 actually began in
Dalry, Dumfries & Galloway, where the sight of an elderly
Covenanter being assaulted by soldiers sparked a riot that spi-
ralled out of control. A more organised band, under the leadership of Robert Maclellan of Barscobe Castle, Balmaclellan,
proceeded to Dumfries, to the Whitesands lodgings of Sir
James Turner, Captain of the Royal Dragoon Guards, whom
they promptly seized. On their way to Edinburgh, to present
a petition, they got as far as Colinton, on the city's southern outskirts (a monument outside Dreghorn Barracks
commemorates this moment), before turning back, having

been persuaded that they weren't going to get anywhere. But 'Bluidy' Tam Dalyell, with 3,000 soldiers, caught them (now 900 strong) at Rullion Green, on 28 November. A couple of score were killed, and 15 of those taken prisoner then hanged as an example. There's a Martyrs' Monument on Lawhead Hill, above the A702.

A far cry from his descendant and namesake Tam Dalyell (1932–), the former Labour MP for West Lothian and Linlithgow, who (some expensive bookcases apart) has offended only by what some have seen as excess of high-minded zeal, 'Bluidy Tam' has gone down in history as a minor monster. Stories of his playing cards with the Devil, though widespread, weren't substantiated, but there's little doubt of the ferocity with which he persecuted King Charles' enemies. He's particularly associated with the use of the 'boot', an instrument of torture which, having been placed around the foot, was then tightened by means of a screw-mechanism, gradually crushing the bones beneath. So perverse are the vicissitudes of history that, in 1681, he was to found what would (from 1707) come to be one of the British Army's most admired regiments, the Royal Scots Greys. By another perverse vicissitude, the Scots Greys would be wound up in 1971 when they were amalgamated into the Royal Scots Dragoon Guards.

Murderers and Martyrs

The year 1679 saw the assassination of James Sharp, Archbishop of St Andrews, whose coach was stopped by Covenanters on the Magus Muir, outside the town. He was cut up in front of his daughter, in what was to be a major coup for the Covenanters, though a major turn-off to less partisan observers. (Sharp, reviled for his loyalty to King Charles II and his repressive policies towards the Covenanters, had survived an earlier assassination attempt in 1668 in Edinburgh's

Blackfriar's Wynd. His would-be assassin, James Mitchell, had been held prisoner on Bass Rock until his execution in 1678, but was regarded as a hero from that time on.) Two memorials near the spot on Magus Muir commemorate Sharp himself and five Covenanters executed in retaliation, after their capture at the Battle of Bothwell Bridge, in 1679. Anything up to 600 Covenanters were killed at this encounter by the bridge over the Clyde between Bothwell and Hamilton. Some 1,200 were taken prisoner, brought back to Edinburgh and held in the open in Greyfriars kirkyard. Of these, a hundred or so died (or were killed): they were buried in a mass grave near the Martyrs' Memorial in the kirkyard.

In 1680, the town square in Sanquhar (Dumfries & Galloway) was the scene of a proclamation by Michael and Richard Cameron and their Covenanting comrades. The Sanquhar Declaration was categorical in its rejection of Charles II, his Church and his government in Scotland and took the crisis to a new pitch of ferocity. In the 'Killing Time' that followed, lots of Covenanters were tortured in Edinburgh's Tolbooth and executed in the Grassmarket – latterly with the 'maiden' (a sort of proto-guillotine). There's a memorial by the site of the old execution spot (as indeed there is on the site of the old Tolbooth).

There's a memorial too on the southeast side of Cathedral Square in Glasgow (in the wall of the Evangelical Church): it records the executions of James Nisbet, James Lawson and Alex Wood, executed not far away in 1684 for their support for the Covenanting cause (though the site itself is now under a raised slip-road of the nearby motorway). Some 17 executions the following year are recorded by a memorial in the grounds of Inveraray Castle. A plaque in the wall outside the garden of the nearby Bank of Scotland shows where the executions actually took place. In 1685, John Graham of Claverhouse, Viscount of Dundee, had the Covenanting farmer John Brown executed in front of his wife and child outside their house when he refused to pray for the king. He's buried where he died, at Priesthill, near Muirkirk, Ayrshire.

The Wigtown (or Solway) Martyrs at least had the benefit of some sort of trial. Their story (and, some scholars say, that's all it is – a story) is certainly shocking. In 1685, Margarets Wilson and McLachlan (aged 18 and 63 respectively) were sentenced to death for refusing to take an oath abjuring the Covenant. Shackled to stakes planted in the Solway sand below the high-water mark, they were left to stand there as the tide came in – the assumption being that they would yield as the waters rose. In the event, they both held firm and were duly drowned. They're both buried in the Old Kirkyard in the town, as is one William Walker, 'without sentence of law hanged' for being a Covenanter that same year. As for the Covenanters' Oak, in Dalzell Park, near Motherwell, that was already half a millennium old when the Covenanters held open-air services beneath its boughs.

Clans and Kings

As in so many other civil conflicts, ideological enmities, however real or deeply felt, could on occasion mask more intimate antipathies. A certain amount of tribal and personal score-settling went on during the 17th century. Such seems to have been the case with the Campbells' killing of the Lamonts. Men, women and children of the clan, captured at Castle Toward, were taken to Dunoon and slaughtered: the Dunoon Massacre claimed over 200 lives.

Clan politics went all the way up to the top in a Scottish society that had clearly only imperfectly incorporated the aristocratic principles of the early-modern age. The religious oppositions and political machinations of the 17th century can all to some extent be seen as wrangling over one key 'conflict': King Stuart vs King Campbell. The Campbells were to be well to the fore in resistance (whether passive or more active, violent even) to the authority of successive Stuart Kings and of an Episcopal Church, which was closely identified with the Crown.

Archibald Campbell, 1st Marquess of Argyll (1607–61), was a stalwart fighter for the Covenanting cause, and the Campbells would continue to defend the Scottish Presbyterian interest. The 1st Marquess was to pay for his loyalty to the Covenanters with his life. After Charles II's Restoration, he was captured and put on trial. Convicted of treason, for collaborating with the Cromwellian Commonwealth, he was beheaded on the maiden in 1661. His severed head then had the dubious distinction of replacing Montrose's, on the exact same spike on which the Royalist hero's had been displayed for the previous decade (see page 102).

The Coffee Question

Whatever the rivalries and hatreds it stoked, religious resistance arguably opened the way, more positively, to a climate of intellectual independence and scepticism. Even to the first stirrings of the much-vaunted 'democratic intellect' of 19th-century Scotland, maybe (see pages 227–28). In 1673, Scotland got its first coffee house, opened by John Row in Edinburgh (Robertson's Land, near the Parliament House). Glasgow got its first a little later the same year: opened by Colonel Walter Whiteford, on the corner of Saltmarket Street and the Trongate. The Edinburgh house was forced to close after four years for fear of sedition.

Scotland's first newspaper, the *Mercurius Caledonius*, had already appeared – for a few issues at least – being published in Edinburgh at the end of 1660 and in the early weeks of 1661. Though its allegiances were Royalist, its tone was irreverent and it was soon suppressed. It was revived at intervals under a number of different titles until, from 1720, it enjoyed a continuous run of 147 years as *The Caledonian Mercury*.

Our Island Stories

English history, it's become modish to point out in recent years, can't sensibly be studied without some sense of the 'archipelagic' dimension, some appreciation of the inter-relation, both complex and dynamic, between the different countries of the British Isles. John of Gaunt's vision (in Shakespeare's *Richard II*) of 'England' as a 'scepter'd isle' makes him the archetypal example of that English complacency that mentally annexes what Lewis Grassic Gibbon was to call 'Scotshire' – and ignores Wales just about completely. Conversely, though, an approach to Scottish history that takes a 'Fog in the Borders, England Isolated' view is hardly going to come up with a convincing version of events.

Ireland, historically harder to ignore than Scotland or Wales, has instead been relentlessly 'othered'. Ironically, one of the things that has marked it out as most alien has been its apparent inability to put its past behind it. Where else would events in 1916 spark such emotive reactions to this day – let alone those of 1690? That, actually, the Easter Rising and the Battle of the Boyne have cast quite a shadow over recent Scottish history only underlines quite how complicated our archipelagic history has been.

As for a 'British' historiography, that starts out at a disadvantage given the absence, for so many centuries, of any such state. And the presence, once a United Kingdom did exist,  of so many forces – not just of nation, but of religion, politics, economics – pulling against the attempt to create a coherent narrative. In so far as there *can* be a British history, though, it starts at about this point, at the end of the 17th century – and starts too in a situation of pretty much generalised conflict. For the 'Glorious Revolution' of 1688, which, it's often been argued, gave birth to a modern, democratic Britain, first brought instability and war.

Billy Boys

Charles II's 'popish' sympathies were a matter of – quite justifiable – rumour; but the Catholicism of his younger brother,
James, the Duke of York, was openly avowed. (His marriage to
the devoutly Catholic Mary of Modena made matters worse.)
Repeated attempts to rule him out of the succession through
'exclusion bills' in Parliament – and even assassination plots –
hadn't ruffled his assurance in the 'divine right' he felt to rule as
a Stuart king. Which he duly did, after Charles' death in 1685.

James VII/II's modern image owes much to that trium-
phalist 'Whig history' which celebrated Britain as a bastion
of Protestant religion and constitutional politics. Despite the
effete image he has in that tradition, the king wasn't short
of courage. During his French exile of the Commonwealth
period, he had seen front-line service against the Fronde
uprising. He showed his resolve quite clearly when, in short
order, he dealt with the rebellion by the Duke of Monmouth
(Charles II's illegitimate son, and James' nephew), who had
hoped to take the throne and reign as a Protestant king.

Having held on to his throne, James immediately set
about consolidating his power by raising a standing army.
Soldiers had always been recruited on an ad hoc basis until
now. Given the climate of discontent, James' decision was
in some ways understandable, but it sent out the message
that he was at war with his own subjects. And if, in 1687,
his Declaration of Indulgence (granting greater religious
freedom for Catholics) caused outrage, the birth of a son –
and, of course, a legal successor – provoked outright panic in
English and Scottish Protestants alike.

A group of Protestant nobles, already in negotiation
with William of Orange, *Stadtholder* of the Dutch Republic,
were now even more eager to have him come, depose James
and reign as William III. His wife (also called Mary) had
the closer claim, but William wanted something more than
Prince Consort status.

His first invasion fleet was dispersed by winds in October 1688; he landed at Torbay a few weeks later. James wasn't fazed – till he found his officers deserting in their droves. There was little actual fighting. James and Mary fled for France, but were captured. Then, rather than have them a focus for royalist unrest, William decided to turn a blind eye while they escaped. A Convention Parliament the following January issued a Declaration of Right: James' attempt to flee had effectively been an abdication, it asserted. William III and Mary II were (unusually) made joint co-rulers in his place. The Declaration of Right had been primarily a stick to beat James II with, though as the Bill of Rights (December 1689) it was to become the blueprint for a constitutional monarchy. The king and queen would be held in the highest respect as heads of state, but not be allowed to disregard the wishes of the people's elected representatives.

The Williamite Wars

In Scotland, John Graham of Claverhouse, Viscount of Dundee, stayed loyal to the Stuarts when James was deposed – the most influential of a number of so-called Jacobites (from *Jacobus*, the Latin form of 'James'). 'Bloody Clavers', as he was known to Covenanters because of the stunts he'd pulled in Ayrshire (see page 107), now became 'Bonnie Dundee' – at least to supporters of the Stuart cause. On 27 July 1689, he negotiated superbly the terrain of the Pass of Killiecrankie, near Pitlochry, and gained a splendid victory over a government force led by General Hugh Mackay. But this triumph was to a large extent tempered for the Jacobites by Dundee's own death – and dashed completely when his army went on to be badly beaten at Dunkeld a few weeks later (21 August).

There's an NTS visitor centre at the Killiecrankie site, though it seems an improbable place for a battle now: the slopes below the A9 road are steep and thickly wooded.

True or not, the legend of the Soldier's Leap made by one of King Billy's Scottish supporters across the rushing River Garry underlines the site's inconvenience as a fighting arena – whatever its importance as a strategic point. (Burns' later song about the battle hints more openly than commemorative verses of the period generally did about the brutal unpleasantness of the encounter: 'An ye had been whare I hae been,/Ye wadna been sae cantie-o;/An ye had seen what I hae seen,/ I' the Braes o' Killicrankie-o.')

At risk of oversimplifying, it seems fair to say that, just as the open, rugged ground had favoured Dundee's Highland troops as they swept down on the government lines at the Battle of Killiecrankie, they were at a disadvantage in the narrow streets of a medieval cathedral city like Dunkeld. Whilst they far outnumbered the government troops and had the initiative to begin with, the first shock of their attack was successfully absorbed and the contest became more equal. And, over 16 hours, as Dunkeld became a sort of mini-Stalingrad, with savage fighting from street to street and from house to house in the city, the Jacobites were gradually worn down.

Whilst the Jacobite army limped on through the Highlands, James VII/II's main focus had moved to Ireland by now. His Scottish army was pretty much routed the following year at the Haughs of Cromdale, a few miles east of Grantown-on-Spey. The defeat of James' army at the Battle of the Boyne, just west of Drogheda, on 12 July 1690, was brought about by an army largely composed of Protestant 'Scots-Irish' from the plantation areas in the north. As in previous 17th-century conflicts in Scotland, a nasty cocktail of religious enmity and clan rivalry had informed the fighting from the start – and lingered some time after the war was nominally won. At Glencoe in 1692, a group of Campbells in King William's service fell upon the MacDonalds, who had taken them into their homes as guests, killing 38. A further 40 women and children died of exposure in the mountains, where they'd fled. The killers were led by the 9th Earl of Argyll, another Archibald Campbell and the son of the Covenanting hero (see page 109). Their 'justification' for the attack was their Stuart-sympathising hosts' reluctance to make an oath of allegiance to the Protestant king – though they seem to have been just as interested in settling their own old scores.

A National Bank

With the end of the century coming up fast, Scotland seemed to be languishing economically. Other countries were carving out colonial empires and modernising more at home. It isn't difficult to see why William Paterson (1658–1719) should have found a receptive audience for what amounted to a national get-rich-quick scheme.

And it wasn't as though he didn't have the credentials. Born in Skipmyre, Dumfries & Galloway, but brought up in Bristol, Paterson had helped found the Bank of England in 1694. When, the next year, he came up to Edinburgh, he had no great difficulty in persuading Parliament to pass an act for the establishment of the Bank of Scotland. Its governor was an Englishman, John Holland (1658–1722); its chief accountant, George Watson (1654–1723), was to found one of Edinburgh's top schools.

The foundation of the Bank of Scotland may have placed the country on a modern financial footing, but as yet it was all dressed up with no mercantile place to go. Over the last century or so, the trading horizons of the major European nations had been much extended: Portugal and Spain had their colonies in the Americas; the Dutch in the Cape of Good Hope and the Indian Ocean, where England's East India Company had also been opening up commercial spheres. England also had its colonies up the eastern coast of America from Virginia to Massachusetts. But Scotland still had only its local British and Baltic trades.

FORT WILLIAM: HOLDING THE LINE

*Inverlochy Castle was built in the 1270s, by 'Black Comyn',
John II, Lord of Badenoch, but it's been gradually going to
rack and ruin since the 16th century. Its siting reflects the
importance of this situation at the southern end of the Great
Glen, which was recognised in 1654 by Cromwell's commander,
General Monck. He saw Inverlochy very much as a frontier
fort for the pacification of the wilder part of Scotland. The
town's Gaelic name An Gearasdan – 'garrison' – is a prosaic
acknowledgement of this function. It got its modern English
name after the enthronement of William of Orange as Britain's
king. Its strategic role only became more crucial with the Jacobite
risings of 1715 and '45 (during the latter of which Fort William
withstood a two-week siege). When peace eventually returned, the
town continued as a local market centre until the expansion of
the tourist industry in modern times.*

Big Plans in Panama

For some time there had been talk of an attempt to move in on the East Indies in competition with the English and the Dutch, but William Paterson had a very different vision. A trading centre in Darien, on the Isthmus of Panama, he argued, would not only establish a foothold for Scottish merchants in the Americas; it would provide an overland corridor to the doorstep of the Pacific and the Indies – so access to two vast trading areas for the price of one. An enticing plan – if under-researched.

In fact, no one from Scotland seems to have so much as set foot in what was to be 'Caledonia'. Beyond the vague assumption that this was to be an Eden-like land of just about unlimited possibility, there seems to have been little sense of what settling in central America would actually involve. Or of how welcome the colonists would be: 17th-century Europeans didn't generally give much thought to the feelings of indigenous peoples in the lands they settled, but it might at least have been anticipated that the Spanish would have views.

At first the scheme was open to English investors as well as Scots, but pressure from the East India Company impelled the London government to prohibit this. If the involvement of English money had reduced the potential profits for participating Scots, it had also spread the risk. Undaunted, Scottish institutions and individuals rushed to invest in a project that had completely caught the national imagination. With shares available for as little as £5, even people of relatively modest means could get involved – which meant that a considerable number of the country's professional and small-tradesmen's classes did.

Unsettling

Others vied to be among the colonists: 1,200 finally set out in a fleet of five ships that left Leith in July 1698. At the end of a three-month voyage, they found their destination: a stinking, sticky mangrove swamp, unfit for cultivation; soon they were sickening by the score, struck down by malaria. In the absence of any fresh water supply but the rain, they built their headquarters – Fort St Andrew – without one. Only a few hundred lived long enough to join the despairing exodus eight months later. A support fleet sent to re-supply the colony and bring new settlers arrived weeks later to find 'New Edinburgh' abandoned. They left without landing – but still lost many lives to fever.

Before word got back to Scotland of the first expedition's fate, a second had already embarked in the summer of 1699. Of the 1,000 fresh settlers who came, only a few were to survive the attacks of the Spanish and the ravages of disease. If those most directly affected by the Darien Disaster were obviously those settlers who'd died in such dismal suffering, the effects at home were profound and far-reaching. It's estimated that over a quarter of the country's liquid capital had been committed in the rush to invest in the project – and it all went up in smoke when the venture failed. Life-savings were lost; families and businesses ruined and the national psyche scarred: the great leap forward had left Scotland on its knees.

It's initially surprising, but on reflection maybe only fitting that no great monument to this pivotal moment should survive. Ironically – perhaps inevitably – the imposing edifice built as the scheme's headquarters, Darien House, subsequently did service as Edinburgh's lunatic asylum. Bedlam, as it was called (after London's Bethlem Royal Hospital, Britain's oldest designated asylum for the mentally ill), stood at the southern end of George IV Bridge, in what's now the triangle between Bristo Place and Forrest Road. The poor house next door was cleared away to become the site of the New North Free Church, which is now the University's 'Bedlam' Theatre.

In the absence of more real estate, Edinburgh's National Museum of Scotland has the next best thing: the Darien Chest, made around 1695 for the safe storage of money and documents relating to the venture. Big and heavy and made of iron, this impressive receptacle shows all the solidity the scheme itself was lacking. An elaborate mechanism inside the lid with 15 spring bolts made it secure. Less directly, the disaster is commemorated in the ruins of Tolquhon Castle, north of Aberdeen. Once a stunning Renaissance-style castle-cum-chateau, it's been slowly decaying since the early years of the 18th century after the Forbes family lost its fortune in the scheme.

FIVE

UNION DUES

SOME WOULD SAY THAT THE MOST ENDURING monument to the Darien Disaster has been the United Kingdom. Certainly, the scheme's collapse hit Scotland with the force of an economic Flodden, not just emptying its coffers but crushing its morale. In these circumstances, the country wasn't best placed to resist the pressure being applied by the beginning of the 18th century for the Union of the Crowns to become an actual union.

Jacobites and Hanoverians

The new century had brought England a new succession crisis, and with it renewed fears of the country falling back into popish hands. In 1702, Queen Anne had ascended the throne, and though no one had felt the slightest anxiety about her loyalties, she was still a Stuart and the daughter of James II. She was also going to die without an heir: her last surviving child, Prince William, Duke of Gloucester, had died in 1700, aged just 11.

In 1701, Parliament had rushed through the Act of Settlement to pre-empt any bid by James II himself, should he outlive Queen Anne, or by his son James Edward Stuart or daughter Louisa Maria Teresa if he should not. Instead, it established that the succession would go to the reliably Protestant (if German) Sophia, Electress of Hanover. Great news for the many who feared a lurch back into Stuart absolutism and Catholicism; not so good for the Jacobites, on the other hand.

Aliens and Rogues

Scotland's Parliament, annoyed at England's arrogance in passing the act without consultation, brought in an Act of Security (1704). This insisted on Scotland's right to choose a monarch of its own. Westminster retaliated with an Alien Act, which marked out Scots in England as foreigners to be discriminated against. This new step only exacerbated the damage to a Scottish economy already reeling at the impact of the Darien Disaster – and left the country in no real position to resist the pressure to accept union with England.

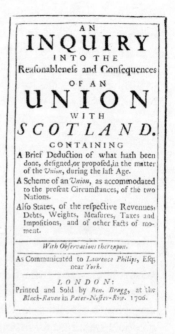

One specific (and highly controversial) provision of the Treaty of Union, agreed in 1706/7, was the compensation for the Darien investors. It's easy to see why this offer should have been seen widely as a 'sweetener'. Burns' later 'parcel of rogues' crack – his claim that Scots had been 'bought and sold for English gold' – was by no means entirely without foundation. There's little doubt that, rogues or not, Scotland's elite had different financial and political priorities from its small tradespeople and poor. Tradition has it that the Scottish signatories put their names to the treaty in the 17th-century summer house of the Earl of Seafield; a lean-to building behind Moray House, Canongate, which is now part of the University's School of Education.

English Espionage

Union certainly suited the English Crown: from the point of view of the monarchy, it made sense that two countries under the same regal authority should be united politically and economically as well. William III's successor (and sister-in-law)

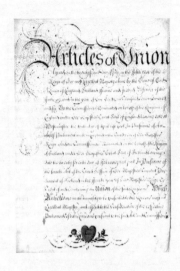

Queen Anne, a niece of Charles II but brought up a Protestant, had been pushing for greater integration for some years. Once the union had been agreed in Edinburgh, her government left no stone unturned in its efforts to nurse it through. Under the soubriquets 'Alexander Goldsmith' and, more exotically, 'Claude Guilot', the novelist Daniel Defoe (approximately 1660–1731) was in Edinburgh and Glasgow as a spy from September 1706, testing the political temperature – and, he claimed, steering Scottish leaders, who trusted him as a dissenter who had famously been (literally) pilloried for his religious beliefs, towards outcomes which would be favourable to the English side. Whatever his exact role, Defoe is known to have lived in Moubray House, 51–53 High St, Edinburgh, for a couple of years from 1710, and he may have lived there during this earlier period as well.

He wasn't short of material. The draft treaty was greeted with riots in Edinburgh, Glasgow and Lanark; over 20,000 people signed petitions across Scotland. Copies of the articles of the treaty were burned by crowds at Stirling's mercat cross and in Dumfries (beside the Midsteeple, then being built). *A Proclamation Against all Tumultuary and Irregular Meetings* ... issued in December 1706, called on householders to take responsibility for the conduct of their sons, their apprentices, their servants and so forth. Defoe described how the Provost of Glasgow had been chased into a tenement by an enraged mob and had escaped murder only by hiding inside a fold-up bed.

FROM FIFE TO JUAN FERNANDEZ

It's ironic, perhaps, that even as Defoe was up in Scotland spying for the English, another aspect of his destiny was being decided – by a Scotsman – far away. For it was at just this time that, with the tumults of human history and society the most distant of memories, Alexander Selkirk (1676–1721) was experiencing his life as a castaway.

Born in Lower Largo, Fife, a fishing village, Selkirk had followed in local traditions by going off to sea. After several years' buccaneering, attacking Spanish shipping around the Americas, in 1704 he had a quarrel with his captain – the English privateer William Dampier (1651–1715) – over the seaworthiness of their vessel. Though they were way out in the Pacific Ocean, almost 700km (440 miles) off the coast of Chile, Selkirk had insisted on being put ashore on the island of Juan Fernández.

Dampier's ship, the Cinque Ports was indeed subsequently to sink, but by that time Selkirk must long since have been asking himself how sensible his stand had really been. For he really wasn't very well equipped for his ordeal. Even so, fending for himself, foraging, fishing and hunting, he eked out a living for the next four years or so before being picked up by a visiting ship.

Hairy and outlandishly unkempt, he was an unrecognisable mess of a man, but – with a rough shelter, basic tools and his own hand-caught and -crafted goatskin clothing – a man who had nevertheless been successfully surviving. A fitting prototype, in other words, for Defoe's great story of human strength and survival – and influential economic paradigm – Robinson Crusoe, *which was published to general wonderment in 1719.*

Slow Progress

The positives of union for Scotland were slower in showing –
at least in the economic sphere. Defoe had always been disappointed, almost distressed, at what he saw as the absence
of any work ethic in 'North Britain'. In a poem written right
on the cusp of union, *Caledonia* (1706), he expresses something close to horror at the country's neglect of its fisheries:

> *What pains has Scotland taken to be poor,*
> *That has the Indies at her door;*
> *That lets her coursest fate of choice remain,*
> *And sees her maker bountiful in vain.*

'Wake, Scotland, from thy long lethargic dream!' he
exhorted, but he was back in the country in the 1720s and
found – in Kirkcudbright, at least – no indication that this
national sloth was significantly closer to being shaken off.
The people there, he reported, were pious and sober, but the
coastal town was pretty much the epitome of backwardness,
with no real sign of industry – or even initiative:

> *Here is a pleasant situation, and yet nothing pleas-
> ant to be seen. Here is a harbour without ships, a port
> without trade, a fishery without nets, a people without
> business; and, that which is worse than all, they do not
> seem to desire business, much less do they understand
> it... They have a fine river, navigable for the greatest
> ships to the town-key; a haven, deep as a well, safe as
> a mill-pond; 'tis a meer wet dock ... But, alas! there is
> not a vessel, that deserves the name of a ship, belongs to
> it; and, though here is an extraordinary salmon fishing,
> the salmon come and offer themselves, and go again,
> and cannot obtain the privilege of being made useful to
> mankind.*

Far from setting Scotland to work, indeed, the union was arguably making some things worse. The suspicion that the (London-owned) Irish linen trade was fiscally favoured over the Scottish contributed to the Fife food riots of January–February 1720. Unemployed linen workers targeted customs and excise offices in their attacks, protesting that their industry was being crippled by tariffs, whilst grain exports were driving up bread-prices at home. Rioting erupted across Fife (in Dysart, Methil, Leven, Elie, Pittenweem, Kingsbarns and Crail), and spread beyond, to Dundee, Valleyfield, Kincardine, Blackness, Bo'ness and Linlithgow. By mid-March there had been flare-ups as far afield as Montrose and Arbroath. After this, though, the unrest slowly subsided.

Crime and Punishment

The criminal code in early-modern Scotland didn't just include what we'd see as crimes – murder, theft and robbery – but more apparently 'moral', private transgressions like adultery. (All these offences, incidentally, could be punishable by death – as, invariably, was blasphemy, which included avowed atheism.) Conversely, the Kirk Sessions (panels of church elders in every parish, meeting regularly) who sat in judgement on such things as church attendance and Sabbath-breaking, also dealt with obviously criminal cases like assault.

The Reformation had only reinvigorated moral zeal and the modern demarcation of 'church' and 'state' still lay a century or so in the future. The penal code was more or less explicitly seen as upholding that which had been lain down in scripture. Hence, in 1661, the passing of legislation to uphold the commandment to 'Honour thy father and thy mother': anyone who 'beat or cursed either their father or mother, shall be put to death without mercy', it ordained.

Imprisonment wasn't generally a punishment in itself: the gaol was just a place of remand before a trial was held, after which other penalties – from execution through flogging down to fines – would be exacted. These last were the 'tolls' that had to be paid to designated officials, who had their own special 'tolbooth' in every town, beside the market.

Capital punishment wasn't just a legal procedure but a set of rituals, from the holding of the prisoner in Edinburgh's Tolbooth through to the final Sunday service in the High Kirk (its sermon specifically directed at the condemned). Then there was the public execution, which was conducted in different places at different times – outside the Castle, down below in the Grassmarket or up on the High Street by the mercat cross. The maiden was used from the end of the 16th century to the beginning of the 18th. You can see this device, an elegant construction in oak and iron, on display in Edinburgh's National Museum of Scotland. It was replaced with the gallows from 1710.

Porteous and the People

When we compare the electoral system we have today with that prevailing in the 18th century, we see how far short the old ways fell in democratic terms. But the people had a voice of sorts: they expected it to be heard, even if it often expressed itself in fairly rough and ready terms. Outbreaks of violent disorder were by no means unusual in those times. One such occurred in the spring of 1736, at a public execution in Edinburgh. The City Guard fired into the crowd to quell the disturbance, killing six. The people were furious, not surprisingly, though their anger was to some extent allayed when the Guard's commanding officer, Captain John Porteous, who had given the order to fire, was tried for murder and convicted that July.

Porteous' execution, scheduled for September, was put back after an intervention by Prime Minister Robert Walpole – sparking suspicions that the establishment was going to look after its own. On 7 September, an angry mob burst into the Tolbooth and dragged the prisoner bodily outside. Beating him as they went, they took him down to the Grassmarket, where they lynched him. He was buried in Greyfriars, where his gravestone may still be seen – as can a memorial in the Grassmarket, near the place where he was hanged. (The Porteous Riots provided the starting point for Sir Walter Scott's 1818 novel, *The Heart of Midlothian*.)

Edinburgh's last public execution did not take place until 21 June 1864, when George Bryce was executed outside the City Chambers for the 'Ratho Murder'. A young man with mental-illness issues, Bryce had murdered Jane Seton, a young maidservant at Ratho Villa, in Baird Road, Ratho, west of Edinburgh. He blamed her for the fact that his girl-friend – another maid in the same household – had thrown him over. Some 26,000 people turned out to experience this edifying event.

Mystic Masons

Stonemasonry is still a visible craft in Scotland, certainly in comparison with England's traditionally brick-built modern cities, where the word 'mason' immediately suggests more secretive and more symbolic meanings. But there's always been a special aura around work in stone. Constructing the country's churches was doing God's work in an espe-cially concrete way. William Schaw, King James VI's Master of Works, is supposed to have been an important figure in the history of freemasonry, which traditionally goes back to the craft guilds of medieval times. The 'Mother Lodge', at Kilwinning, Ayrshire, actually claims to have been estab-lished in the 12th century. (There is, indeed, a sort of West

Coast version of Rosslyn Chapel (see page 57) at Kilwinning Abbey, which is supposed to have been a headquarters of the Knights Templars.)

Number 0 on the roll of Scottish lodges, St Mary's Chapel Lodge, in Edinburgh, appears to have had a pivotal role in the movement's history. The first initiation, under its auspices (in 1634), of a man who wasn't actually a working stonemason, marked the start of the order's transition from its ancient role as a workers' fraternity to its modern one as an organisation dedicated to philosophical speculation – interpreting the works of the creator, or 'Grand Architect' of the Universe. The Grand Lodge of Scotland was founded in 1736 – so very much a product of the Enlightenment. Its present premises, on Hill St, in Edinburgh's New Town, were built in 1820.

Old Pretensions

The struggles of the Stuarts to reclaim the Crown – for themselves and for Catholicism – continued through the early decades of the 18th century. The ousted dynasty came back to haunt the Hanoverians in a series of rebellions that rocked the state, at the same time reminding Britain of what had so nearly been.

James Francis Edward Stuart (1688–1766) was the man who would have been King James VIII (James III of England) – the rightful 'King Over the Water' as far as Jacobites were concerned. Others said that James VII's 'son' was actually an impostor – smuggled into Mary of Modena's bedchamber in a warming-pan, after her own baby was stillborn. Whisked away weeks later, he grew up in France.

He came back to claim his throne in 1708, with the help of a French invasion fleet. There was support for him in Scotland:

Union Dues

*Never was seen so universal a joy at Edinburgh as that
which appeared in everybody's countenance for three or
four days before the King's arrival. The loyal subjects
thronged together, and those of the government durst not
appear in public.*

Universal? Everybody's countenance? Jacobite Charles
Fleming (1673–1744), the future Earl of Wigtown, was obviously exaggerating (what, otherwise, of those government-
supporters who 'durst not appear in public'?) but there's
no doubt that enthusiasm for a Stuart restoration was running high. In the end, though, it was all to end in anticlimax:
the Royal Navy was waiting for them in the mouth of the
Firth of Forth, frustrating their plan to put troops ashore
at Burntisland. Beaten back before he could even land, the
'Pretender' (so called for his pretension, his claim to the
throne) had to retire in ignominy, his rising having concluded
before it had even begun.

He was back seven years later to try again. Once more,
though, circumstances were against him. Louis XIV's
France and Britain had both been signatories to the Treaty
of Utrecht (1713) and the French didn't want to risk another
war. It hadn't even been James' idea to mount this rebellion
in the first place: his Scottish representative, John Erskine,
22nd Earl of Mar, had got over-excited and raised the standard unilaterally. He had called the clan chiefs together for
the traditional summer hunt at Braemar (they assembled at
Invercauld Castle, outside the town: it was the seat of the
Farquharsons, Mar's supporters). The 'Hunt of Braemar',
accordingly, was on this occasion much more than a sporting and social gathering, and James had little alternative but
to make the best of things. As quickly as he could, he sought
French help and set to sea – inevitably, though, it was going
to take some weeks for him to get to Scotland; in the meantime, 'his' rising would have to proceed without him.

Fifteen Fiasco

As it turned out, 'the Fifteen' – or Jacobite rising of 1715 – started promisingly, with Mar's men quickly gaining ground in the Highlands and establishing a base in Perth. But John Campbell, Duke of Argyll, a government supporter, was occupying Stirling and in no mood to give it up to the rebels. He wasn't wild about the Hanoverians, but liked the idea of Jacobitism even less, and he favoured the union with England. Meanwhile, an anticipated rising in southwestern England failed to take place – broken up by government agents before it had begun. Whilst a smallish force of Northumbrian supporters rose up in support, marched south with the help of a band of Highlanders, and even took Preston, they were halted there and forced to surrender.

In Scotland, the rebellion in the Highlands was still strong. Clan loyalty still came before all others: the lords who supported the Stuarts were also chiefs. In the Lowlands too, big magnates like James Maule, Earl of Panmure, could call up support at will among a tenantry (in the withering words of one contemporary) 'for the most part ignorant and inured to slavery'.

So Mar had no business losing the Battle of Sheriffmuir, outside Dunblane, on the eastern side of what's now the A9 road on 13 November 1715. His army was twice as big as Argyll's, but his dithering beforehand and the shambolic nature of his eventual advance allowed the smaller force to stand strong and even to some extent take the initiative. The resulting stalemate (actually, the left wings of both armies were defeated) ended up feeling much more like a Hanoverian win. Much of the battlefield has now been wooded over, but, by the roadside at the forest's southern edge, there's a monument to those members of the Clan Macrae who fell at Sheriffmuir. And, in a clearing further north, the Gathering Stone, where the Jacobite standard is supposed to have been raised before the battle – and where the dead were laid to rest when it was done.

Enthusiasts see the Fifteen as the rising the Jacobites 'should' have won. Mar really made a mess of things, in everything from his timing to his tactics in the field. By the time the Pretender landed at Peterhead on 22 December, it was all over bar a bit of shouting (from his Highland supporters, angry that a cautious French Crown had sent no troops or armaments). It was all up, and, with Argyll pushing steadily up towards Perth, a matter of damage-limitation.

And, for the elite, escape back to France – or a nerve-racking period lying low in Scotland. Many were rounded up and shipped from Liverpool, destined for indentured service on the plantations of Trinidad, though some were sold during stops in England's American colonies en route. James VIII/ III and his courtiers returned to France, to live increasingly difficult lives on aristocratic charity, as the government broke Jacobite power in Scotland by confiscating their old estates.

Taming the Highlands

In 1716, a Disarming Act was passed: this did what its name implies, depriving the Highlanders of their weapons. It was, though, a cultural attack as well as a military one, since the dirk (long dagger), claymore or broadsword and target (a small round shield) were not just essential kit but an integral part of Highland dress. Even so, there was an attempted Jacobite rising in the spring of 1719. This one relied on Spanish help, the French having now made their peace with England. But the main England-bound invasion force was dispersed by the weather, rather as the great Armada of 1588 had been.

What was never supposed to have been more than a diversionary force of 270 marines was successfully landed under the leadership of Lord George Keith, the 10th Earl Marischal (see page 94), and managed briefly to occupy Eilean Donan Castle, before being bombarded out by the

Royal Navy. They didn't give up, though, but struck inland to Glen Shiel with those Highlanders who'd risen up to help them. On 10 June, the government troops arrived armed with mortars: they were able to sit at a safe distance and lob these at the Jacobites, who held firm for a creditable few hours before withdrawing, in greater or lesser degrees of disarray. Abandoned by their Scottish supporters, the Spanish marines ended up surrendering. Another Jacobite rebellion ending in indignity.

ROB ROY

The historic Rob Roy MacGregor (1671–1734) fought for the Jacobite side at Glen Shiel and was badly wounded. His life, memorably fictionalised in the novel by Sir Walter Scott (1817), illustrates how far – even between Jacobite risings – some Highland chieftains could end up living outside the law. Though his image as Scotland's Robin Hood was much romanticised, this veteran of Bonnie Dundee's first rebellion (see page 112) had seen some reverses in the years that followed and pursued a way of life as a cattle-raiding brigand.

Glengyle House, beside Loch Katrine, is believed to stand on the site of the cottage in which Rob Roy was born. You can still see the foundations of the cottage he stayed in for a while in Glen Shira, and his grave in the churchyard at Balquhidder. And, if you're more enterprising, and want to get a sense of the Scotland he saw about him on his travels in the hills, you can walk the 'Rob Roy Way', running between Drymen and Pitlochry.

Digging In

The rising of 1719 may have been a failure, but it had come close enough to success to spark anxiety in London – especially given that the Disarming Act should have made this sort of thing impossible. To secure the Hanoverian hold on the Highlands, existing forts were strengthened and garrisons were established. Later that same year, for example, work started on the construction of Bernera Barracks in Glenelg (see page 23). Ruthven Barracks were also built, on what had previously been the mound of a medieval castle, just south of Kingussie, in Strathspey. (The ruins left by the retreating Jacobites who came this way in 1746 still present an imposing sight on the higher ground east of the railway and the A9 road.)

An inspection of 1724 by General George Wade (1673–1748) recommended large-scale infrastructural improvements. Fort William was strengthened; Fort Augustus built further up the Great Glen and Fort George on a promontory northeast of Inverness. (This earlier fort was destroyed during the later Jacobite rising of 1745; the one we see now was built in the course of the 1750s.)

Wade's Bridge, over the Tay at Aberfeldy, which was designed by William Adam, father of the more famous Robert, is perhaps the most handsome enduring memorial to this time. But General Wade is most famous for 'his' roads. Whilst some sections have been overbuilt by modern highways (itself a compliment of sorts) and others washed away or otherwise lost, many fragments may still be seen around the Highlands. Among the most famous are those by Bernera Barracks, Glenelg; beside the A82 in Glen Falloch and just south of Tyndrum; beside the A83 at Rest and Be Thankful, and over the Corrieyairack Pass between Laggan and Fort Augustus.

Efforts to 'domesticate' the Highlands continued with the establishment of the Black Watch regiment in 1725. Very much a Highland band in its organisation and tactics, it was at the same time firmly loyal to the Crown. (Through a great many conflicts around the world, it was, of course, to become one of the British Army's most famous regiments: its glories and tragedies are commemorated in the regimental museum beside the North Inch Park in Perth.)

Riotous Assembly

It wasn't just the Highlands that were wild. Scotland's Lowland cities had their moments too. The year 1725 saw the Malt Tax Riots in Glasgow. The London government's introduction of a tax of threepence a barrel of beer brought about a general hike in the price of what was (in an age before decent drinking water on tap) not just a popular tipple but a near-necessity. Daniel Campbell (approximately 1670–1753) was closely associated with this new levy. A wealthy business-man and politician, he'd not long since built himself a flamboyantly expensive house in the city centre. Completed 13 years earlier and fitted out and furnished in sumptuous style, Shawfield Mansion (at the corner of Trongate and Glassford Street) seemed to sit there, a provocation to the poor.

As temperatures soared that summer, public feelings became inflamed and, one night in June, a crowd stormed the city garrison, rang the fire bell and grabbed weapons then rushed off to Shawfield Mansion, which they also took by storm. Ransacking the place completely, they set it ablaze. Soldiers were sent in from barracks outside Glasgow, but their presence only exacerbated the situation. Especially when their commander, Captain Bushell, decided to dispense with the reading of the Riot Act (an official proclamation, read out at any serious breakdown of order, warning that – potentially deadly – action will be taken if people don't disperse). Instead, he ordered his troops to open fire, which they duly did, killing nine and wounding a further 16 before the soldiers were withdrawn. There were more casualties as they fired to cover their retreat.

To add insult to injury, London took the view that Glasgow's city fathers had fostered unrest over the Malt Tax and that they should take responsibility for the damage to Campbell's house. The corporation was, accordingly, ordered to pay the MP £9,000 in compensation, an enormous burden for the city as a whole. As for Campbell, he came out of the whole thing well ahead, buying the Isle of Islay with his proceeds. This enabled him to cash in on the rise of whisky, which was finding favour now as it wasn't so badly affected by the tax he'd helped introduce. Never trust a Campbell? The old Scottish saying is a bit rough on innumerable blameless Naomis, Neves and Sols, but it's true that a few bad'uns have borne the name. Daniel Campbell died in 1753; Shawfield Mansion was pulled down in 1792; but whisky's ascendancy has continued to this day.

WATER OF LIFE

'Scotch' and whisky are synonymous: the spirit has been distilled for more than a millennium. It takes its name from the Gaelic uisge beatha, *'water of life'. That description was originally a wry joke, of course, but it doesn't overstate the importance of distilling to modern Scotland and to local economies from Skye to Speyside and from Islay to Orkney.*

That said, the ancient Gaelic name does perhaps imply a more historically enduring importance than the spirit we know as whisky actually has. Until the 18th century, it seems, most Scots – like people in England – drank mostly beer. Whilst whisky, made from malted barley mash, was also subject to the Malt Tax, it relied much less heavily on this ingredient. It was, in any case, as a concentrated spirit, a great deal easier to transport than beer – and consequently easier to smuggle. The black-market trade in untaxed spirit, distilled illicitly in the Highlands, transformed a minority taste into the national drink of Scotland.

The Young Pretender

'Bonnie Prince Charlie', Charles Edward Stuart, was the son of 'Old Pretender' James VIII/III. He set his sights on succeeding his father to the Stuart birthright and to reigning in the United Kingdom as Charles III. By the 1740s the French were again in a mood to make mischief for the British (as, of course, they had been in 1708 but not in 1715). Louis XIV now agreed to provide naval backing for an invasion of England, but this fleet was broken up by storms beforehand. France lost interest, but a fired-up Charles kept planning. In July 1745, he turned up virtually unannounced (and without French troops) on the island of Eriskay, before being taken by boat to the mainland on the shores of Loch nan Uamh, south of Arisaig. A few weeks later, his standard was raised on the mainland at Glenfinnan, on the northernmost banks of Loch Shiel (there's a monument).

Despite much scepticism among the Highland chiefs, the Bonnie Prince seems to have had a real gift for swaying hearts and minds. In the days that followed, he managed to muster 3,000 troops. The Jacobites received a welcome omen when a group of MacDonnell clansmen on their way to join them won a skirmish with government forces by the old High Bridge over the River Spean a couple of kilometres downstream of present-day Spean Bridge. Setting off towards the east, the Prince was able to take Perth and Edinburgh without resistance.

Rather than pressing his advantage, though, he lingered there, apparently enjoying the opportunity of posing as a reigning monarch, while many of his troops dribbled gradually away. Then, remembering his purpose, he led what was left of his force to an unexpected triumph at Prestonpans, East Lothian, on 21 September. (Traces of musket shot and other finds have revealed the presence of a battlefield between the southern edge of Cockenzie and the A198, a little way inland. A viewing point at Meadowmill is signposted.) *Hey Johnnie*

Cope are ye wauking yet?, the derisive Jacobite song asked the defeated English general, Sir John Cope (1690–1760), who does indeed seem to have been utterly unprepared for the fight – and only too ready to 'take wing' like an 'ill scar'd bird' before the Highlanders' advance. (A campaign for a fully-equipped modern visitor centre at the scene of what, in the popular imagination, has come to seem one of Scottish history's more upbeat moments has been led by the novelist Alexander McCall Smith in recent years. In the meantime, some re-enactments and other events are staged at the nearby industrial museum of Prestongrange, and a 100m+ Prestonpans Tapestry has been created by enthusiasts.)

Despite this victory, there was still no sign of a popular rising in Prince Charlie's support. But the Crown forces were getting organised by now. And dissension was splitting the Jacobite camp: Lord George Murray (1694–1760), a real general, with experience in the field, disagreed with the Prince on just about everything. Not least on the whole idea of invading England. Even so, in November the Jacobites headed south via Carlisle and Manchester, where a group of English supporters joined them. But there was no great rush to rally to the Jacobite banner, and the Highland troops were uncomfortable so far from home.

At Derby, a government agent persuaded the Highland chiefs that a formidable defence was being mounted around London and that they'd be wasting their time by pushing further south. (On the contrary, as the novelist William Walpole said in a letter of 27 September, the English elite had been filled with consternation by their army's defeat at Prestonpans. 'We are sadly convinced that they are not such raw ragamuffins as they was represented ... This defeat has frightened everybody but those it rejoices.') To Charlie's disgust, the chiefs voted to withdraw to Scotland – supposedly to consolidate their position, though in practice, having lost the initiative, they quickly found themselves in full retreat.

Lord George Murray managed seemingly to turn things round when, the next January, Prince Charlie laid siege to Stirling against advice. Murray, with 8,000 Highlanders, beat off a relief force led by General Henry Hawley (approximately 1679–1759). An important triumph – but the Jacobites weren't able to make much use of the time it bought.

Bogged Down

By April 1746, William Augustus, the Duke of Cumberland, and his army had Prince Charlie and his supporters backed into a corner at Culloden Moor. (There's an NTS visitor centre at the battlefield, a little to the east of Inverness.) But they did not have to fight a pitched battle on this (disadvantageous) ground. Both field and tactics were the Prince's choice, against Lord George Murray's strenuous objections: he favoured a low-level guerrilla war.

Murray's own idea for a night attack on Cumberland's camp southwest of Nairn, on 15 April, was badly botched, however. Back at Culloden, the Jacobites were exhausted, hungry and in disarray as Cumberland advanced early the next day. Confusions among the Jacobite commanders led to its front line becoming overstretched. And then the Prince left his men standing, exposed to fierce artillery fire, while he waited for the 'right moment' to attack. When it finally came, the Highlanders' charge – till now the Jacobites' 'secret weapon' – quickly lost its cohesion over this rough and marshy ground.

'Their front had nothing left to oppose us but their pistols and broadswords,' reported one of Cumberland's officers, Captain James-Ashe Lee. Most were shot down as they pressed forward. By the time Murray could bring up the French-trained Royal Écossois regiment, his left wing had broken and fled. Victory was out of the question now, though the professionalism of the Écossois allowed an orderly retreat – and gave Bonnie Prince Charlie a chance to flee.

On the Run

The rising collapsed. The Prince, a wanted man, had a price of £30,000 on his head. Even so, he was helped by loyal supporters. Now a little bit of Scottish history in his own right, the polymath Walter Biggar Blaikie (1847–1928) pieced together the fugitive's entire route and published his *Itinerary of Prince Charles Edward* in 1896. It was a long, arduous and dangerous journey, much of it necessarily undertaken in the hours of darkness and under constant pressure from the pursuing redcoats. A cairn marks the spot, on the banks of Loch nan Uamh, where he'd first set foot on mainland Scotland, and from which, some 10 days after his defeat at Culloden, he set off to lie low in the Hebrides. During that time, he was still the subject of a manhunt – once, notoriously, having to slip away in disguise as serving-maid to Flora MacDonald. Finally, five months later, he returned to Loch nan Uamh once more to be picked up and whisked away to exile by the French frigate *L'Heureux*.

There was to be no happy ending for Prince Charlie, growing less 'bonny' by the year as, drunken and debauched, in a continental exile from which there was never to be any realistic chance of his returning, he sank deeper and deeper into depression and resentment. He died in Rome (where, as it happened, he'd also been born) in 1788.

Hard Times in the Highlands

There had been grim times to be endured by the Highlands in the meantime as 'Butcher' Cumberland carried out his reprisals. Quite how far his atrocities went is disputed – as these things invariably are; and what was till recently a Jacobite-leaning popular romantic tradition had an interest in talking up the Butcher's crimes. There doesn't seem to be much doubt, though, that it was a difficult time to have the wrong clan-allegiance. Innocent civilians were caught up in the slaughter as suspected Jacobites were put to the sword; cattle were confiscated, crops were destroyed and villages burned.

More than a thousand Jacobite supporters were banished into exile – or actually shipped out and sold into indentured slavery; others were held in Scottish prisons, or in floating hulks on the River Thames. Over the longer term, the government redoubled its efforts to suppress the clan culture in all its aspects, outlawing traditional weapons and Highland dress.

Some chiefs are thought to have 'stayed out', living outside civil society as drovers and beyond the law as cattle-raiders, rather as Rob Roy MacGregor had before. They were, suggests historian Stuart McHardy, waging what amounted to a guerrilla war, though it would have been a self-perpetuating conflict, its ultimate aims unclear. There was also a perfectly lawful tradition of droving, though this too was inherently nomadic. Herds were regularly driven all the way from the western Highlands and Islands to Lowland markets (especially in Crieff): this custom is commemorated in the Highland Drove Walk.

Others emigrated, as the Irish 'Wild Geese' had in the wake of the Williamite Wars. Strong links had already been established with Charles XII's Sweden, several Jacobite émigrés having offered their support through the period since 1715, in return for his blessing on Stuart claims to the British throne. Scots were also involved in the activities of the Swedish East India Company, founded in 1731 in Gothenburg by Nicklas Salgren and Henric König, with help from Colin Campbell (1686–1757), a Stuart-sympathising Scot.

'Other' Countries

Historians have, quite rightly, been at pains to remind us that Prince Charlie's was by no means a nationalistic struggle and that Scots fought on both sides of the Jacobite conflict. In his study of *Rebellion and Savagery* (University of Pennsylvania Press, 2005), however, Geoffrey Plank points out that, despite this truism, the 'Forty-Five' did at least in its aftermath take on some of the characteristics of a race war, with 'wild' hold-out Highlanders being branded as a barbarian 'Other'. This suppression of the 'savage' was deemed wholly necessary and was to provide a moral basis for British empire-building in North America and beyond over the subsequent decades.

As far as the English were concerned, in any case, Scotland was quite remote enough to have an exoticism all its own. Government engineer Edmund Burt, working in the Highlands in the 1720s, saw himself very much as an explorer, 'for there has been less, that I know of, written upon the subject, than of either of the Indies'. A character in Tobias Smollett's *The Expedition of Humphry Clinker* (1771), Jeremy Melford, observes that 'the people at the other end of the island know as little of Scotland as of Japan.' In the same novel, maid Win Jenkins is surprised to learn that she doesn't have to cross the sea to get to Scotland. She's been persuaded by 'some wag, that there was nothing to eat in Scotland, but oat-meal and sheep's heads' (though, as she herself subsequently acknowledges, 'if I hadn't been a fool, I mought have known there could be no heads without kerkasses.').

The Highlands seemed another country again, alien even to Scottish Lowlanders. As Dr Johnson remarked: 'To the southern inhabitants of Scotland, the state of the mountains and the islands is equally unknown with that of Borneo and Sumatra.'

From Rude to Romantic

Cultural differences were underlined by linguistic ones: to Johnson, Gaelic was 'the rude speech of a barbarous people', though he was perhaps on the wrong side of history – or at very least behindhand – in these views. The advent of a new aesthetic that prized the 'wild', the 'free' and the 'sublime' above the classically-disciplined was bringing about what was to prove a seismic shift in attitudes.

This new view was most strikingly evidenced in the response to James Macpherson (1736–96) and his great Ossian imposture. 'Ossian' was supposedly an ancient Gaelic bard, the son of the mythic Irish hero, Fingal or Finn McCool (see page 10). Macpherson maintained that a series of poetic fragments he published in 1760 were derived directly from original Gaelic manuscript sources he had discovered, and of which he had been no more than the translator.

'As rushes a stream of foam from the dark shady steep of Cromla; when the thunder is rolling above, and dark-brown night on half the hill. So fierce, so fast, and so terrible rushed on the sons of Erin...' This sort of nonsense writes itself – or, at least, it would do now, with the benefit of Romantic hindsight. Dr Johnson saw straight through Macpherson's claims: the poems of Ossian weren't just rubbish, he said, but a 'gross imposition' on the reading public.

For the most part, though, the public was only too happy to be imposed on. Ossian's poems came upon the educated world with the force of revelation. They created a sensation, sweeping Europe and North America, their fans including US President Thomas Jefferson (1743–1826) and France's Napoleon Bonaparte (1769–1821). And it wasn't just the public: composers like Felix Mendelssohn (1809–47) and Franz Schubert (1797–1828) were to find deep inspiration in Ossian's works.

Given, moreover, that Macpherson's 'dupes' included such great poets as Johann Wolfgang von Goethe (1749–1832), you have to wonder how far Johnson's contempt was warranted. Pastiche they may have been, but they found a way of reading a remote romantic past that spoke with thrilling immediacy to the sensibility of their own time. A readership tiring of classical correctness, restraint and balance, wanted to be transported by wild rhetoric, uncontained emotions, 'primitive' passions.

Classical Hankerings

Not that this sort of pre-Romanticism was the only poetic game in town. Far from it: the overwhelming mood of Scottish literature (as of English) in the earlier part of the 18th century had been a deep nostalgia for classical symmetry, ease and grace. Allan Ramsay (1686–1758) was arguably to make Scotland seem still more exotic, evoking in its landscape the verdant fields and purling streams of classical pastoral. He himself was the product of a much more workaday rural scene, having come to Edinburgh from Lanarkshire, where his father had managed Lord Hopetoun's lead mines at Leadhills. A wigmaker by trade, he first set up in a shop in the High Street, dabbling in writing verses in his spare time. His hugely successful poem *The Gentle Shepherd* (1725), a pastoral interlude that four years later was to be made into Scotland's earliest opera, is set in the valley of the Logan Burn, above what's now the Loganlea Reservoir, north of Penicuik. At most times of the year, in truth, the windswept Pentlands make a most improbable Arcadia, but on certain spring and summer mornings, with some effort, it can be imagined.

In his new prosperity, Ramsay was able to move to a larger shop in the Luckenbooths (a line of tenements which, till the early 19th century, ran down the centre of the High Street, opposite the Tolbooth), where he was able both to sell books and rent them out by the week – making this the first known 'circulating library' in Britain. He also held little literary gatherings attended by such luminaries as Tobias Smollett, and visitors from London like John 'Beggar's Opera' Gay (1685–1732). In 1733, he built himself a house on the edge of the Castle Rock: 'Ramsay Lodge', as it was known, later formed the basis for Charles Geddes' Ramsay Garden (see page 248). The poet's son, also Allan Ramsay (1713–84), grew up to be one of the foremost portrait-painters of his age.

In Praise of Industry

Pastoral poetry was conventionally set in what classical myth had regarded as the world's first 'Golden Age', in which there had been no death or sickness (or property or wealth); the earth had given up its abundance without labour, and rustic men and women just had to exchange rhyming compliments, do country dances and tend their sheep. As the 18th century went on, this particular idyll was coming to seem less appealing. James Thomson's long poem *The Seasons* (1730) suggests that Scottish thinking was beginning to catch up with that of Defoe, who bemoaned the lack of industry in the country (see page 124). The sight of the summer countryside awaiting harvest sparked this flight of rapture:

> *These are thy blessings, Industry, rough power!*
> *Whom labour still attends, and sweat, and pain;*
> *Yet the kind source of every gentle art*
> *And all the soft civility of life:*
> *Raiser of human kind! by nature cast*
> *Naked and helpless out amid the woods*
> *And wilds to rude inclement elements;*
> *With various seeds of art deep in the mind*
> *Implanted, and profusely poured around*
> *Materials infinite; but idle all,*
> *Still unexerted, in the unconscious breast*
> *Slept the lethargic powers ...*
> *Aghast and comfortless when the bleak north,*
> *With winter charged, let the mixed tempest fly,*
> *Hail, rain, and snow, and bitter-breathing frost.*
> *Then to the shelter of the hut he fled,*
> *And the wild season, sordid, pined away;*
> *For home he had not: home is the resort*
> *Of love, of joy, of peace and plenty, where,*
> *Supporting and supported, polished friends*
> *And dear relations mingle into bliss.*

But this the rugged savage never felt,
Even desolate in crowds; and thus his days
Rolled heavy, dark, and unenjoyed along—
A waste of time! till Industry approached...

Nature is nothing here until it's taken in hand and made productive. Thomson's (underrated) poem takes an unquestioningly upbeat view of progress, development and industry, both as economic activity and as human virtue. Thomson, who also wrote the lyrics to the song *Rule, Britannia!*, for which the Englishman Thomas Arne (1710–78) was to write the music, was the uncle of James Craig, designer of Edinburgh's New Town.

Enlightened Values

A classical aesthetic that laid emphasis on the human ability to impose order and symmetry on chaos ... A can-do spirit that energised innovation and industry ... Both these things may be seen as aspects of a wider European interest in the capacity of humanity to comprehend its universe, to come to terms with its existence and to rationalise it – literally so, for it trusted increasingly during the 18th century to the power of (capital-R) Reason. No longer was religion to be the guiding light that led scholarly and scientific enquiry – for many, indeed, it was starting to seem a superstition, a source of darkness. Instead, intellectual endeavour, freely directed and unhindered by antiquated spiritual taboos, was to bring about a better world in which 'Enlightenment' would reign. Conventionally, this new way of thinking was for a long time seen as having originated on the Continent, and especially in France – home first to Descartes, then to such prophets of modernity as Voltaire and Rousseau. But more recent researches have painted a more complex picture. At the very least, it's been appreciated that Scotland was anything but a backwater in this period. Some scholars have felt justified in making much grander claims.

Though the Scottish Enlightenment was most obviously associated with Edinburgh, its roots were in the west. In an area with absolutely no consensus, the nearest thing to a generally agreed starting point for the whole phenomenon was the work of the Glasgow-based philosopher Francis Hutcheson (1694–1746). Born in Drumalig, County Down, but of Scots-Presbyterian ancestry, he studied at the University of Glasgow as an undergraduate. After some years teaching in Dublin, he came back to take up a chair in moral philosophy in 1729. An Aberdeen graduate, Thomas Reid (1710–96), was a successor in the same position, whilst John Millar (1735–1801) made Glasgow an important centre for the study of the law.

Meanwhile, however, intellectual Edinburgh was also on the march. David Hume (1711–76) is obviously up there among the greatest thinkers of all time, with works like *A Treatise of Human Nature* (1739) and *An Enquiry Concerning Human Understanding* (1748). He's believed to have been born in a tenement on the north side of the Lawnmarket, but spent his boyhood at his family's ancestral home at Ninewells House, near Chirnside in Berwickshire (unfortunately, the house no longer survives). Hume went to Edinburgh University at the age of 12. Although he did go back to Berwickshire to live with his sister for a while after graduating, he missed the excitement of the capital. Around 1753, then, they moved to Edinburgh, to 'Riddell's Land, in the Lawnmarket, near the West Bow'. (To make sense of this description in Edinburgh's modern geography, we have to remember that the West Bow went all the way up the hill in those days – there'd been no Queen Victoria, so there was no Victoria Street back then.) A few years later, they moved a little way down the Royal Mile to Jack's Land in the Canongate. The success he'd sought so long came only with the publication (in stages, from 1754) of *The History of England* – which became a big best-seller, though it's now not much more than a curiosity, alongside the philosophical works.

Himself a historian of distinction, William Robertson (1721–93) probably made his greatest contribution to the new climate of ideas in his time as Principal of the University of Edinburgh (1762–93). A Presbyterian minister's son, he was born in Borthwick Manse, southeast of Gorebridge in Midlothian (though today's 'Old Manse' was only built in 1815). One of his first appointments, Hugh Blair (1718–1800), holds the dubious distinction of having been the world's first English professor. In 1762 he was awarded a new chair in Rhetoric and Belles Lettres, multi-tasking meanwhile as the Minister of St Giles' High Kirk. Dugald Stewart (1753–1828) was Professor of Moral Philosophy for three decades from 1785.

At gatherings of the Philosophical Society of Edinburgh and (from 1754) the Select Society, academics from the university would come into contact with like-minded laymen such as the jurist Henry Home, Lord Kames (1696–1782) and William Smellie (1740–95), first editor (from 1768) of the *Encyclopaedia Britannica*. It was the Select Society that, briefly, in 1755–6, first published the influential intellectual journal, the *Edinburgh Review*, revived versions of which ran from 1773 to 1776, and from 1802 to 1929. (In its 19th-century manifestation, the *Edinburgh Review*'s Whiggism, its support for economic liberalism and strictly constitutional monarchy, alienated old-style Tories, who from 1818 rallied around another Edinburgh journal, *Blackwood's Magazine*.)

Enlightenment in Stone

The principles of civilisation, reason and thoughtfulness for which these illustrious thinkers argued were given concrete form in Edinburgh's George Square, just south of the Old

Town. Most visitors find it a bit depressing that the heirs of Robertson, Blair and Stewart in the university preferred to pull half of this down to give their principles glass-and-concrete form in the 1960s. That said, at least we can still see some of it: another elegant development built in 1766, Brown Square (behind the Royal Museum of Scotland), has been demolished and built over long since.

These schemes constituted a sort of dry run for one of the 18th century's most ambitious building projects, the New Town. Impressive as it is, the New Town reflects only imperfectly the original vision of its original architect, James Craig (1739–95). That's probably just as well, though: his vision of a grid with diagonal as well as cross-streets in the approximate form of the Union Jack would have produced all sorts of awkward corners and angled walls.

Even in the simplified form in which it came to be constructed from the second half of the 1760s, the New Town embodies elegance, order and symmetry – all essentially unionist virtues to Craig's way of thinking. The earth dug out to prepare the foundations (over a million and a half cartfuls, it was calculated) was heaped up across the Norloch – now drained – to connect the New Town with the Old. Quite quickly, though, it seemed that the life of the Old Town was seeping away downhill, leaving the cramped, dark tenements and closes of the past for the spacious vistas of the future. Connie Byrom's book on *The Edinburgh New Town Gardens* (Birlinn, 2005) makes clear how integral a part of the project this greenery and open space was from the very start, the sense of *rus in urbe* as important as that of order.

On the back of his new, post-*History of England* prosperity, David Hume is believed to have built his own house in the New Town in the 1770s, on the corner of St Andrew's Square and what's now South St David Street. He designed his own resting-place as well ('built after the simple and solemn fashion of the old Roman tombs', according to his 19th-century biographer John Hill Burton, another New Town resident), in Old Calton Cemetery on the side of Edinburgh's Calton Hill.

Glasgow too reflected these values: it was 'one of the prettiest towns in Europe', as far as Matthew Bramble, an English visitor in Smollett's *The Expedition of Humphry Clinker*, is concerned, and 'a perfect bee-hive in point of industry ... The streets are straight, open, airy, and well paved; and the houses lofty and well built of hewn stone.'

One family more than any other put Enlightenment principles into architectural practice around Scotland: William Adam (1689–1748) and his sons John (1721–92), Robert (1728–92) and James (1732–94). William's monuments include Craigdarroch in Dumfries & Galloway (1729), Banff's Duff House (1730s) and Robert Gordon's College, Aberdeen (1750). He built Mellerstain House, northwest of Kelso, in 1725, though it was renewed and extended by his son Robert in the 1770s.

ABERDEEN: A TALE OF TWO BURGHS

Old Aberdeen, at the mouth of the River Don, dates back to the 6th century as an ecclesiastical – and, later, consequently, educational – foundation. St Machar's Cathedral and the University are both there. St Machar, reputedly a companion of Columba on Iona, was told in a vision to build his church on this site – where the river loops like a bishop's crosier. New

Aberdeen, on the north bank of the Dee, was founded as a fishing settlement and trading port by William the Lion from the 1130s. It was given its charter by David I in 1179.

A Handbook of Scotland's History

*When Dr Samuel Johnson came north with James Boswell in 1773 (*A Journey to the Western Islands of Scotland, *1775), the city seemed to present a Janus face:*

> *Old Aberdeen is the ancient episcopal city, in which are still to be seen the remains of the cathedral. It has the appearance of a town in decay, having been situated in times when commerce was yet unstudied, with very little attention to the commodities of the harbour.*
>
> *New Aberdeen has all the bustle of prosperous trade, and all the shew of increasing opulence. It is built by the water-side. The houses are large and lofty, and the streets spacious and clean. They build almost wholly with the granite used in the new pavement of the streets of London, which is well known not to want hardness, yet they shape it easily. It is beautiful and must be very lasting.*

Aberdeen as the 'Granite City' was, initially at least, a creation of the late-18th century, a parallel development to Edinburgh's New Town. Union Street and Union Bridge (named, in this case, for the 1800 act bringing union between Britain and Ireland) were built in 1801 and 1805 respectively. John Smith (1781–1852), burgh architect from 1807, did much to shape the city: his list of landmarks ranges from the North Church (1831) to the St Devenick's Bridge (1837). From 1813, he found himself in competition with Archibald Simpson (1790–1847), Aberdeen-born but based in London for the last few years, having been apprenticed there to Robert Lugar (1770–1855) and then to David Laing (1774–1856). His St Andrew's Chapel, built 1817, has been Aberdeen's Cathedral since the early 20th century. The Assembly Rooms (now the Music Hall) went up in 1820. The North of Scotland Bank building (1844) is now the Archibald Simpson pub. The two burghs were officially joined in 1891.

Market Leader

A native of Kirkcaldy and a student of Francis Hutcheson's at Glasgow, Adam Smith (1723–90) won a scholarship to Oxford in the 1740s but ended up disenchanted with what he saw of academic England. That he said so in several of his later works – arguably helping to launch the whole mythos of the Scottish Enlightenment and the 'democratic intellect' (see page 227) – has endeared him to Scottish intellectuals, who might feel less comfortable with his current status as the patron saint of free-market economics.

The late Lady Thatcher, who's said to have carried a copy of his pioneering work *The Wealth of Nations* (1776) around with her in that handbag, must have been delighted that the name of its author's mother had been Margaret. He lived with her during the late-1760s and early-1770s, in a house just behind the High Street, Kirkcaldy, roughly opposite the bottom of Kirk Wynd. That house was demolished in the early 19th century, its site largely covered by a new building, which now houses a row of shops and constitutes numbers 218–222 High Street. It seems to have been there that the famous philosopher-economist wrote most of *The Wealth of Nations*.

From 1778 he lived in Edinburgh. Even when he went to the capital, Smith seems to have bucked the trend by establishing himself in the Old Town. Efforts are currently under way to restore Panmure House, 129 Canongate, as a headquarters for Heriot Watt University's Edinburgh Business School. An L-plan tower house, it was originally built in 1691 for the Earls of Panmure. Among the guests Smith entertained there were the university's Principal William Robertson and Adam Ferguson (1723–1816), philosopher, historian and social theorist. David Hume had been a longtime friend, but he had sadly died before Smith settled there, though his younger brother John (1709–86), a playwright, was a frequent visitor.

There too came distinguished Scottish scientists like Joseph Black (1728–99), discoverer of latent heat. James Hutton

(1726–97), the founder of modern geology, had, since 1770, owned a house at St John's Hill, just off the Pleasance, with views across Holyrood Park to Salisbury Crags (there's now a little memorial garden where his house was). Hutton made observations there, but his most famous breakthrough came with what he found at Berwickshire's Siccar Point, south of Cockburnspath. Seeing that strata of what were clearly different origins and ages adjoined and overlay each other among the rocks, he suggested that this evidence of what he called 'unconformity' confirmed his Uniformitarian theory – that the Earth had been formed in a single continuous (and continuing) process of rock-formation, erosion and sedimentation and so on and so forth, cycling over ad infinitum through countless millennia. His work was popularised by John Playfair (1748–1819), son of the manse of Benvie, a village in the Carse of Gowrie, west of Dundee, but in later life a maths

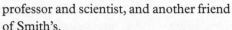

professor and scientist, and another friend of Smith's.

James Hutton is not to be confused with the English mathematician and cartographer Charles Hutton (1737–1823), who in 1772 invented contour lines. It's easily done, though, given that Playfair knew this Hutton too, helping him with his work in estimating the mass of the Perthshire mountain Schiehallion as a first step in the calculation of the mass of the Earth itself – and the other planets, moon and sun.

Athenian Aspirations

New accommodation – now, paradoxically, known as the Old College – on the city's South Bridge was designed for Edinburgh's university by Robert Adam in 1789. By the time it was finished, modifications had been made by

William Playfair (1790–1857; the scientist's nephew), though the spirit of Adam's classical conception had been preserved. Scotland's capital was by now becoming known as the 'Athens of the North', though it's not clear how far this title related to its now-impressive collection of neo-classical architecture and how far to the sense of a city-wide symposium of intellectual exchange. Either way, what should have been its Parthenon, the National Monument to the dead of the Napoleonic Wars, built in 1818, was left unfinished, so looked like a ruin from the start. In fact its incompletion stemmed from a failure to raise sufficient funds, so it stands now as an emblem of Edinburgh's unfulfilled ambitions.

From Reason to Rationalisation

Adam Smith's writings represent an obvious bridge between Enlightenment thought and Enlightenment economic practice, but there had long been signs of a new approach to real-world problems on the ground. 'The Honourable the Society the Improvers in the Knowledge of Agriculture' had been founded in 1723, at which point no fewer than 300 landowners in Scotland had signed up. 'Improving' landlords like these were, in a certain sense, inscribing new values on the Scottish landscape – most obviously in great new castles (maybe more *châteaux* – they were more ornament than military use) such as that of Culzean, west of Maybole on the Ayrshire coast (1777–92), or Inveraray (1740s–80s).

Less visibly, but more importantly in the long term, they manifested themselves in agricultural methods and in land-use. The greatest 'Agrarian Revolution' since the Neolithic was taking place. In southern England, these changes were already well advanced. Scottish farming too was transformed between the 18th and the 19th centuries. (The whole story can be followed at the National Museum of Rural Life, outside East Kilbride.) The changes encompassed everything from the introduction of new crops, from rye grass to turnips and (in 1739) the potato, to ideas of field rotation, fertiliser-use and selective breeding. Swamps were drained to expand the cultivable area and roads built to facilitate transportation.

Green Fingers

Haddo House, in Aberdeenshire, shows improvements both in agricultural arrangements and in the landscaping of its parkland and gardens. So do the grounds at Culzean Castle and at Dawyck House, south of Peebles (and now a 'regional garden' of the Royal Botanic Garden of Edinburgh). The famous gardens at Tyninghame House, East Lothian, were the work of Helen Hope, Countess of Haddington (1677–1768).

Gardening and botany were to become a Scottish 'thing', of course, but the development of this field was very much an aspect of the Enlightenment. William Aiton (1731–93) was, from 1759, the first director of the Royal Botanic Garden at Kew, London. Christian Ramsay, Countess of Dalhousie (1786–1839), made an important contribution as a collector of new plant species, first as the wife of the Lieutenant-Governor of Nova Scotia, and then afterwards in India. She sent specimens home to Dalhousie House, and to the Edinburgh Botanical Society.

Charles M'Intosh (1794–1864), from Abercairney, near Crieff, was celebrated both as horticultural practitioner and as author: Lord Buccleuch's head gardener, he created famous gardens at Dalkeith Park. Robert Fortune (1812–80) worked in the Edinburgh Botanics: it was he who brought the tea plant from China to India – and irrevocably changed the shape of the British working day. Frances Jane Hope (1822–80) pioneered 'natural gardening' at her home in Wardie Lodge (now St Columba's Hospice, 15 Boswall Road, Granton, Edinburgh).

Improvement – for Some

None of these reforms would even have been imaginable without far-reaching changes in land ownership. For centuries, the ancient 'run rig' system – which saw each community's land redistributed among families every year – had prevailed across much of Scotland (see page 50). An admirably equitable system, it also arguably militated against the spirit of improvement or enterprise: no one felt any incentive to invest time or effort in land they'd never own. Now, however, in the course of the 18th century, it was starting to give way to more modern landlord–tenant arrangements, whilst common land was being systematically enclosed (fenced in to make it private property). Again, this had been happening in England since Tudor times, though the process had accelerated into the 18th century.

For Scotland, though, it came as more or less a total shock. Evidence of what was to be a wave of 'Lowland Clearances' may be seen at, for example, the abandoned village of Polmaddy (off the A713 north of New Galloway, Dumfries & Galloway). Replicated across much of south and central Scotland, these changes prompted what Dr Johnson, a recent visitor, was in 1773 to characterise as an 'epidemical fury of emigration'. His phrasing is deceptively elegant, but – as always – the great lexicographer was choosing his words carefully: the results of enclosure were, indeed, a demographic 'fury' (madness, frenzy), with all the force of a fearful disease. Apocalyptic language, then, but by no means necessarily exaggerated given the human costs these 'improvements' were bringing in their wake.

It's difficult, of course, to identify precisely the point at which 'Improvement', seen as (broadly) good, gives way to 'Clearance', which has at one time or another been seen as representing everything from regrettable development to Highland Holocaust. It's true that those who carried out the 'Lowland Clearances' could point to actual and enduring gains in agricultural efficiency, whilst the later 'Highland Clearances' didn't leave much more than empty glens.

Both movements were obviously in large part driven by a desire for greater profitability: the building and upkeep of big houses with beautiful grounds required a great deal of money. The sort of absentee landlordism that left a Scottish estate ticking over whilst the family enjoyed itself in fashionable Edinburgh or London, with a costume-drama's worth of servants, dresses, carriages, entertainments and so on to be provided every year, required even more – and not in capital but in big cash sums. Stana Nenadic has written interestingly (in *Lairds and Luxury*, Birlinn, 2007) on the new social imperatives that drove this consumerist rage among the Highland aristocracy – even as their tenants (once, of course, their clansmen) and their families went hungry or were 'cleared'.

Kelping on the coasts – the harvesting of seaweed for processing into soda-ash – was an early example of this rush to profit (the MacDonald estates on North Uist, for example, funded the development of properties on Skye); other examples are to be found in Moidart, Arisaig and elsewhere. There isn't much doubt that run rig had been an inefficient system, but the sort of sheep farming introduced into the Highlands was hardly better, after the first fast buck. And for the people on the ground in such situations, this sort of 'improvement' didn't improve anything at all. Not surprisingly, opposition had started early: in 1782, in Letterfinlay, Lochaber, a crowd of women had beaten up a prospective sheep farmer.

HOW ENLIGHTENED? HOW SCOTTISH?

Ownership of the Enlightenment has in recent decades been hotly contested in Britain – which is odd, given the efforts of its traditional proprietors to slough it off. Time was when every schoolboy knew that the Enlightenment had been made in France, where philosophes *like Voltaire (François-Marie Arouet, 1694–1778) were out to* écrasez l infâme *('crush*

the infamy'): namely, the benighted superstition sown by the
Church and the political slavery imposed by the ancien régime.
Whilst the Encyclopédistes, *under the leadership of Denis*
Diderot (1713–84), set out to catalogue the world, Jean-Jacques
Rousseau (1712–78) was going to set it free. Since the 1960s,
though, followers of Michel Foucault (1926–84) have come to
see this supposedly liberating movement as a deeply damaging
one of imprisonment, repression – this 'Age of Reason' the dream
that (in Francisco Goya's famous words) would 'bring forth
monsters'.

It's no bad thing, perhaps, that the English-speaking nations
should have got over their intellectual and cultural cringe, but
it's hard to avoid the note of UKIP-esque defiance, even in
so brilliant a book as Roy Porter's Enlightenment *(Penguin,*
2000). If Porter protests too much, that may be because he's
kicking against a consensus view that no longer exists – that
the Enlightenment was overwhelmingly, if not exclusively, a
French production. American author Arthur Herman was
even more specific in How the Scots Invented the Modern
World *(Crown, 2001). In the small-print of his subtitle, far*
from walking back this hyperbolic claim, he simply doubled
down: 'The True Story of How Western Europe's Poorest Nation
Created Our World & Everything in it.'

Again, there's no harm in a bit of patriotic pride. What's
known as the Scottish Enlightenment was certainly a time of
extraordinary intellectual, scientific and cultural creativity. But
before we get too nationalistic about it, it's as well to remember
how closely this episode followed on from the formation of
the United Kingdom, and how far its wider British aspects
are commemorated in everything from the street names of
Edinburgh's New Town to the Encyclopaedia Britannica.
Scottish it may have been, but there's really no denying that it
took place under the auspices of a greater Britain – or that it
may have derived much of its energy from the fact of union.

A Handbook of Scotland's History

Lairds and Lords

The extent to which the 'invisible hand' of Adam Smith's market upset old hierarchies can quite easily be exaggerated. Certainly in this early stage of agrarian reform: to be an 'improving landlord' you had to have land. Rather than 'new money' at this stage, then, Scotland saw the enrichment of 'old'. And to some extent, those same ancient families were to remain at the top, where they'd just about always been.

In the days when the Ascendancy (the historically dominant landowning families) were really in the ascendant, a great many important British statesmen came from the landed class – and a great many of these were of Scottish origin. Dalmeny House, a couple of kilometres east of the Forth Rail Bridge, was built in 1817 as seat of the Earls of Rosebery. The 5th Earl (1847–1929) was to be Prime Minister in 1894–95. Whittingehame House, East Lothian, was birthplace of another Prime Minister, Arthur Balfour (1848–1930). As Foreign Secretary, in 1917, he had been the author of the Balfour Declaration ordaining a 'National Homeland' for the Jews in Palestine. Hirsel, Coldstream, was the home of the Douglas-Homes; the house isn't open today but the estate's a country park. Alec Douglas-Home (1903–95) was Conservative Prime Minister in 1963–64 – though the Earls of Home had been movers and shakers since the start of the 17th century.

Meanwhile, others had been making the transition from industrialist to laird – like John Roebuck (1718–94); Sheffield-born but Edinburgh-educated, he'd developed the large-scale manufacture of sulphuric acid at Prestonpans. Having bought the Carron Company, the ironworks (whose late-Victorian gate and clock tower are still to be seen outside Falkirk), Roebuck set up home in the old Hamilton family seat, Kinneil House, near Bo'ness. It's a stately home with beautiful gardens – but it also has in its grounds the remains of the workshop used by engineer James Watt (1736–1820) when he was developing his steam engine under Roebuck's sponsorship.

158

Drovers and Desperadoes

The tumults of the '19 and the '45 now firmly in the past, British politics became a much more meek affair. Even so, there were strong oppositions, albeit for the most part peacefully expressed at Westminster. Indeed, these oppositions were at least analogous to those that had gone before.

One faction, which followed the banner of parliamentary rule under a constitutional monarchy, became known as the 'Whigs', an originally insulting – and originally Scottish – label derived from 'whiggamore', one of those (supposedly uncouth) Highland drovers who brought the herds of cattle down to Leith. The Whigs could clearly be seen as the political heirs of those who'd supported the Hanoverian state in the wars of the early century.

Named after a different set of savages from the wilder Celtic fringe, the 'Tories' (originally Irish brigands) were now those in British politics whose instincts were to support the authority of the Crown and of the hereditary aristocracy. Whilst any ambition to reinstate the Stuarts had long since been abandoned, this party could clearly be seen to uphold some of the same principles as the Jacobites had fought for in times gone by. Basically (if, admittedly, a bit crudely) the Tories saw Parliament as existing to rubber-stamp the decisions of the monarch, to formulate legislation and raise revenues on his or her behalf. For the Whigs, on the other hand, the king or queen was to have a largely ceremonial status in a realm that should essentially be governed by its MPs.

Neither the Whigs nor the Tories were ever really 'political parties' as we'd understand the term today, with a wider presence beyond Parliament in 'the country'. Within the Westminster chambers, though, the opposition between these two sides was to dominate debate well into the 19th century.

JEKYLL AND HYDE

Robert Louis Stevenson's famous book wasn't actually written until 1886, but its supposed model, Deacon William Brodie (1741–88), was a man of the Enlightenment. By day a respectable cabinet-maker, the deacon of his guild, at night he deployed his locksmith's skills in burgling houses. And his taste for excitement by maintaining a number of mistresses – in some accounts a number of separate households. A crowd of 40,000 turned out to see his execution. He was buried in an unmarked grave in Buccleuch Churchyard, Chapel Street. (Such had been his ingenuity in life, though, that there were inevitably stories that he'd cheated death by slipping a copper tube inside his throat to keep an airway clear and that 'his' coffin had been buried empty. It was even claimed that he'd been sighted, alive and well, years later in the Borders – whether this was true or not, his story certainly caught the public imagination.)

A certain strange duality seems to have been inherent in this newly Enlightened Scotland. It was embodied most strongly of all in Edinburgh, in the opposition of New Town vs Old Town; Modern vs Medieval; Enlightenment vs Unreason. And, of course, in that of scientific medicine vs bodysnatching. Extreme forms of Scottish Calvinism appeared to allow a coexistence of good and evil: in theological theory, the 'elect' would be saved however bad their conduct (this idea is explored in James Hogg's novel The Confessions of a Justified Sinner, *1824). These more lurid dualities apart, the prosaic fact seems to have been that the New Town drained some of the life out of the Old, as respectable people didn't have to go there much. The opening of the Edinburgh Academy in 1824, in Henderson Row on the New Town's northern edge, shifted the focus of the city still further away from the Old Town for the 'better sort', leaving a more conventional duality between rich and poor.*

Medicine and the Macabre

Edinburgh's Royal College of Surgeons was given its licence as a craft guild as early as 1505, under James IV, but surgery still had no real scientific pretensions at this stage. Professionalisation came later, at the time of the Enlightenment. Playfair's Surgeon's Hall was built in 1830.

Well into early-modern times, even the most advanced medical practitioners had shown what we'd see as an astonishingly insouciant disregard to the scientific facts. The 'authority' of ancient sources such as Hippocrates (5th century BCE), Aristotle (4th century BCE) and Galen (2nd century BCE) trumped anything that might be gleaned from observation. Imbalances of the different 'elements' and the 'humours' in the blood were blamed for most distempers and were 'cured' by a range of extravagant and exotic methods which, however, always had a way of coming back to 'bleeding' – the removal of quantities of blood.

Edinburgh's emergence in the 18th century as a centre for the study of medicine started to change all this – in many ways, obviously for the better, but there were less agreeable aspects of the new discipline as well. The expectation that students would now examine actual bodies at first hand brought with it a demand for cadavers. Since at this stage (as till recently) Christian believers looked forward to the resurrection of the body, not just the soul, for eternal life, they weren't too keen on the idea of being dissected and left un-whole.

Hence the fear of dying destitute; hence too the most dreadful aspect of the death penalty – since those who were executed had no right to a Christian burial. And hence the practice of grave robbing: fresh corpses were dug up in the dead of night by 'Resurrectionists' for sale to students and to medical researchers. There was a brisk black market in bodies, and reports of students actually paying for their courses in dead bodies.

Those who could afford it had themselves interred in armoured coffins. The posher cemeteries and churchyards had high-security arrangements so the dead could sleep in safety: there's a watchtower at the corner of St Cuthbert's churchyard, in Edinburgh's West End.

But where there's a demand, the market shall supply. And Brian Bailey, in his book *Burke and Hare: The Year of the Ghouls* (Mainstream, 2002), describes the attempt to send 11 corpses from Liverpool to a Mr G.H. Ironside of Edinburgh in 1826. Dock workers, noticing a 'dreadful stench' from three barrels they had loaded on to a vessel bound for Leith, found the bodies pickled in brine. The police investigation led to a nearby house, where 22 corpses were discovered in the cellar, some severely decomposed. At the subsequent trial, it was revealed that 'a tierce of brine in the cellar had been found to contain the bodies of babies, and this evidence made the foreman of the jury feel so ill that he had to leave the court to recover'.

It was only a matter of time, perhaps, before someone thought of cutting out the Grim Reaper as middleman. The moment came with Burke and Hare's campaign of murder in 1828. William Burke (1792–1829) and William Hare (approximately 1792–?) were both Irish immigrants to Edinburgh who'd come to work on the Union Canal, then under construction not far away from where both were living in the West Port, off the Grassmarket. Hare's wife, Margaret, ran a lodging house in what was, then as now, a slightly seedy district, and their first cadaver seems to have come to them by natural causes when an elderly resident died still owing rent. After that, though, rather than wait on nature, Burke and Hare started enticing homeless and hopeless individuals – male and female – off the nearby streets with offers of hospitality, disorientated them with drink and then suffocated them to death.

Their next step was to take their victims' bodies – there were eventually to be 16 in all, it's thought – to the house of the respected surgeon Robert Knox (1791–1862) in Newington Place (behind what's now 17 Newington Road). There they were paid for their labours, no awkward questions apparently being asked, though Knox was to swear at the murderers' trial that he hadn't had a clue what they'd been doing. Once they were caught, Hare turned against his partner, so he was spared whilst Burke was hanged. And, of course, dissected: his remains were carefully preserved and now have pride of place in the exhibition in the Surgeon's Hall. The Edinburgh mob, never convinced of Knox's innocence, was later to attack his house: he went down to London to work there.

Burns, Baby, Burns!

The French Revolution of 1789 sent a shockwave across Europe. Its radical fervour is famously reflected in Robert Burns' poetry (a' that *A Man's a Man for a' That* stuff). Burns' genius was all his own, of course, but the cult of his celebrity that had followed the publication of his *Poems, Chiefly in the Scottish Dialect* in 1787 can't completely be separated from his romantic (if distinctly stereotyping) status as a low-born and unlettered 'Ploughman Poet'.

But if Burns personified the new democratising impulse – and indeed articulated many of its values – he can be seen as reflecting the ambivalence of his age as well. It was partly the mercurial spirit of the man that, in his writings, he should have hailed (the monarchical absolutism of) Jacobitism one moment and (the revolutionary republicanism of) French Jacobinism the next. Just as in life he denounced aristocratic privilege one moment and grovelled to noble patrons the next; and just as he attacked the union and then went to work for the Excise. But it was also maybe the mixed-up feelings of late-18th-century Scotland. It's fascinating to visit Robert Burns House, Dumfries (where he lived during his later years), and – even more – the Birthplace Museum in Alloway. (The museum itself is a short walk from the actual birthplace – the Burns' cottage, carefully preserved – but it's right next to the 'auld haunted kirk' outside which, in Burns' classic poem, Tam o' Shanter witnesses the witches' sabbath and has to ride pell-mell to safety across the 'Brig o' Doon'. The latter may also still be seen, just a little way upriver from the modern road bridge.)

More generally, the radicalism fired by the French Revolution found eloquent expression in Tom Paine's *Rights of Man* (1791). A double whammy of Paineism and high bread prices (caused by the corn laws, which kept grain prices high as a favour to aristocratic landowners) led to the 'King's Birthday Riots' in Edinburgh, in 1792. On the night of 4 June, a mob rioted in the Royal Mile: they took a sentry box from the High Street and carried it down the street to burn it at the Netherbow. Dragoons were brought in from Musselburgh: they charged through the streets, swords drawn. Next night, an effigy of Lord Advocate Henry Dundas was burned in front of his mother's (Lady Arniston) house in George Square. The house was attacked with missiles and windows broken, before a detachment of marines was brought in from Leith, the Riot Act read and at least one person killed in the shooting that ensued. The young Walter Scott was living in the Square (number 25) at this time, but he makes no mention of these events in his later writings. On 6 June, for a further (and final) night of rioting, the focus moved to St Andrew's Square, where the then Lord Provost, James Stirling, had a house.

The following year brought another long, hot summer, during which a military call-up among the miners of Tranent met with resistance. The official suspicion was, as always, that this popular opposition could not conceivably be spontaneous. The dangerous radicals in this case were the 'United Scotsmen', a republican movement modelled on the United Irishmen of Theobald Wolfe Tone (1763–98). They were led by lawyer Thomas Muir the Younger of Huntershill (1765–99). After a meeting on 29 August, militiamen were sent in and shot or cut down anywhere between 10 and 20 people. The 'Massacre of Tranent' has been commemorated by a statue in the High Street since 1995.

BROSE BEFORE HAUTE CUISINE

Doctor Johnson's notorious definition of oats as 'a grain which, in England, is generally given to horses, but in Scotland supports the people', may have been mean-minded but could not be said to have been untrue. Tougher and more tolerant of the cold and damp than the namby-pamby wheat the English diet relied on, oats had been a Scottish staple for centuries.

Not only could they be cooked with water and a pinch of salt for porridge; they could be mixed raw with a dash of water to make a soggy mess and carried around cold as brose. Indeed, at all but the highest levels of society, it was pretty much oats with everything. If an army marches on its stomach, that of Scotland's soldiers was filled substantially with brose; its scholars attained Enlightenment on an oatmeal diet (a day each term – 'Meal Monday' – was actually set aside for students to go home to their villages and replenish their supplies of oats to eat and peat to heat their rooms).

Oats featured in haggis too, though the 'Scottishness' of this preparation of mutton offal, onion, spices and herbs served up in a sheep's stomach has been relatively recent, and firmly established only in the time of Burns. Again, it's an example of England opting for more refined foods: similar dishes seem to have been popular south of the Border in medieval times, only to be marginalised in the modern era.

Revolutionary Wars

The American Revolution came to the Firth of Forth in 1779 (in improbable alliance with the reactionary Bourbon monarchy in France) in the form of a Franco-American fleet commanded by (Kirkcudbright-boy) John Paul Jones (1747–92). A storm frustrated his plan to capture – and hold to ransom – the port of Leith. There was much more to come in the years that followed, however, after the French Revolution. The new regime – and the dictatorship of Napoleon Bonaparte (1769–1821), which came quickly after – found it convenient to direct domestic discontent into foreign wars. In the face of persistent harassment of local shipping, the island of Inchgarvie in the Firth of Forth was built up as a defensive bastion (though the fortifications there now were mostly built a great deal later).

Small circular forts – Martello Towers – were a major feature of Britain's coastal defences at the time of the Napoleonic Wars. Leith's Tally Toor stood on rocks at the outer edge of the harbour, supervising its approaches; since the big breakwater was built in the 1930s, changing the shape of the shoreline there, it's been absorbed into the dock complex onshore. Other Martello Towers can be seen in the

Orkneys, overlooking Scapa Flow, at Crockness, Hoy, and at Hackness, on South Walls, where the tower is just part of a larger defensive complex, with battery.

The need for naval crew to fight in the wars prompted the government to give incentives to the fishing fleet, which was seen as a perfect training school for seafarers. When sufficient crewmen didn't sign up willingly (to escape from difficult domestic situations, dead-end jobs – or just to see the world) they had to be coerced. Or, as the official terminology had it, 'impressed' – though victims would have been anything but. The 'Press Gang' made a nuisance of itself not only in Britain's big seaports, but also smaller fishing centres around the coast, and it had a disproportionate impact on Scotland's island communities, according to J.D.M. Robertson's *The Press Gang in Orkney and Shetland* (Orcadian, 2011).

During the Napoleonic Wars, French prisoners were held in the Midlothian town of Penicuik, whilst more captives were held at the depot that later became Perth Prison; others were confined in Edinburgh Castle. Officers were allowed a degree of freedom, being billeted in 'parole towns' like Kelso, Peebles and Dumfries, where they were able to lead comparatively normal lives.

Democratic Domesticity

The way people packed into Edinburgh's Old Town tenements was remarked on by bemused visitors from England – like Jeremy Melford in Smollett's *The Expedition of Humphry Clinker*:

> *The first thing that strikes the nose of a stranger, shall be nameless but what first strikes the eye, is the unconscionable height of the houses, which generally rise to five, six, seven, and eight stories, and, in some places (as I am assured), to twelve. This manner of building, attended*

> *with numberless inconveniences, must have been origi-*
> *nally owing to want of room. Certain it is, the town seems*
> *to be full of people: but their looks, their language, and*
> *their customs, are so different from ours, that I can hardly*
> *believe myself in Great-Britain.*

Scots had long been accustomed to living cheek by jowl. Gladstone's Land, Lawnmarket, in Edinburgh, has six storeys, and was built in the 17th century. There wasn't necessarily anything utopian about this sort of living, but it still involved the different classes coexisting in close proximity. The construction of the New Town 'opened out' conditions in the Old to some extent. John Lockhart, writing in 1819, reported: 'I have a tailor for my neighbour immediately below me – a cobbler – a tallow-chandler – a dancing-master – a grocer and a cow-feeder ... and above, God knows what store of washerwomen – French teachers – auctioneers – midwives – seamstresses – and students of divinity.'

SIX

LAND OF THE
SLAG HEAP AND
THE CANAL

'THERE IS,' WROTE SIR WALTER SCOTT in 1814, 'no European nation which, within the course of half a century, or little more, has undergone so complete a change as this kingdom of Scotland.' He meant, he explained, the political and social transformation brought about by the defeat of the Jacobite cause; 'the destruction of the patriarchal power of the Highland chiefs – the abolition of the heritable jurisdictions of the Lowland nobility and barons', and the old attachments and loyalties that had gone along with these. But these were just the start of the changes: with the Agrarian Revolution had come the first stirrings of the Industrial; Scotland would never be the same again.

Moral Fabric

The 18th century had seen the establishment of a woollen textile industry in towns in the Borders (such as Hawick and Selkirk) and of cotton manufacture further west. The reliance of this industry on water power (and on the availability of water for other processes, like washing and dyeing) often meant new start-up centres at out-of-city sites. The sense of new beginning this brought perhaps made an element of utopianism inescapable. These new industrial complexes were often to be planned along 'model village' lines.

One such planned settlement was that of Gatehouse of Fleet, in Dumfries & Galloway, founded by local landowner James Murray in the 1760s. The cotton mills he and his family established were eventually to employ 500 people; their Cally Hotel would later open up this beautiful part of Galloway to tourists. Sir William Douglas' Castle Douglas, built on a grid-plan beside Carlingwark Loch, was also founded (in the 1790s) with cotton manufacture in mind. Further east in Dumfries & Galloway, Langholm also owes its modern form to the textile industry, both cotton and wool. George Ludovic Houston's Johnstone was deliberately established as a centre for coal mining and cotton-weaving; as was another Renfrewshire settlement, Alexander Montgomerie's Eaglesham.

Now a World Heritage Site, the cotton mills at New Lanark were founded in 1786 by David Dale (1739–1806), but it's with his son-in-law, Robert Owen (1771–1858), that they're now most closely associated. This planned settlement had four seven-storey factory buildings, their machinery driven by water diverted from the nearby Clyde; some 2,000 people lived in the workers' housing just nearby. So far, so rational: business efficiency was served as much as social idealism, though it mattered to Dale that his 'hands' and their families should be comfortably accommodated and well cared for. When Robert took over in 1800, he pushed his father-in-law's socialist project that much further, creating what are believed to have been Britain's first infant schools. He set up a co-operative store and community health insurance and democracy, with elected representatives and regular meetings for the discussion of grievances and issues of the moment. Within the workplace itself, he improved conditions, shortening hours and introducing incentives for quality and productivity – over time, these enhanced the mills' performance and profitability.

New Lanark was by no means unique: Owen himself had other mills – at Stanley, Perthshire, for instance; whilst there were other idealists, like James Finlay, who had model mills at Deanston and at Doune. These last outlasted other cotton mills in southern Scotland as they produced specialised textiles that remained in some demand. At Gairbraid, northwest of Glasgow, a cotton-printing mill was founded in the late-18th century by Hew Hill, the local landlord; the surrounding accommodation was built up into a new town by his daughter Mary (1730–1809) and her husband, Robert Graham. They gave it Mary's maiden name, so it's since been known as Maryhill.

In Scotland as in England, the textile industry was the first really to take off to any appreciable degree, but manufacture in other fields was also getting going. Albeit on a comparatively small scale – and in what in hindsight seem like quite strange places. One of Scotland's first important industrial iron foundries, for example, was the Lorn Furnace at Bonawe, on the northern shore of Loch Etive, Argyllshire – the middle of nowhere, as far as the later map of industrial Scotland would be concerned. The site made sense, though, because, whilst ore could be brought in by sea from Cumbria, northern England, trees could be felled and burned for charcoal, and limestone quarried in the region around. Between the 1750s and the 1870s, this foundry turned out over 700 tonnes of iron a year.

The Telford Effect

Adam Smith himself had underlined the importance of infrastructure in advancing economic development:

> *Good roads, canals, and navigable rivers, by diminishing the expence of carriage, put the remote parts of the country more nearly upon a level with those of the neighbourhood of the town. They are upon that the greatest of all improvements.*

Thomas Telford (1757–1834) was probably the most famous of a whole generation of Scottish engineers. He may have first made his name in Shropshire, where he now even has a town named after him, but Telford was born in Glendinning, outside Langholm, Dumfries & Galloway. (There's a 'Telford Trail' around Langholm, taking in some of the places that figured in his early life.) He was to have an immeasurable impact on his native country with his roads, bridges, canals and harbours. What is now the A74 between

Glasgow and Carlisle was originally built by this 'Colossus of Roads', as were the road across the centre of Arran and the Caledonian Canal (completed in 1822).

Telford's work is often good to look at – function and form came together with perfect grace in the Craigellachie Bridge (1814) on Speyside – but utility always came first with an engineer whose works embodied a new Caledonian can-do spirit. It was Telford who developed the harbours at Gourdon, Banff, Peterhead and Aberdeen, bringing these ports into the modern age. At Pultneytown, near Wick, he created what was arguably the world's first industrial estate. His extraordinary range extended into the ecclesiastical: the 'Telford Church' was pretty much a model kit. Over 30 of these iron-framed churches were built in the Highlands and Islands in the 1820s. They were also known as 'Parliamentary Churches', as they were funded by a government grant.

Peterhead Harbour.

ULLAPOOL: FISH WITH EVERYTHING

This town on the west coast of Ross and Cromarty was founded in 1788 specifically as a centre for the herring fishery. It was built on an area of flat land alongside Loch Broom where there was space for the accommodation, workshops and warehousing needed not just to land herring, but also to process, pack and export the fish.

Thomas Telford was brought in to conjure a community into being. It was constructed along conspicuously rational, modern lines. The regularity of its gridlike street plan contrasts with the rugged unevenness of the surrounding landscape. A boxy 'Telford Church' now houses the town museum.

The herring fishery boomed – so much so that, by the 1830s, stocks were declining and catches diminishing. By 1900, the settlement was pretty much ruined. World War II brought a brief revival (the North Sea was plagued by mines, which favoured Atlantic fishing), but stocks again declined after this until herring fishing had to be banned in 1978. Life went on, with a switch to mackerel, Scottish fishermen servicing Russian, East European and even West African 'Klondyker' factory ships, till these stocks too began to dwindle and quotas were enforced in the 1990s. Fishing continues, but has been restricted in its scope and scale.

Industrial Arteries

James Watt's Monkland Canal (1771) now survives, improbably enough, as a subway under Castle Street at Glasgow's Royston Road – and as the course of the M8 motorway east of the city. You can also see a section at Coatbridge's Summerlee Industrial Museum. Watt's Crinan Canal, which opened in 1801, created a short cut across Kintyre, linking the Firth of Clyde (via Loch Gilp) with the Sound of Jura and the Hebrides. As its name suggests, the Forth and Clyde (1790) connected the two great rivers of Scotland's eastern and western coasts, whilst Telford's Caledonian Canal (1822) also linked east and west, in this case following the geological faultline of the Great Glen.

Also opened in 1822, and designed to connect the capital up with the Forth and Clyde at Falkirk, the Union Canal was conceived as a 'contour canal', constructed along a single continuous height-contour. The great thing about this was that no locks – a major cause of aggravation and delay – would be required, although elaborate engineering design was needed to make it possible. Aqueducts had to be built, like the one at Slateford and those over the Almond and Avon west of Edinburgh, and tunnels like that through Falkirk's Prospect Hill. The Linlithgow Union Canal Society has a Canal Centre with boat trips and a museum for visitors, where the history of this extraordinary enterprise is documented.

That history is of course a human one, not just one of engineering or economics in the abstract. A resident's letter – written in 1818 – evokes the impact of the Union Canal's construction on Falkirk life:

> *They are cutting a tunal belaw grany from west side of our moar all the way to the glen burn about half a mill … they sunk pits about 100 yards from each other to the level of the cannal and then cut east and west till they met below taking all the stuff up by windlasts … a great deal of Irish men came over and is employed at it and several accident has happened at it and 2 was killed by the face of the brea faling down on them … few of our countrymen is at it as in general they cannot stand the work … they are mostly irish young men and a bad set they are.*

As for the impact of such projects on the Scottish land-scape, that might seem to go without saying, but the indirect consequences have to be considered too. For example, a whole town, Grangemouth, grew up around the lock at which the Forth and Clyde Canal connected with the sea. (Other factors kicked in later, of course: the new canalside settlement made an ideal headquarters for James 'Paraffin' Young when he was establishing his West Lothian oil-shale industry (see page 205); this in turn helped set up the town for its later role with North Sea Oil.)

Some canals came and went quite quickly: the Aberdeen-shire (Aberdeen–Inverurie) opened in 1805, but in 1854 it was filled in and became the course of a railway line. Pretty much the whole section of the East Coast Main Line between Aberdeen Harbour and Inverurie follows this route. You can see traces of the old canal construction alongside Elmbank Terrace, Kittybrewster, and beside the Great North Road, in Woodside, Aberdeen.

Canals were mainly for moving freight, but passenger 'fly' boats also plied up and down – mainly to offer excursions and day trips across country. Sedate as these little jaunts may sound, they could prove surprisingly risky: this was a very new industry, and many safety issues weren't yet understood. In 1810, the Paisley Canal Disaster cost 84 lives when one such boat capsized after a stampede of passengers. In the 1880s, this canal was drained to provide a course for the con-

struction of the Paisley Canal Line to Glasgow Central. What had been the canal basin in Paisley – the scene of the 1810 disaster – became a coal yard attached to Canal Street Station; now it's all been subsumed into the Castle Gait housing development.

Darkness of Heart

The Atlantic slave trade is now regarded as one of the great enormities of modern history. But whilst there's unanimity over its significance as a crime, and as a human tragedy, there's no consensus on its ultimate importance as an economic force. For some scholars, though, this was the commerce that underwrote the Industrial Revolution; another example of modern civilisation as a gentle Dr Jekyll with a dark and cruel Mr-Hyde heart.

The indications are that the great Enlightenment thinkers had only pragmatic reservations about this trade. Hume, whilst seeing slavery as a brake on general progress, seems to have been ethically unperturbed; for Adam Smith it was an encumbrance on the free market. Although the trade in slaves in the British Empire was abolished in 1807, slavery itself remained allowable until 1833. Glasgow and Dumfries both sent ships in the trading times; thereafter slave-gathered cotton was still spun and woven in all the textile centres of the southwest (not excluding utopian New Lanark). Glasgow was also important for tobacco – again, this was slave-produced until the 1830s. Scotland wasn't implicated on anything like the scale of Liverpool and the Lancashire textile towns, but even so, the country's hands were hardly clean.

For decades, the ethics of the business went unquestioned except by a small minority, though the strength of the abolitionist movement grew as the decades went by. Otherwise decent and high-minded people took the trade for granted. In 1786, for instance, Robert Burns – in many respects a radical – had been planning to go to Jamaica to work as an overseer on a plantation. Only the success of the Kilmarnock Edition of his poems changed his plans.

White Slavery

If the Atlantic slave trade failed to shock, that was presumably because the actual transportation of the 'product' took place so far away. A ship setting out from Dumfries, say, would carry only finished goods from Britain – anything from printed fabrics and household goods to guns. Bought in one of the West African ports and then shipped direct to the Americas, the slaves themselves would (with rare exceptions) never come within a thousand miles of Scotland. Having sold its cargo in the New World, the ship would then come back to its home port with a load of cotton, the traffic in people out of sight and out of mind.

The moral impact may also have been dulled by the memory of a pattern of indentured servitude. Many of America's English and Scottish settlers in the early days had had their passage paid by landowners whom they then had to repay with years of work. They still weren't chattel slaves to be traded like livestock. But the fate of the hundred or so men, women and children abducted from settlements on Skye on the orders of Chiefs MacDonald of Sleat and MacLeod of Dunvegan in 1739 and shipped to the Carolinas to be sold, can't perhaps have felt too different from that of those many thousands of Africans who were sold as slaves.

After the Jacobite risings of the first half of the 18th century, hundreds of Highlanders had been shipped to the West Indies to work on plantations there (this theme is touched on in Robert Louis Stevenson's famous 1886 novel, *Kidnapped*). The story of 'Indian Peter', though unusual, is not unique. Peter Williamson was abducted in Aberdeen in 1743, and spent seven years in slavery in the West Indies (sold to another Scottish former slave who'd earned his freedom) before returning to Scotland in 1756. He opened his own coffee house in Edinburgh's Parliament Close.

Sweetness of Tooth

In addition to imported cotton, considerable quantities of slave-produced sugar were brought to Scotland. Greenock was the country's Sugaropolis from 1765. This in turn provided the basis for a major confectionery and sweet industry – and, of course, in part, Scotland's terrible and ongoing dental health problems. Tunnock's of Uddingston, Lanarkshire, was founded in 1890 (though, that said, its iconic lines – teacakes, snowballs – didn't appear until 1950).

Rum was another sugar-based import, its consumption encouraged by West Indian interests. Scotland had a special stake in Jamaica – the source for some of the finest rum – where an estimated 30 per cent of the estates were Scottish-owned. Tea came first from China and then afterwards from India, but was served with Caribbean sugar. When the campaign against slavery began in earnest at the end of the 18th century, it found itself having to contend with powerful business interests: boycotts of sugar by middle-class women and children were a way of fighting back. William Dickson (1751–1823), the Moffat-born secretary to Britain's Governor of Barbados, became a powerful ally of William Wilberforce (1759–1833), Britain's leading abolitionist campaigner. So shocked was Dickson by what he saw at first hand in the Caribbean that, on returning to London, he committed himself to the abolitionists' cause. As their emissary to Scotland, he spoke at meetings around the country and co-ordinated the preparation of petitions and the organisation of letter-writing campaigns.

A few slaves did end up in Scotland. Born in about 1753, Joseph Knight was originally from West Africa but was brought to Scotland by his master, Sir John Wedderburn of Ballendean (1729–1803). In 1778, emboldened by James Somerset's successful suit in England for freedom (against, as it happens, another Scottish owner, one Charles Stewart, in 1772), Knight left Wedderburn and went to work in

Dundee. Sir John took legal action, attempting to enforce his ownership, but his action was rejected by the court in Perth, which ruled that slaveholding was contrary to Scottish law.

The Clearances

The labour pool in the newly industrialising urban centres was meanwhile being swollen by the arrival of Highlanders dislodged from lands their forebears had previously farmed for generations. The Highland Clearances can be seen as the conclusion (and perhaps the only logical one) of the 18th-century 'Improvement' movement (see pages 155–56). The process reached its most intensive pitch in the early 19th century, when landlords started turning extensive areas over to the grazing of large flocks of sheep. The existing human inhabitants were surplus to requirements in these new circumstances, and they found themselves being evicted in their thousands.

Some were relocated by their landlords to new settlements around the coast, where they had to find new ways of subsistence, involving fishing. One such place was Helmsdale, Highland, which was visited by Robert Chambers (1802–71) in the 1820s, and described in glowing terms. 'It has an excellent harbour,' the young Edinburgh writer and publisher reported, 'to which immense armadas of fishing-boats resort during the herring season.' A Lowlander, Chambers had no reason to consider the cost of this prosperity in human terms. The fishing port had been established by the Duke of Sutherland in 1818, as part of a wider redevelopment involving the expulsion of over 15,000 tenants from his lands. Only a few found employment in Helmsdale: the rest were forced into emigration and into starting new lives in North America, Australia and New Zealand (these were boom times for the owners of shipping lines).

The Highlands themselves were drained of human life and bustle. The empty desolation of the 'wilderness' we see today is anything but 'natural' – rich as this country may be in scenic beauty and in wildlife. Rather, it's for the most part a direct result of this policy of expulsion. Deserted villages abound, like the one at Arichonan, northwest of Lochgilphead, Knapdale, Argyll and Bute, or at Camasunary, Strathaird, southwestern Skye. More examples are evocatively described and documented in David Paterson and David Craig's beautifully illustrated book, *The Glens of Silence* (Birlinn, 2004). Cock Farm, on Arran, was the home in the 18th and 19th centuries to the crofting ancestors of the modern Macmillan publishing dynasty – and, of course, one of our seemingly posher Prime Ministers, Sir Harold Macmillan, Earl of Stockton (1894–1986). The house they lived in is just a heap of rubble in a hollow now, having finally been abandoned in 1912.

Was there a sectarian strand to these expulsions, perhaps a hangover from the Jacobite risings? It has been suggested by some scholars, and it was the case that the landlords involved were overwhelmingly Protestants whilst the majority of those 'cleared' were Roman Catholics. That said, the economic argument for clearance – however short-sighted, and however ethically reprehensible – was obviously seen as compelling in itself. Religious differences may have been one of several factors that made it easier for aristocratic landowners to see their villagers as alien, in some way 'other', and consequently easier to regard without empathy. Language would have been another: many of these communities were Gaelic-speaking, with all the cultural differ-ences that went along with that. Comparisons between the Scottish Clearances and the Irish Famine of the 1840s are fraught with all sorts of danger, but they do appear to have had these two things in common.

Hunger and Help

In fact, Scotland was to experience the 'Irish' famine for itself, when potato blight hit Highland fields in 1845. Like Ireland, Scotland continued to export grain, and this raised the emotional temperature among an increasingly angry and desperate populace: troops had to be deployed during disturbances at Cromarty, Wick and Invergordon.

But the scale of the problem was much smaller than it was in Ireland, and relief was much more readily forthcoming. The Protestant Work Ethic was still very much in play, though: those same Christian principles that wouldn't let the more comfortably-off just watch while their less fortunate brethren starved also made them fear the creation of a culture of dependency and ease. So the poor and hungry were made to earn their assistance. To give just one example, what is now the A832 between Dundonnell and Braemore Junction was in large part constructed as a so-called 'Destitution Road'. Local crofters had to work on it for six eight-hour days a week in return for a regular oatmeal ration. This allowance was half that allowed to prisoners at the time, and to secure it people didn't just have to work full days: they had to be able to demonstrate that their house was 'clean, and the pool of water or dirt removed from before the door, or else their meal will be stopped'. (Krisztina Fenyő's *Contempt, Sympathy and Romance* (Tuckwell, 1997), is interesting on all this.) The bridge at the eastern end of Kinlochewe, carrying the road over the A'Ghairbhe River, has always been known as the 'Hunger Bridge' because of this origin.

Some landlords had sheer 'follies' built, just to keep their clients busy while they were on this kind of assistance. Scolpaig Tower, on an island in Loch Scolpaig, North Uist, went up in circumstances like these (albeit during an earlier famine period, around 1830). Similar projects were undertaken much later in times of recession and unemployment. 'Knockbrex Castle', near Borgue, Dumfries & Galloway, was built in the

1900s by the Manchester magnate James Brown, owner of Knockbrex House, as a garage for his little fleet of cars.

Enlightenment at Sea

For most of us, perhaps, the modern lighthouse is more emblematic than it is functional – especially in these days of GPS. There can, though, be few more heroic symbols of a thinking, ordering humanity in its confrontation with a wild – and ultimately uncontrollable – cosmos. The first lighthouse to be built on the Scottish mainland, Kinnaird Head, Fraserburgh, which went up in 1787, is now home to a Museum of Scottish Lighthouses.

The construction of the Bell Rock Lighthouse, off the Angus coast, by Robert Stevenson (1772–1850) and his men, was an epic engineering achievement. The light, built between 1807 and 1810, rested upon a partially-submerged rock foundation – an important first. A majestic sight, the finished lighthouse was memorably portrayed by J.M.W. Turner (1775–1851) in a painting of 1819. Robert Stevenson was also responsible for the Mull of Galloway Lighthouse (1830), dramatically situated at the southernmost extremity of Scotland. His son Alan (1807–65) designed the lighthouse on Skerryvore, southwest of Tiree: rising 48m (157ft) above the surrounding rocks, its tower is Scotland's tallest. Its construction, like that of the Bell Rock Light, was difficult and dangerous: it took almost six years, from 1838 to 1844. Thomas Stevenson (1818–87) also went into the family business. He's probably best known now for his light at Muckle Flugga, north of Unst, in the Shetlands. This great Victorian monument was built in 1854 at the time of the Crimean War, which, despite its name, was fought partly in these northern waters. With the rise of Russia, the North Atlantic, the Baltic and the White Seas had become more strategically important.

Scottish Inventors

The Enlightenment spirit was continued throughout the Industrial Revolution and well after by a just-about endless list of Scottish scientists and inventors. James Watt (1736–1819) was among the earliest examples. This great engineer, who transformed steam technology, was one of the original industrial revolutionaries. Watt was to hone his skills under the patronage of English entrepreneurs like Matthew Boulton (1728–1809) of Birmingham, and John Roebuck of Carron, Falkirk (see page 158). But he wouldn't have achieved what he did had it not been for the start in life he'd been afforded by the Greenock Grammar School (on a site at the corner of Smith's Street and the Vennel, now cleared and built over) – even though it really wasn't much more than a glorified village school. Even so, like other young Scots of his time, Watt had the advantage of high-quality and committed teachers. Greenock's principal, Robert Arrol, was a genuine scholar who'd published translations from Erasmus and other Latin authors; John Marc was a specialist in maths.

William Murdoch (1754–1839), widely hailed as the inventor of gas lighting, was born in the cottage beside Bello Mill, on the banks of Lugar Water, Ayrshire. His father was the miller there, and had introduced important improvements to the mill machinery. His son grew up mechanically minded: an employee of Boulton and Watt in Birmingham, and in Redruth, Cornwall, where he designed steam-driven pumps for draining mines.

John Loudon McAdam (1756–1836) was born in Ayr, in Lady Cathcart's House in the Sandgate. Named for the wife of its builder, Lord Elias Cathcart, it's now a tourist office and (as one of the burgh's oldest buildings) a tourist attraction in itself. After his father lost his fortune in financial speculation, John went off to make his own in America, where he lived through the War of Independence, before returning to Britain where he worked as a road engineer. It's difficult

The dramatic glaciated profile of Suilven, from Glencanisp, Assynt.

Loch Coruisk, at the foot of the Black Cuillin, Isle of Skye.

Rubh' an Dùnain, Isle of Skye, site of many neolithic finds
and this 12th-century so-called 'Viking Canal'.

Excavation at Skara Brae, Orkney *(© John Burka).*

Detail of the central group of standing stones at Callanish
(Calanais), Isle of Lewis (© *Marta Gutowska*).

The Antonine Wall, northernmost Roman frontier (© *Kim Traynor*).

Pictish stone at Aberlemno.

Madonna and Child, *Book of Kells*.

Iona Abbey, 1890s, shortly before it was rebuilt.

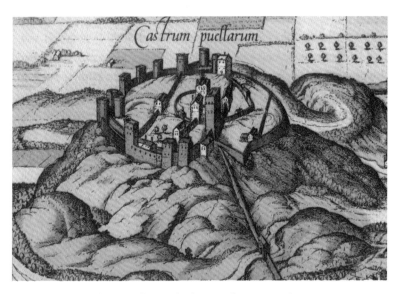

Edinburgh Castle, late 16th-century image.

Balmoral Castle, in a late Victorian view.

The Battle of Culloden *(David Morier)*.

The Highland Shepherd *(Rosa Bonheur)*.

Robert the Bruce and Isabella.

Mary, Queen of Scots.

'Bonnie Prince Charlie'
(*portrait by Allan Ramsay*).

Robert Burns.

View toward Arthur's Seat, an Edinburgh landmark
and a Site of Special Scientific Interest (© *Lauren van Buren*).

View of the Clyde in Glasgow, with the Finnieston Crane, left,
and the Clyde Arc, or 'Squinty Bridge, centre (© *Sara Hunt*).

now to imagine how revolutionary his method of 'macad-amising' once seemed – given that, the addition of tar apart (to make 'tarmac'), it's more or less the way we do it now. Briefly, McAdam built up his highways in successive layers of stone, with big rocks on the bottom and finer pebbles and gravels above; finally cambering the surface so they'd read-ily drain off rain. It's claimed that part of Culzean Road, in Maybole – where the newly-wealthy McAdam had bought an estate – was the world's first stretch of macadamised high-way. Drumcrieff House, near Moffat, where the engineer lived in later life, is now let out as an upscale holiday home.

The roll of inventive honour goes on and on – albeit, per-haps, a little randomly. Born in Arbroath, but based for much of his adulthood in Dundee, publisher James Chalmers (1782–1853) is believed to have come up with the idea for the adhesive postage stamp. He had an office on Castle Street, and lies buried a stone's throw away in the Howff burial ground. The pioneer of the pneumatic tyre, John Boyd Dunlop (1840–1921) was born in Dreghorn, Ayrshire (he trained as a vet at Edinburgh University's Dick Vet school). James Clerk Maxwell (1831–79), whose work on electromag-netism was to make him one of the very foremost modern physicists, was born at 14a India Street in Edinburgh's New Town but brought up mostly in the southwestern countryside. The family home, Glenlair House, north of Castle Douglas, Dumfries & Galloway, lay in ruins for most of the 20th cen-tury, after a succession of fires, but efforts are being made to have it restored. Alexander Graham Bell (1847–1922), who in 1876 secured the first US patent for a working tele-phone, was born at 16 South Charlotte Street, in Edinburgh. Helensburgh's John Logie Baird (1888–1946) was born at the Lodge, 121 West Argyle Street. He was helped in devel-oping his television prototype by his fellow-townsman Jack Buchanan (1891–1957): the actor, singer and director fea-tured in the world's first outside broadcast in 1928.

Inventor of Scotland

Even as this new, modern, high-tech Scotland was taking shape, though (and as traditional ways of Highland life were being destroyed by the Clearances), Walter Scott (1771–1832) was promoting a whole new mythologising cult of Romantic Scotland. First a poet, then a novelist, and, eventually, what amounted to a sort of national impresario, Scott made his home country fashionable around the world.

He was born in College Wynd, a narrow alley between Edinburgh's Grassmarket and what was then the University entrance. It was demolished to make way for the 'Old College' (see page 152), and is not to be confused with the College Wynd off the Cowgate, now lined with backpacker hostels and student flats. Sent away from the city for his health in boyhood, Scott spent several years with his paternal grandparents at Sandyknowe Farm, near Smailholm Tower, a 15th-century tower house he was to make famous in his writings. By the time he went back to Edinburgh, his family had moved, joining the genteel rush to George Square – just built (see p.age 148); the Scotts were to occupy number 25.

Scott-associated places abound in Edinburgh. A plaque on a wall in Sciennes House Place, Newington, marks out the site of the house in which, as a young and star-struck man of Scottish letters, he met his hero Robert Burns at an evening gathering. At 50 George Street, there's the flat in which he lived with his wife Charlotte in the first months of their marriage, before moving on to number 10 South Castle Street, whence they moved up to 39 North Castle Street – a house that Scott himself had built. The failure of the publishing house that Scott had helped to launch with his schoolfriend James Ballantyne (1772–1833) in 1813 left Scott ruined, despite the popularity of the collections of Border ballads he'd compiled and of his own narrative poems. It was for this reason that he then embarked on a second literary career as a novelist, with works like *Waverley*

Land of the Slag Heap and the Canal

(1814), *Rob Roy* (1817) and *The Heart of Midlothian* (1818).

Scott wasn't the first author to write a historical novel, but he was *among* the first – and he made the form his own. His history, though highly coloured, has a ring of truth. Even in so melodramatic a narrative as that of *The Bride of Lammermoor* (1819), which was, Scott said, based on the story of he'd heard of a young woman in the Machars, Wigtownshire, who'd pined away after being forced to wed against her will. Novelistic license allowed the author to switch the action from Scotland's southwest corner to its far southeast – the Lammermuir Hills. *Lucia di Lammermoor* (1835), by the Italian composer Gaetano Donizetti (1797–1848), was only one of six operas based on this single novel of Scott's alone. Its success is a reminder of how far Scott-mania spread in Europe. Russia, France and Italy all fell in love both with Scott's writings and with the country he made clear had been his inspiration.

So important had Scott become to his country's image that he was given a special role in organising the royal visit of King George IV in 1822. Scott ordained that His Majesty should be kitted out in full 'Highland Dress' (actually a confection of Scott's own design). King George, himself caught up in the excitement of it all, commissioned his own costume at a cost of more than £1,300 – in today's money well over £100,000. Concerned that any unfortunate embarrassments should be avoided, Scott prepared his own pamphlet full of scheduling details, dress codes and etiquette advice, entitled *HINTS addressed to the INHABITANTS OF EDINBURGH AND OTHERS in prospect of HIS MAJESTY'S VISIT by an old citizen*.

Scott was also on the committee of 'great and good' which oversaw the foundation of the new Edinburgh Academy. Its façade fitted out with an impressive array of Doric columns, as befitted the *Akademia* of the Athens of the North, it opened its doors to its first students in 1824. Meanwhile, on the back of his works' astonishing success, he started building himself a country home at Abbotsford, on the southern bank of the Tweed, outside Galashiels. What started as a cottage was extended and improved so many times between 1817 and 1825 that by the time it was completed it was one of Scotland's grandest houses. It differed from the standard stately home, however, in being a Caledonian fantasy made concrete, incorporating stones and fittings from a wide variety of historical ruins the length and breadth of Scotland, and filled with Scottish curiosities of every kind. A second publishers' failure in 1826 left him insolvent at the very zenith of his success: he pledged all future income from his works to pay his creditors, and worked flat-out on his fiction to make good his debts. Eventually they were all paid off – though not until 1847, when his remaining copyright was sold. By that time, Scott had been dead for 15 years, his grave in the grounds of Dryburgh Abbey, amidst the historical heritage he'd done so much to bring to life.

Abbotsford House.

FAIR MAIDS, FULMINATIONS & FLOODS

Catharine Glover, the protagonist in Sir Walter Scott's novel of 1828, The Fair Maid of Perth, *may be fictional, but the story was inspired by the true-life Battle of North Inch. The field on which this was fought (in 1396, between the loose collection of clans known as the Chattan Federation and a now-uncertain enemy, perhaps the Clan Cameron) remains an area of open parkland, running along the west bank of the Tay, just to the north of the centre of Perth. Catharine's sympathies with Lollardy (a medieval 'heresy' first promulgated in the 1380s by the English reformer John Wycliffe) would have made her seem acceptably proto-Protestant to Scott's first audience.*

Perth was certainly to play its part in Scotland's religious conflicts: John Knox's sermon against idolatry at St John's Kirk on 11 May 1559 is often seen as the start of Scottish Reformation (see pages 79–80). The city's Greyfriars Burial Ground has some stunning gravestones, dating back to the 18th century.

Floods have always been a feature: one in 1209 carried away the castle's foundation and washed the Tay Bridge away completely. Rebuilt versions of the bridge were destroyed in the 1580s and 1640s, and flooding caused serious damage again as late as 1993.

Posthumous Scott

The Scott Effect was both far-reaching and enduring. The composer Felix Mendelssohn (1809–47) was typical of a new type of tourist, making a Scott-inspired pilgrimage in 1829. His tour took in Abbotsford and Melrose before following the Road to the Isles through to Mull and Staffa, where he was of course to find his inspiration for the overture *Fingal's Cave*. The German novelist Theodor Fontane (1819–98) made a similar tour of Scotland in 1858. Scott's influence in the American South was more sinister, though he can hardly be blamed for the fact that the white supremacist Ku Klux Klan was a 'Klan' in tribute to his romancing of the tribal instinct and the doughty fight to defend old ways (the KKK's burning crosses are an allusion to his 1810 poem *The Lady of the Lake*). It extended further than this, though: the whole antebellum South, Mark Twain complained, had been afflicted with an acute 'Sir Walter disease', its symptoms an exaggerated taste for titles and an obsession with caste and rank.

Rumours of a Scott revival have so far proven exaggerated – at least as an author to be read for fun. There have certainly been signs of his being studied more. As long ago as the late-1940s, the Hungarian Marxist critic György Lukács (1885–1971) was, whilst damning Scott as a reactionary, acclaiming him as a revolutionary despite himself. Scott's conscious views and attitudes may have been staunchly conservative, but – said Lukács – the analysis of history he made in his fiction showed a real engagement with the economic and political forces that drove change. By the same token, Scott is one Dead White Male who's succeeded in engaging recent critics of the 'postcolonial' persuasion – all those struggles for hegemony, the subduing of 'native' tribes.

The Jewels in the Crown

Viewed from a longer historical perspective, it's interesting that, at a time when nationalism was on the rise in the rest of Europe, all this Scottishness was enlisted in the service of the British Union. It's interesting too that a comparatively unrepresentative (and actually still-marginalised) part of the country, the Highlands, was being taken to stand for Scotland as a whole. Just as Scotland, peripheral as it might have seemed, was the jewel in the crown of a United Kingdom whose identifying essence was its plurality. By the kind of compromise that would one day come to be considered 'very British', the more extravagantly Scottish this sort of patriotism was, the more strongly it affirmed the connection between two countries that seemed self-evidently 'better together', to coin a phrase.

Scott's campaign over the so-called 'Honours of Scotland' – or Scottish Crown Jewels – is a case in point. Indeed, in some ways it can be seen as paralleling Scotland's story at this time. The independent kingdom's Crown Jewels had stayed in the country after the Union of the Crowns but then been hidden away in Dunnottar Castle during the Cromwellian period. Though retrieved after the Restoration of Charles II, they had been rendered redundant by the union of 1706/7 and put to one side – almost forgotten – in a corner of Edinburgh Castle. Walter Scott was one of a group of concerned Scottish citizens who, in 1818, launched a campaign for them to be brought out, dusted off and publicly exhibited, then to be incorporated into the British Crown Jewels as an emblem of Scottish kingship within the union. (Since 1999, the Crown has been brought out regularly for the monarch to wear at the State Opening of the Scottish Parliament.)

Highland Games

It was Romantic Scottishness that Queen Victoria (1819–1901) and her Prince Consort Albert (1819–61) were playing at when, in 1852, they set about building Balmoral Castle as a summer residence. The 16th-century tower house already on the site wasn't big or characterful enough – hence the baronial pile that quickly went up in its place. The German-born Prince Consort took charge of the interior, which ended up being pretty much tartan wall-to-wall. It's easy enough to point to the absurd aspects of Queen Victoria's life up on 'Royal Deeside' and see comparisons with that of Marie 'shepherdess' Antoinette, at Hameau de la Reine, her village at Versailles, but the royal couple were hardly alone in their mania for Romantic Scotland.

The institution of the Highland Games is another legacy of this period: sporting competitions in tossing the caber or the wheatsheaf, or throwing the hammer or the stone, had already existed, but they were comprehensively repackaged and promoted at this time. It was a similar story with dancing. Since the late-18th century there'd been a vogue for 'Scottish Country Dancing' of the type to be seen in any decent Jane Austen costume-drama: now these were joined by wilder, solo dances, expressive of an indomitable – and excitingly uncivilised – spirit, like the Highland Fling. It was at about this time that the stereotype started to take hold in the wider world that, first, every Scotsman was a Highlander, and that, second, he invariably went about his daily business in a kilt.

TARTANRY

The vogue for tartan ironically started at a time when real Highlanders were at their most vulnerable, being pushed off their ancestral lands and forced into emigration in their thousands. Tartan fabric was real, of course; and there were genuine local variations – dyers stuck to tried and trusted formulas and weavers to well-established patterns. But the idea that each clan had its own uniform tartan was very much an 'invented tradition', fostered in the 19th century by an enterprising (and overwhelmingly Lowland-based!) textile industry.

An elaborate pseudo-scholarship of tartan history soon arose, complete with cod-conventions over who was 'entitled' to wear what pattern and for what purpose. The rest is kitsch-history: today, the range of institutions with their own tartan extends from the Clan Campbell to the Metro Detroit Police and Fire Department; superstars like Madonna have strutted their stuff in plaid.

From Tartan to Tweed

Tartan plaid was not the only distinctly Scottish textile product to become popular at about this time. A cottage industry in spinning and weaving had existed in the Hebrides for centuries, but it only really developed on a larger scale from the 1840s when Catherine Murray, Countess of Dunmore, saw the true potential of the cloth the weavers on her Harris estate produced. Not only was it comfortable and hard-wearing: it was beautifully coloured and textured, with an extremely distinctive 'natural', earth-toned look. The Countess decided to take charge of organising and training the island's weavers, sending some to serve apprenticeships in modern factories in the Lowlands, so that traditional skills in spinning, weaving and colouring with natural dyes could be combined with the best of modern industrial practice. She then took upon herself the task of marketing what she called 'Harris Tweed' (the precise etymology of 'tweed' is uncertain: however, the use of the name of a river from right down on the English border does seem to suggest that, for the Countess' customers, one bit of Scotland was much like another). The whole operation was a triumphant success.

Home knitting was another age-old tradition that took on a new lease of commercialised life in the 1850s with the opening of an ordering and marketing agency in Edinburgh. The ornately-patterned 'Fair Isle sweater' was to receive a major boost from the patronage of the Prince of Wales (and future Edward VIII) in the 1920s, but this was just one of a wide range of attractive island knitwear. The industry endured a long – and seemingly irreversible – decline through the latter half of the 20th century but is now enjoying something of a revival thanks to the vogue for hand-made prestige items.

Whisky Galore

Scottish *uisge* had of course been distilled for hundreds of years (see page 135), and made the transition from local hooch to common tipple in the 18th century. Even so, excise duties had been such as to constitute a major disincentive for legitimate suppliers, so it had remained a clandestine business, carried out largely on a local and small-scale level. The Excise Act of 1823 allowed producers to buy a licence to set up a still for a relatively small sum and then to pay a much more manageable duty on what they distilled thereafter.

The introduction of the 'column still' in the 1830s made whisky production truly industrial. It also resulted in a product that was smoother – and, for most, more palatable. For many, though, this drinker-friendliness had been achieved at the expense of distinctiveness. From the 1850s, blended whiskies were introduced: makers mixed in a certain amount of more characterful 'malt' whisky distilled the old way to give a better product at a still-affordable price. The original Johnnie Walker (1805–57) had a grocery business in Kilmarnock. The blend he developed was built into a big commercial brand in the 1860s by his sons. The Haig family had been distilling whisky since the 17th century and had industrialised in the 1820s, building a big modern distillery at Cameronbridge in Fife, but they also moved into more widely marketable blended whiskies at about this time.

So too did the Chivas brothers, proprietors of the upmarket Aberdeen grocery store that supplied Her Majesty at Balmoral, down the road. Their blend, Chivas Regal, made no concessions to the common pocket. This was a whisky for connoisseurs. The very idea that there might be such a thing as a discriminating whisky drinker might have seemed a little absurd not so long before, but suppliers were working hard now to build up a sense of glamour and mystique around certain brands. The blighting of the French grape harvest by the phylloxera aphid in the 1880s represented a second chance for the more expensive single (unblended) malts. Both wine and brandy were for a while in short supply. Malt whisky was to some extent able to step into the breach, and the prestige varieties have, ever since, had something of the sort of cachet once confined to vintage wines.

Local distilleries were able to create highly branded whiskies, employing an advertising rhetoric rich in ideas of ancient tradition, hand-crafted quality and (at a time of rapid urbanisation) a near-poetic sense of place. Not that the notion of a whisky's distinctive character was entirely bogus, by any means. All sorts of factors – from the amount of peat in the water used, to the length of ageing after distillation; from the kind of wood used in the casks it was aged in, to their previous use for storing other drinks like sherry – could have a bearing on the whisky's final taste. These fine malt whiskies were international in their appeal: the continuing vogue for all things Scottish created a demand in the outside world for a product that really would be the 'spirit of Scotland', as high in romantic symbolism as in alcohol.

Abstention and Ideology

The original Johnnie Walker was, ironically, a teetotaller. The rise in the drinks industry was paralleled – paradoxically or not – by the emergence of a temperance movement. It was in Maryhill, Glasgow, that, in 1829, a Presbyterian Minister, John Dunlop (grandson of the original Mary Hill – see page 171), founded what was probably the world's first society dedicated to the abjuration of 'ardent spirits'. Dunlop's was, quite literally, a 'temperance' society, in that its message was all about moderation: whilst strong liquor was banned, light beers and wines were all right in Dunlop's book. Interestingly, he'd had his anti-alcohol epiphany during a tour of France – a soft, southern, Catholic country he'd expected to despise. Instead, he'd returned an early advocate of the view that was much later to be so fashionable that the Gallic way with drink (moderately with meals, watered-wine for children...) had a great deal to recommend it. But later collaborators, who were to include the printer and publisher William Collins (1817–95; his father, also William (1789–1853), had founded the famous firm), took a tougher line, insisting that alcohol had to be renounced completely and forever. ('Teetotallism' meant 'T-for-Total' abstention.)

Puritanical sobriety and the Protestant Work Ethic went together – and both upheld the aims of Industry. Not just with a small 'i', as a moral concept (drink was the enemy of work and purposeful living), but with a capital 'I', as an economic force. Attitudes ran, to some extent, along party-political lines. The Liberals led the temperance movement and marched in lock-step with the industrial employers, who were exasperated at the amount of work-time lost to drunkenness and its consequences, such as absenteeism or industrial unrest. As with coffee, a couple of centuries before (see page 109), the bars and taverns where alcohol was served were seen as places in which people might come together, talk and bond against those in power in their lives. The Tories – traditionally the party of the jolly, red-faced English squire – favoured the farmers and the brewers, who benefitted more.

There was at least the whiff of a double-standard: women's drinking – and the sexual licence it might lead to – certainly occasioned a special horror. In fairness, though, for the most part, the temperance campaigners were equal-opportunity killjoys: drunkenness was seen as being 'swinish' in either sex. Women were an important part of the workforce in a great many Scottish textile mills – their lost hours were potentially as disruptive as men's.

Liberals and Conservatives

There was of course much more to Toryism than an easy-going attitude to drunken festivity and fun: since 1834, indeed, there'd been a fully organised 'Conservative Party'. Even so, the continuities were clear: in a changing Britain, they were quite literally conservative, and stood for the interests of the old aristocracy and gentry, and their traditional allies in the Anglican (and Episcopalian) clergy in the countryside. Whilst the welfare of the rural poor wasn't necessarily at the top of their list of priorities (and they barely even acknowledged the existence of the growing industrial working class), they saw a place for concern of a paternalistic sort.

The Whigs had changed more obviously, though their instinct to uphold the privileges of Parliament in the face of the overweening power of the monarch and his or her traditional elite, the landed aristocracy, made them the 'natural' choice of an emergent urban middle class. And of England's religious nonconformists – a category, of course, which often overlapped with the former: their sense of exclusion only strengthened their will to work hard and to succeed by their own efforts (if, perhaps, also to deprecate the character of those who failed). Stereotypically sober – not just in their approach to alcohol but in their approach to personal, social and economic life – they believed in charity but also in self-help. As entrepreneurs and industrialists, they learned to value free trade, the free market, the free movement of labour from the land to the factories: hence the formation of the Liberal Party in 1859. They weren't for the most part all that liberal in the more recent and 'social' sense of showing bleeding-heart compassion, touchy-feely tolerance or 'open-minded' moral views.

To acknowledge that the giants of Victorian parliamentary politics were English doesn't tell quite the whole story. Scotland was more strongly represented than may first appear. Though born in Liverpool, William Ewart Gladstone

(1809–98), who served as Prime Minister four times between 1868 and 1894 – not to mention terms as Chancellor of the Exchequer and Lord Knows What Else – had Scottish parents. Whilst his mother's Episcopalian views were reflected in his foundation of Glenalmond College (not far from Methven, Perth and Kinross) in 1847, his father's early Presbyterianism arguably showed in the evangelical streak running through the earnest Anglicanism of his later life.

Gladstone's great rival, Conservative leader Benjamin Disraeli (1804–81), first came to Scotland at the age of 20, long before his first election as Prime Minister in 1868. Sir Walter Scott, polite in his presence, subsequently dismissed his visitor as a 'sprig of the rod of Aaron', a view undoubtedly shared by all too many. Born in London, and an Anglican, but the descendant of Sephardic Jews from Italy, Disraeli's was a strangely double-edged success. One of the dominant figures of Victorian politics, he was at the same time never to be fully accepted; his loyalty to Britain continually questioned. Even Gladstone, famous (if not notorious) for his high-mindedness, wasn't above playing the 'cosmopolitan' card against his opponent on occasion.

Antisemitism apart, Scotland had long been inhospitable territory for the Tories – and their Conservative successors. In the first place, because of the importance of the Kirk. The assumption that the Conservative Party was the Episcopalian Church at the polls was to be difficult to shift – and, for that matter, for a long time no one really tried. Increasingly, too, those who had the vote in an industrialising Scotland (a propertied elite, but a predominantly urban one) were coming to feel that their best interests were served by the Liberals – a party that seemed to stand for economic progress, the modern way.

Interesting (and, broadly, justifiable) as such demographic discussion may be, it's wildly anachronistic in certain key respects. It's difficult for us to imagine just how utterly tiny some of the electorates involved in these decisions were. When 'the People' spoke, it was in a whisper, if at all. Prior to 1832, the entire electorate in Scotland was less than 5,000 strong. That meant, in a large rural constituency like Sutherland, an MP being returned by a total poll of 128 voters. In Edinburgh – at a time when the Scottish capital had a population of some 160,000 – a total of 33 voters got to decide on one MP. The 'Great Reform Act' of 1832 may not seem so great from today's perspective, but it did increase the electorate to about 65,000 (out of an overall population of a little over two million) – approximately thirteenfold, in other words. Further Reform Bills in 1868 and 1884 improved things further – though the continuing property qualification still left almost half the country's men without a vote; and, of course, no prospect whatsoever of women's suffrage.

Against the Machine

Industrial Scotland was well and truly on the march by now – albeit staggering a little from time to time as its population gradually adjusted to the disciplines of mill and factory work. It's true that in pre-industrial Scotland the agricultural year had exacted enormous amounts of back-breaking toil at ploughing and planting time – and weeks of frantic work, from dawn to dusk, in the summer harvest. But it had also included lengthy lulls; days severely shortened through the dark of winter and slack periods over the course of the growing year. Following a horse-plough was hard slog but slow; work with a spade or hoe went to a human rhythm – there was none of the sense of running on a treadmill that was to be involved when men and women had to keep up with a machine.

The feeling that the operative was just another cog in that machine was something new. The idea of the working classes as an abstraction was taking root. Karl Marx (1818–83) was soon to articulate his idea of alienation. Modern industrial workers, he suggested, didn't have the sense of satisfaction available to the old-style craftsman – or even the farm labourer – of having brought into being something of real value. Along with losing their sense of genuinely shaping what they produced and their feeling that they had some real say over where their wages went, they had also lost all sense of agency, of autonomous involvement in and real engagement with their world.

But the dehumanising effects of industrial labour had been appreciated long before, from a conservative-paternalistic point of view. 'He is very near dried up,' noted the physician Jacob Pattison, horrified by the skeletal, hollowed-out appearance of a foundryman he saw at work in 1780. 'The heat will certainly one day catch him like touchpaper or tinder and crackling, he will disappear.' Charles Dickens (1812–70), with his unerring eye for the grotesque in 19th-century society, noted the metaphorical dismemberment involved in the description of industrial workers as 'hands'. They would, he wrote in *Hard Times* (1854), 'have found more favour with some people, if Providence had seen fit to make them only hands, or, like the lower creatures of the seashore, only hands and stomachs'.

Dickens was an English novelist, of course, and the action of *Hard Times* unfolded in central Lancashire, but the book was dedicated to a Scottish thinker, Thomas Carlyle (1795–1881). In his latter years, the 'Sage of Chelsea' was to be known for the literary gatherings at his house in London's Cheyne Walk, but he was actually a son of Ecclefechan, Dumfries & Galloway – his birthplace in the village may still be visited; as may the farmhouse at Craigenputtock, where he and his wife and fellow-writer Jane Welsh Carlyle (1801–66) spent several unhappy years early in their marriage. Jane Welsh was from East Lothian: her childhood home in Lodge Street, Haddington, has been made into a museum. But a plaque marks the house at 22 George Square (a couple of doors down from the home of much of Sir Walter Scott's Edinburgh youth) in which she'd been living when Thomas came to court her.

It isn't easy to imagine Carlyle as a lovesick swain or dashing beau, so arresting is the bad-tempered tone of his writerly persona, its predominant register that of the jeremiad. Carlyle writes with extraordinary fire and flair, but he spent much of his working life railing against what he saw as the evils of his age. In his ideas, he was pretty much the antithesis of Marx, articulating a whole philosophy of anti-materialism, in opposition to that of economics, which he notoriously described as 'the dismal science'. But he matched the famous revolutionary in his radicalism, and arguably outdid him in the eloquence with which he called on his contemporaries to forsake 'mechanistic' rationalism in favour of 'organic' faith. The economic imperative to which his society had subjected itself was destroying everything that made life worth living, Carlyle believed. 'To what shifts is poor Society reduced, struggling to give still some account of herself, in epochs when Cash Payment has become the sole nexus of man to men!'

Were these prophecies exaggerated? Well, possibly: Carlyle and Dickens wouldn't have found such an immediate and ardent response in so many of their readers if the spirit of human sympathy and solidarity had been truly dead. There's no doubt, though, that the Industrial Revolution was bringing real transformation to the face of Scotland and to the texture of Scottish life. From cobbling to canning, from printed wallpaper to Paisley-patterned cotton products: everything you could think of was in the throes of dramatic change. In terms of its abruptness, though, the transition wasn't strictly speaking quite revolutionary. Aspects of industrial development had already been taking place for quite some time.

An Industrial Epic

The monks of Dunfermline Abbey had quarried coal at ground level in medieval times. By the end of the 16th century, indeed, the merchant and engineer Sir George Carnock (approximately 1550–1625), relying on a pump-drainage system of his own devising, had built the first mine in the world to extend underneath the sea. No less a personage than King James VI was given a tour of its tunnels, at Culross on the northern coast of the Firth of Forth.

There's no doubt, though, that the late-18th century had brought so sudden an escalation in industrial technology and economic strategy that it really did seem, to all intents and purposes, a revolution. The scale of operations was growing rapidly, for a start. Compare the 18th-century mine that is now the focus for the (fascinating) Lead Mining Museum in Wanlockhead, Dumfries & Galloway, with what is to be seen at the National Mining Museum, based in what was the Lady Victoria Colliery, Newtongrange, Midlothian, south of Edinburgh. The latter gives a vivid impression of how immense a modern industrial enterprise could be. First opened in 1895, the complex ceased production as a coalmine in 1981. Its Victorian winding gear towers above a handsome cluster of buildings into which the coal was brought for grading and sorting and for pouring into the giant hoppers, through which it was loaded into railway wagons on special sidings in the arched brick undercroft below.

The exhibitions there embrace just about every imaginable aspect of mining life – including the home lives of the miners and their families as well as their daily battles at the coalface. Work down the mines, backbreaking and unpleasant at best, could at times be downright dangerous. Accidents in these dark, cramped conditions were all too frequent. 'Firedamp' – a highly flammable gas build-up – was an ever-present danger. Blantyre Colliery, outside Hamilton, Lanarkshire, was in 1877 the scene of an explosion in which 207 miners died.

A decade later, it was the turn of next-door Udston Colliery to be hit: a blast there killed 73 miners in 1887. The costs of hewing coal could be as heroic as the work itself.

The New Antiquities

Epic? Heroic? There are clearly dangers in romanticising work that wrecked men's health, even when it wasn't actually taking their lives, and which wrought such destruction on the Scottish environment as well. It's impossible to dispute the awe-inspiring scale of the undertaking, though, or the magnificence of what was achieved – even if, for an eco-conscious age, it seems these deeds of derring-do were performed in a sustained war between humanity and nature. Now, though, that working miners are as rare as knights-at-arms, it's possible to see their labours as the stuff of legend.

In his essay 'The Sentimental Scot' (1915), G.K. Chesterton contrasted the Scots, who had embraced industry, with the Irish, who, he said, had 'clung to agriculture with claws of iron'. This, Chesterton insisted,

> is because the Irish, though far inferior to the Scotch in art and literature, are hugely superior to them in practical politics. You do need to be very romantic to accept the industrial civilisation. It does really require all the old Gaelic glamour to make men think that Glasgow is a grand place. Yet the miracle is achieved; and while I was in Glasgow I shared the illusion. I have never had the faintest illusion about Leeds or Birmingham. The industrial dream suited the Scots. Here was a really romantic vista, suited to a romantic people; a vision of higher and higher chimneys taking hold upon the heavens, of fiercer and fiercer fires in which adamant could evaporate like dew. Here were taller and taller engines that began already to shriek and gesticulate like giants.

He's being ironic, clearly, and deliberately perverse, though it's uncanny the extent to which a chapter of history that not too long ago appeared to have marked Scotland's Central Belt so obviously and indelibly, should now seem more like a misty memory of Ossianic myth. It's sad that so much of Scotland's industrial history should have been so firmly consigned to the museum. It does make it easy to visit, though, these days.

West Central Scotland had already been well on its way to industrialisation by the end of the 18th century, thanks to the early success of its textiles industry (see pages 170–71). In the 19th century, however, in association with its mining industry, it was becoming important for the production of iron – the basis for the region's later fame as a centre for heavy engineering. Coatbridge's spectacular Summerlee Industrial Museum occupies an old ironworks (it also has its own bits of tramway and rail siding, complete with locomotives and rolling stock – not to mention a section of the old Monkland Canal). Other aspects of Scottish transport history are celebrated in the Riverside Museum, in Glasgow Harbour, Partick, on the site of the old A. & J. Inglis shipyard.

The Clyde was of course to be world-famous for the construction of ships – an industry that encompassed not just heavy engineering work in wood, iron and steel, but a range

of associated trades from upholstery to fancy glasswork. But the Riverside Museum (which incorporates the old Glasgow Museum of Transport, formerly of Pollokshields) has a great many other exhibits, from city trams to classic cars. More ships are to be seen at the Scottish Maritime Museum, Irvine, Dumbarton (but see also the Trinity House Maritime Museum, in Leith). Much older trades and crafts were susceptible to industrialisation too. Hence the boost given to Scottish fishing by the advent of steam drifters, which could get a catch back to port so much faster than their sail-driven forerunners – and then see it distributed the length and breadth of Britain by rail. The Scottish Fisheries Museum, in Anstruther, Fife, provides an enthralling portrait of centuries of Scottish fishing and of the technological and social changes which helped to shape it as time went by.

Men and Mountains

The Industrial Revolution 'got under the skin' of Central Scotland in particular, leaving a lasting mark on a previously agrarian Lowland scene. Slag heaps or 'bings' abound, most of them built up over decades from colliery-waste and long since abandoned, overgrown and – in recent years – often landscaped. The 'Blue Billy' Bing, in Irvine, Ayrshire, takes its name from the colour of the waste that made it – a by-product of local chemical processing. In World War II an observation post was established atop this man-made mountain, which offered uninterrupted views across the Firth of Clyde.

Few industries impacted on the landscape so arrestingly as that of oil shale extraction – built up almost single-handedly in West Lothian by Glasgow-born James 'Paraffin' Young (1811–83). Having invented a method of distilling out paraffin oil from coal, he helped set up a big new plant at Bathgate in 1851. Some 15 years later, he bought out his fellow investors, to start afresh at Addiewell, outside West Calder: he'd found a way of extracting oil from the torbanite shales to be found there. The plant he built at Addiewell came complete with model village for his employees, along the lines of the one created by the Cadbury family at Bournville, Birmingham. And with the impressive Five Sisters bings.

As local supplies were exhausted, Young expanded the scope of his operations through West Lothian, his progress marked by a succession of bings like those at Greendykes or Faucheldean outside Broxburn. He also, less directly, left a memorial in the shape of the modern petrochemical industry of Grangemouth and environs. Whilst Young himself had no involvement in a development that took place some time after his death (and burial in the churchyard at Inverkip, Inverclyde) the pool of skilled labour at his works made West Lothian the obvious place to establish oil refineries. There's a Museum of the Scottish Shale Oil Industry in Millfield, Livingston.

Out Into the World

It wasn't quite an industry, perhaps, but Scotland was certainly over-represented in the field of exploration – of which the 19th century was a golden age of sorts. The Luskentyre House, Stornoway, in which Alexander Mackenzie (1764–1820) was born, has now given way to Martin's Memorial Church. Mackenzie grew up to cross Canada, all the way to the Pacific (1793), and to have a great river named in his honour.

An upbringing in the islands seemed a natural preparation for a life of work outdoors in the far north. As we've already seen, the majority of the Hudson Bay Company's employees were Orcadians, and they were later joined by another, John Rae (1813–93), who became an explorer on the Company's behalf. And, in 1854, the solver of the riddle of what had become of Sir John Franklin's Northwest Passage expedition, which had set out nine years before and disappeared. His revelations, which included reports that the desperate explorers had been reduced to cannibalism before they finally starved, understandably horrified the nation. If Sir John's widow's indignant denial was perhaps to be expected, Charles Dickens' vociferous outrage was less so, and the campaign of vilification he launched against Rae was unforgivable.

Land of the Slag Heap and the Canal

It didn't help Rae's case – though it seems intriguing now – that he had learned to survive in what were otherwise impossible circumstances by, effectively, 'going native' with the Inuit, learning their ways and adopting many of their strategies. The fact that he took the word of these supposed 'savages' over the fate of British officers was regarded as utterly indefensible at the time, though it's been borne out by modern investigators. Not only was Rae never to receive the just-about-obligatory knighthood; he was more or less completely disgraced, though he continued with his work as an explorer. He was buried in the churchyard of St Magnus' Cathedral, Kirkwall; there's also a memorial to him inside.

Others went to warmer climes. Mungo Park (1771–1806), a product of the Enlightenment, was born in Foulshiels, near Selkirk, in the Borders. You can still see the cottage in which he was born, on the banks of the River Yarrow, though it's rather the worse for wear now – despite some restoration work, it's essentially a ruin. Park, a farmer's son, received a good education at Selkirk Grammar School and went on to study medicine and botany at Edinburgh University. In 1795, he made history by becoming the first European to travel up the Gambia River to the Niger, in West Africa. During a second expedition to the region in 1806, his party came under sustained attack by hostile tribesmen and Park jumped into the Niger to escape and drowned.

A complex mixture of motives drove the missionary-explorer David Livingstone (1813–73): wanderlust; curiosity; Christian evangelism; a desire to stop the slave trade ... Starting out in 1851, he traced the course of the upper Zambezi; he then walked to the Atlantic coast at Luanda. Retracing his steps to the source of the Zambezi, he followed it down to the Indian Ocean, the first European to cross Africa from west to east. And to see what the Scottish explorer named as 'Victoria Falls' (locally known as the 'Smoke that Thunders'). In all, he's estimated to have covered a distance of 47,000 km (29,000 miles) in the course of his African explorations, opening up approximately 2.6 million square km (1 million square miles) of territory. David Livingstone died deep in the African interior after years of failing health, and though his body was brought back to Britain, it was interred in London's Westminster Abbey. But his birthplace in Shuttle Row, Blantyre, Lanarkshire, a tenement attached to the cotton mill in which his parents worked, has been made into a museum about his life and explorations.

DUNDEE

A Royal Burgh since the 13th century, Dundee was fought over in the Wars of Independence and then again in Cromwellian times, when it was attacked in turn by the Royalist Montrose and Cromwell's general George Monck (1608–70). In 1689, it became famous as a centre of Stuart resistance when John Graham, Viscount of Dundee – 'Bonnie Dundee' – raised the Jacobite flag at the top of Dundee Law.

In the latter part of the 18th century, Dundee emerged as 'Blubbertown' – Scotland's leading whaling port. The government encouraged this new industry as a way of training able seamen for the Royal Navy. Whaling also made Dundee a natural centre for polar exploration: hence the preservation there (in a partitioned-off section of Robert Telford's 1821 Craig Harbour) of RRS Discovery, *the ship taken to the Antarctic by the ill-fated Captain Robert Falcon Scott (1868–1912). An earlier expedition of the 1890s had left the city its legacy in the form of a 'Dundee Island' – off the northernmost tip of the Antarctic Peninsula.*

It was actually whaling, and more specifically the surplus supply of whale oil it left the city with, that led to the decision to turn to jute-processing. Jute fibres, though strong and durable, were at the same time extremely coarse and rough: only when

well-lubricated could they be mechanically spun and woven. (The Verdant Works, on West Henderson Wynd, a former mill, has been painstakingly restored to house a museum about the history of the jute industry.) After jute came jam – on the back of fruit production in the nearby Carse of Gowrie, a fertile sun-trap sheltered from the worst of the rain-bearing west winds by the Sidlaw Hills.

The third of Dundee's J's was journalism, specifically the published works of D.C. Thomson, whose headquarters are still in the old Courier *building on Meadowside, off Marketgait. Purveyors of wholesome and heartwarming entertainment via the* Sunday Post *(first established in 1814) and* My Weekly *(founded in 1910), D.C. Thomson were reputed to be deeply conservative in their attitudes, not just as publishers but as employers, suspicious alike of trades unionists and Catholics. It's difficult to deny their contribution to the gaiety of the Scottish nation, though, in the cartoon antics of* Oor Wullie *and* The Broons *– even if these strips seem chiefly comic now for their datedness. Generations of children both in Scotland and beyond grew up with D.C. Thomson titles like* The Dandy *(1937),* The Beano *(1938) and, a bit more recently,* Jackie *(1964–2003).*

Imperial Ambiguities

Harsh as it may seem to see men like Mungo Park and David Livingstone as trailblazers for imperialism, there's little doubt that where European explorers went their countries' armed forces had a way of following. Britain's 'first empire' in North America may have been largely lost (though a great many Scots were, of course, to follow Alexander Mackenzie to Canada) but the power of London's East India Company had steadily been growing. The Company was nominally an independent venture, and it wasn't until after the 'Indian Mutiny' of 1857 that its authority was curbed and India brought under direct rule as a British territory. Queen Victoria was crowned 'Empress of India' in 1876. Britain had for some time been quietly establishing itself in what was, oddly enough, only now – as the colonial opportunities were becoming clear – beginning to be referred to as the 'Dark Continent'. But the real 'Scramble for Africa' began with the Berlin Conference of 1884.

Britain made the most of its head start, of course, building an empire on which the sun would not set for several decades. Scotland's role in what's become an increasingly controversial episode is difficult to assess. That Scotland shared the honour (or the blame, or both) can hardly be disputed; neither can the country's junior status in the supposed partnership at the imperial centre. Whilst the suggestion that Scotland was itself a victim of English colonialism has only ever been advanced by the most excitable and historically illiterate of nationalists, the country's relationship with the widening empire was undoubtedly a complex one. For example, should those who went out to settle Nova Scotia or New Zealand have posterity's compassion for what they'd lost in the Highlands, or its contempt for the part they played in the occupation of what had been others' lands? Should those thousands of young men who enlisted in the Scottish regiments or who joined the Colonial Service (as everything from District Commissioners to veterinarians and clerks) be praised for their contribution, or condemned for complicity in oppression? Or something in between?

Some certainly got to live like conquering kings and queens: the parents of writer Roddy Martine, for example, as recalled in his memoir, *A Scorpion on the Ceiling* (Birlinn, 2005). Scots they may have been, but it was an idealised England that they established in the improbable environment of the Malayan jungle in the 1920s and '30s. Martine's father was managing a rubber plantation there. The strictest standards were observed, a man typically taking a bag of six stiff white collars to an evening ball, so he could change them between dances as each grew limp in the sweltering heat. Dressing less formally was unthinkable: starch was one of the symbols of Anglo-Saxon ascendancy; discomfort just a part of the White Man's Burden.

There were compensations, of course: 'Everything was fetched and carried for them,' Martine says. 'Clothes were pressed, shoes polished, drinks served. My father felt as if he had been catapulted into an indulgent promised land, where every demand was satisfied by simply shouting "boy".'

The reality is that, one way and another, Scotland stood in an ambiguous relation to the entire imperial enterprise, its subaltern status within the British union even resulting in what might be seen as an over-representation in the history of the building and the running of the British Empire. That imbalance was to register at home in Scotland itself, in a way that would remain in evidence well into the years of imperial decline. Historian Richard Finlay has pointed to the comparative (and comparatively surprising) strength of Scottish support for the government at

the time of the Suez Crisis (1956), an Empire's-end humiliation viewed more cynically by the British public as a whole. Much more recently, in 2006, Whitehall was caught off-guard by the reaction to its resolve to axe famous Scottish regiments like the Black Watch, the Argyll and Sutherland Highlanders, the Royal Scots and others. Though these were indeed subsequently amalgamated as battalions of a new Royal Regiment of Scotland, they were allowed to keep their old names and insignia – and some of their old autonomy.

SEVEN

'ACHIEVE!
ACHIEVE!'

'THINK OF YOURSELF AS on the threshold of unparalleled success,' exhorted Andrew Carnegie. 'A whole, clear, glorious life lies before you. Achieve! Achieve!' A son of Dunfermline, born in 1835, Carnegie found his destiny in the United States. And if it was a life by no means without its glories, it also exemplified the darker side of industrial capitalism: Carnegie became one of America's most notorious union-busting bosses. But his personal rallying cry and promise of 'unparalleled success' might not have served too badly for an industrialising Scotland. Just as he himself didn't serve too badly as an emblem for those times. If no one individual back home could quite match his achievements, Scotland still followed in his footsteps. Carnegie was exemplary in many ways: one of so many Scots to make the leap of faith required to make it as an emigrant; an early practitioner of what would come to be categorised as 'self-help'; as a steel- and railwayman he succeeded in the same sort of sphere as Scotland. And, as bitter as the irony may have been to some, he did in his final years dedicate himself to philanthropy – and specifically to the spreading of enlightenment and education through his libraries.

Even so, he was obviously unusual. At a time when Scottish emigrants were streaming to America and the Antipodes, when Scottish whalers were sailing far and frigid seas and Scots explorers were trekking across exotic continents, back home their countrymen were by and large a lot less intrepid. Such were the advances in transport technology and the wider social changes these brought with them, though, that, collectively, they clocked far greater distances than their forebears had. As soldiers, sailors and merchants, Scots had always travelled round the world; now, though, they were tracking back and forth across their own country.

Today, Scotland's railways show no sign of being relegated to the museum (though there *is* a terrific Museum of Scottish Railways in Bo'ness). Granted, a great many lines were lost to cuts during the post-war era – of which those brought in by Beeching in the early Sixties were only the best known. But, with the opening of a new Borders Line from Edinburgh to Tweedbank (taking in sections of the old Waverley Line between the capital and Carlisle), there have been a few more hopeful signs, and the main lines are just about as busy as they've ever been. The little tin-box trains trundling up and down much of today's network may lack the romance of the great locomotives and Pullmans of the past, but they keep the old idea of the railway alive and offer a great way of experiencing scenic – and historic – Scotland.

Scotland on Track

The first Scottish railway ran between Kilmarnock and Troon: it opened in 1807 – though its trains were drawn by horses until 1841. By that time, the Liverpool–Manchester Railway had been fully operational for 11 years. Horse-drawn trains were subsequently to operate on a number of other lines as well, mainly for hauling coal to Scotland's cities. Hence the Monkland–Kirkintilloch line, which was opened in 1826; the Garnkirk and Glasgow line, which started oper- ations in 1831; and Edinburgh–Dalkeith, which also opened that same year. Lines like these had an immediate impact on industrial development more generally as they brought about an instant reduction in the cost of coal. By 1837, Aberdeen engineer Robert Davidson (1804–94) had designed the world's first electric locomotive. Its performance was fairly feeble, and it used unwieldy and un-rechargeable batteries, but it was still a start.

Passenger services were introduced from the beginning of the 1840s: the line linking Glasgow, Paisley and Ayr was opened in 1840, for example; that between Glasgow and Edinburgh in

1842. By 1850, Dundee and Aberdeen had been connected; by 1863 there was an onward link to Inverness; the Forth Bridge was under construction from 1883. The railways had an enormous effect on industrial advancement, bringing important economies to the movement of raw materials, finished goods – and, sometimes, of labour. But they also brought less obvious changes: milk production and fishing, for example, gained immeasurably from the way the railway facilitated the speedy distribution of fresh produce. (The advent of the fish supper is directly attributable to the coming of the railways: fish could be shipped to every part of Scotland – and Britain – overnight.)

And as time went on and passenger lines proliferated, the railways had an immeasurable impact on town planning. Stations were typically built on city-centre slum-sites where the land was at that time cheap. These new developments obviously dislodged many thousands of poor inhabitants, but at the same time they gave an immediate economic uplift to what had previously been impoverished zones, creating new commercial and shopping districts. New arcades opened for retail: Glasgow's Argyll Arcade in 1828, for instance – just two years after the construction of Paris' Galerie Vivienne. Department stores suddenly became viable: Jenner's, on Edinburgh's Princes Street, opened in 1838; Glasgow's Arthur and Fraser (now House of Fraser) in 1849.

Beyond the established city limits, commuter villas sprang up in purpose-built places like Lenzie, Dumbartonshire, a stop on the Glasgow–Edinburgh line. It was in the later decades of the 19th century that Glasgow made the transition from big city to conurbation. It is difficult to be certain what caused what: urban growth was following a complex chicken-and-egg expansion, with new suburbs springing up alongside the new suburban lines. Opened in 1886, the Cathcart Circle Line brought extensive tracts of what had been countryside into the city. By that time, Glasgow's suburban lines were carrying over 25 million passengers a year – though, closer to the centre, horse trams (electrified from 1898 onward) were already coming to the fore. Around Edinburgh, too, local lines were helping to transform a wide sweep of outlying settlements into suburbs: from 1884, for example, Abbeyhill, Portobello, Duddingston, Newington, Blackford and Morningside were linked with Waverley by a loop line owned by the North British Railway Company, while the Caledonian Railway Company had a line running round the north of the city from Leith via Newhaven, Pilton, Craigleith and Murrayfield to Princes Street. In Edinburgh too, however, these local commuter railways were soon to face stiff competition from city trams.

Already a successful resort, Helensburgh also became a viable dormitory for Glasgow commuters once the railway reached it in 1858. One such commuter, Andrew Bonar Law (1858–1923), living with his wife Annie at Kintillo House (36 Suffolk Street) early in the 20th century, was a partner in a Glasgow iron firm and then a Conservative MP, before becoming 'the unknown Prime Minister' as he is now (un)known. North Berwick, along the coast from Edinburgh, had a similar experience to Helensburgh when a railway branch opened in 1849, transforming what had been purely a resort into a commuter town also.

Tourism was important too: a new sort of railway touring gave a new lease of life to little towns like Oban and Callander; the two were linked by their own rail connection from 1880. The journey mattered as much as the destination: lines like this and the later West Highland Line (from Fort William to Mallaig, 1901) offered panoramic views of some of the most celebrated scenery in the world. Dornoch, on the Moray Firth, had its heyday as a resort from the 1900s after a light railway was built to connect it to the East Coast Main Line. Strathpeffer, in Easter Ross, grew up as a spa on the back of its railway link.

'From a Railway Carriage'

Rail travel, wrote Robert Louis Stevenson in his famous poem, was 'Faster than fairies, faster than witches...' The effects of technology could seem like enchantment, machine-worked magic. The railways brought a real shift in perception, the landscape flashing by too quickly to be mentally ordered, a succession of random scenes: 'each a glimpse and gone for ever!'

But if travel by train could be bewildering in its effects, dissolving certainties in the speed with which it surged through the world and brought together the country's farthest corners, it also had the effect of fixing things. Only now, for example, was any necessity acknowledged for a standard time. Till then, each town had followed its own local clock. And even when the need to synchronise watches was eventually accepted, it was to be implemented with an ironic lack of urgency. It took almost 40 years for 'Railway Time', introduced by the Great Western Railway in 1840, to be adopted by all the other railways in Great Britain (though the Caledonian Railway was a comparatively early adopter, signing up in 1847). 'The train, like "time", waits for no one,' wrote English tourist Harry Underhill, having had to cut short a visit to Killiekrankie in the summer of 1868. In fact, before this, however inexorable Fate's final summons, 'time' itself seems to have been a fairly easy-going sort of master. This truth, however, could only now begin to be appreciated from a position of hindsight, for only now had the railway timetable really started regimenting life.

The train was impressive in itself, of course. The steam locomotive, belching fire and hissing steam as it thundered its way across country, with its long tail of clanking carriages, seemed a mechanical dragon – the biggest, most powerful beast that most ordinary people had ever seen. In size, strength, speed – not to mention noise – it had a scale that dwarfed the human. And yet it was the creation of humankind. The very limitations of rail travel underlined man's mastery over nature. Modern roadbuilders had for the most part respected the irregularities of the topography they found – going up hill, down dale and skirting the more rugged outcrops and softer marshlands. By contrast, the railway ran straight and true along embankments, across viaducts, through tunnels and deep cuttings gouged out of rocky mountainsides.

Full Steam Ahead

The railway-effect was to some extent pre-empted in the area around the Firth of Clyde by the boom in steamboat-travel – for tourism and even to a degree commuting. As early as 1778, a paddle steamer built by the banker Patrick Miller (1731–1815), its engine designed by William Symington (1764–1831), made its maiden trip on Dalswinton Loch, just north of Dumfries. Among its crew was the engineer and inventor James Nasmyth (1808–90) – whose artist father Alexander (1758–1840) was on shore, recording proceedings in a drawing. Henry Bell (1767–1830) of Helensburgh built the first steamboat to go into regular passenger service. The *Comet* sailed from Helensburgh to Greenock and Glasgow from 1812.

By the 1830s, over 30 paddle-steamers were plying the waters round the Firth of Clyde. Resorts like Dunoon, and Brodick on the Isle of Arran, were re-born in the rush of tourism that the steamers brought; towns like Gourock were both resorts in their own right and steamer ports. Glaswegians who didn't feel like a trip 'doon the watter' could always take the train to Balloch, from where steamers set out regularly to tour the waters of Loch Lomond. (The first steamer there, the *Marion*, had begun its cruises as long ago as 1816, a paradoxically high-tech response to an essentially conservative interest sparked by the works of Walter Scott.)

Steam ferries from Wormit, Tayport and Newport-on-Tay made the daily commute from northern Fife to Dundee practicable – and it was all the more so from 1879, when the Newport Line was opened. Its trains, which crossed over the new Tay Bridge (1878), were in open competition with existing ferries and often raced them. Some suggested that excessive speeds were a factor in the terrible Tay Bridge Disaster of 28 December 1879, when a central span collapsed in a storm, and a train pitched into the water with 75 people on board. (A replacement bridge was built: much more sturdy in construction, it was opened in 1887. You can still see the bases of some of the pilings of the first bridge from the second, near the Angus shore.)

Civilisation and Celebrity

This was a time of prosperity, albeit not for everybody. All the A-list stars came to Scotland's cities on their tours. In 1831, for instance, the violin virtuoso Niccolò Paganini (1782–1840) played the Glasgow Theatre Royal (this venue in Dunlop Street was unfortunately destroyed by fire in 1863). He also appeared at the Assembly Rooms in both Edinburgh and Aberdeen, as well as in Perth's Theatre Royal, and halls in Dundee and Ayr. He hadn't arranged an appearance in Kilmarnock, but when his carriage broke down there on his way back from Ayr, the local theatre owner found he was staying in the George Hotel and booked a performance. Franz Liszt (1811–66) performed at Glasgow Merchant's House, West George Street, and at Edinburgh's Assembly Rooms, in January 1841.

Six years later, on 27 September 1847, Frédéric Chopin (1810–49) didn't go down quite so well at the Merchant House. Was there anything more than East Coast snobbery in the view of contemporary observers that the quiet subtlety of Chopin's playing underwhelmed the Glasgow audience, whilst Edinburgh loved his concert a few nights later? He had stayed with a fellow Pole, Dr Lyszcynski, in his house at 40 Warriston Crescent – but the merely bourgeois comforts there could not meet Chopin's exacting standards. Even so, he rose above this adversity to achieve the great (and perhaps the only) triumph of that autumn's tour in the performance he gave on 4 October at the Hopetoun Rooms (68–73 Queen Street). He stayed a couple of nights at the Douglas Hotel (73 St Andrew Square) before being whisked off to Lord Torphichen's place at Calder Hall, Mid Calder, West Lothian. There he was able to stay more in the sort of style to which he'd by now become accustomed.

The following November, his fellow-megastar (and reputed lover) the soprano Jenny Lind (1820–87) was in Edinburgh, performing at the Theatre Royal, at the east end of Princes Street. In the mania around another visit of the 'Swedish Nightingale' to Scotland, in November 1861, Charles Dickens wrote to a friend recording his disgust that his agent had managed to lose all the handbills he had been going to distribute at Lind's concert, promoting Dickens' reading dates the following week. He finally reassured himself that a few pages from *David Copperfield* would have his hearers hooked – and bring in the crowds by word of mouth. (Dickens was no stranger to the city: his wife had Edinburgh connections, and he'd first gone there in 1841 for a reception in his honour at the Waterloo Hotel, Waterloo Place – where he would often stay thereafter.) Lecture tours by famous authors were a popular attraction: William Makepeace Thackeray (1811–63), who delivered a sell-out series in Edinburgh in 1857, added up his gates and worked out that he must have entertained some three per cent of the city's population. In 1867 Clara Schumann appeared in Glasgow and Edinburgh 'to tempestuous applause'.

The Free Degrees

By the 19th century, 'tempestuous' might be an apt description of religious life in Scotland. The Church of Scotland is by no means the same entity as the Church of England, though both have as their head Her Majesty the Queen. The nearest equivalent to Anglicanism in Scotland is the Episcopalian Church. But even that can't strictly speaking be described as the Church of England in Scotland – even if it is a member of the worldwide Anglican Communion. The Episcopalians have their own Primus, who doesn't answer to Canterbury.

Even Presbyterianism isn't one single, simple thing. In 1690, the Reformed Presbyterian Church of Scotland broke away. In keeping with their founding values of individual conscience and ecclesiastical democracy, the rebels didn't feel comfortable forming part of an 'established' – officially supported – church. Dundonian John Glas (1693–1722) started his own 'Glasite' breakaway movement in the 1720s. This ultimately became a separate Church of Christ. Not only did Glas in principle reject the possibility of a truly Christian 'national church' but he followed a sort of ecclesiastical anarchism, rejecting all institutional structures of authority and recognising only that of Jesus in the Gospels. Among other idiosyncrasies, the Church of Christ commemorated the Last Supper in its services not with bits of bread but with proper meals with kale broth. Glas is buried in Dundee's Howff. (His son-in-law Robert Sandeman, who came from Perth, took up his message and developed it: from 1764, he took his mission to America.)

Not that the disputations ended there. The 19th-century Presbyterians would have given 20th-century Trotskyists a run for their money, arguing endlessly and splitting at the slightest provocation. In the 'Disruption' of 1843, the Free Church of Scotland ('Wee Frees') broke away. The Free Presbyterian Church of Scotland (the 'Wee Wee Frees') splintered off from them 50 years later. This history helps explain what to the non-believer is the utterly bewildering range of places of Christian worship found in the typical Scottish town or city – and the wonderful array of church halls available as venues for the Edinburgh Fringe.

Rich and Poor

'Industry' in the Christian world was in the first instance a moral virtue: that combination of hard work and frugality that the Bible's Book of Proverbs associated with the tireless labours of the ant (6, 6). Modern capitalism, the economic expression of what Max Weber (1864–1920) characterised as the Protestant Work Ethic, tended towards a rhetoric that didn't acknowledge any distinction between diligence and reward. If the 'self-made' were deserving of praise for the hard work, enterprise and prudence which had got them where they were, the poor – by implicit contrast – had been kept down by their own idle and feckless ways.

The reality was that economic success was cyclical at best. Even the wealthiest plutocrats had their ups and downs. And for most in Scottish society, the downs were a permanent state: mass poverty was an unfortunate by-product of the massive wealth-creation of the Industrial Revolution. During one downturn in 1830, a local minister observed, 'a whole population was turned adrift on the world.' These conditions fostered radicalism: as early as 1787, the 'Calton Weavers', from Glasgow's East End, had come together to form one of Scotland's first 'combinations', or trades unions. Calling a strike, they'd gathered for a meeting on nearby Glasgow Green. Soldiers fired into the crowd, killing six, who were finally commemorated with a memorial a century later in the Abercrombie Street Burial Ground in which they'd been laid to rest in unmarked graves.

Glasgow Green became Ground Zero for Scotland's explosive labour history in the century or so that followed.

Glasgow's Town Council was quick to see its significance for the urban poor and banned all public meetings on the Green in 1816, when economic depression and discontent followed the mass-demobilisation after the Napoleonic Wars. So it was that, when the English radical William Cobbett (1763–1835) came to speak in Scotland, local magnate (and shoemaker's son) James Turner gave him a site on lands of his own at Thrushgrove, Royston – just outside the city limits. No fewer than 40,000 people turned out to hear him speak.

But when 1820 brought the 'Radical War', Glasgow Green once more became the focus – though there were demonstrations as far afield as Ayr and Renfrew. Some were bold enough to announce the secession of Scotland from the union under its own Provisional Government: they called on Britain's soldiers not to obey any orders to attack their own kind. Anything up to 60,000 workers joined a general strike, though planned musters on the Cathkin Braes (southeast of Glasgow's Castlemilk) and Campsie Fells (outside the city to the north) were frustrated when these areas were swamped with troops. Meanwhile, after a meeting on Glasgow Green, a small 'army' set off to march to Carron to occupy the ironworks there (see page 158), but was disrupted by confusing warnings issued by government agents among the demonstrators. As momentum ebbed, the majority of the marchers thought better of the plan and headed home. Only a few dozen freedom-fighters stayed the course – the press were greatly to enjoy their sense of *schadenfreude*. Even so, the authorities took the demonstrators seriously enough to meet their arrival with a cavalry charge.

Glasgow Green was again to be the scene when, in 1838 the Chartist leader Feargus O'Connor addressed a meeting of 150,000 supporters there. The 'charter' he was calling for was one of electoral enfranchisement: Britain's working class should have a democratic voice, O'Connor argued. On the face of it, the British political system had seen a succession of radical reforms, culminating in the Great Reform Act of 1832. As we've seen, though (page 199), with property quali-fications still the norm – necessary to prove some 'stake' in the fortunes of the nation – the mass of working men (and women of all classes) were unrepresented.

Two Scottish Nations

Even in the good times, though, there was extreme poverty in the rapidly expanding cities. Disraeli's 'two nations' crack served just as well for Scotland. In 1842, indeed, the social observer Edwin Chadwick, in his report on the *Sanitary Condition of the Labouring Population of Great Britain*, noted that Glasgow was 'possibly the filthiest and unhealthiest of all the British towns'. (And this, of course, at a time when that was a very fiercely contested title.) He added that 'in the courts of Argyle Street there were no privies or drains and the dung heaps received all the filth which the swarms of wretched inhabitants could give'.

It's interesting to encounter (even in the writing of this philanthropist) such dehumanising language as we see with 'swarms'. The Scotland of the rich felt little kinship with the Scotland of the poor.

Under such conditions, major epidemics were just about inevitable. There were serious outbreaks of cholera, especially in 1830. Death wasn't much of a lev-eller: Glasgow's Necropolis is by no means the only enduring monument to the city's 19th-century plutoc-racy, but it's one of the most impressive – and eloquent,

in its way. Whilst the tombs and monuments to those self-made men who made the Victorian city are extraordinarily rich in interest, the poor – in their unmarked mass graves – have been erased from view.

A tablet in a corner of Kilmarnock's Howard Park marks a mass grave dug for the victims of a cholera epidemic of 1832 (250 died in that outbreak). A monument in St Michael's churchyard, Dumfries, marks the grave of 420 casualties of an epidemic the following year. Now known as 'Deid Mans Plantin", the site of a cholera pit at South Barr Farm, Barrmill, in Ayrshire, has been lovingly restored by local conservationists.

Though famously his breakthrough came with his researches into mortality in the areas around the Broad Street Pump in London, in 1854, the studies of John Snow (1813–58) also considered mortality in Scottish cities such as Glasgow and Dumfries. In fairness to the Victorians, they didn't hang around once they understood what was at issue. The Loch Katrine project, aimed at supplying fresh water and enhancing sanitation in the city of Glasgow, was undertaken in 1855 and up and running four years later.

An influx of Irish immigrants aggravated existing problems in poorer neighbourhoods – and added new, sectarian, ones. Also competing for space in the slums by now were 'cleared' Highlanders. As for the lives endured in these areas, we can only really guess: jerry-built dwellings by definition don't last; vast swathes were subsequently cleared and few would really mourn their passing. Glasgow's Tenement House, at 149 Buccleuch Street, was a middle-class home built in 1892, and by the standards of its time perfectly comfortable, despite seeming fairly basic to us now. (The word 'tenement' may mislead the visitor: in much of the English-speaking world, a tenement is by definition some sort of slum; in Scotland it can be any multi-occupancy dwelling, however genteel.)

A Democratic Intellect?

The phrase 'democratic intellect', which was coined in 1961 by the philosopher George Davie, referred specifically to the Scots' pro-equality-of-opportunity attitude to university education in the 19th century. These days, though, it's generally interpreted much more widely. The tradition of the local minister or dominie (from the Latin *dominus*, or 'master') tawseing education into generations of young lads o' pairts (clever boys of humble origin) is important mythically – and at very least partly based in fact.

The principle of Universal Education had been set out in the Church of Scotland's *First Booke of Discipline* (1560). Girls' education had not been seen as so important as boys', but still they were expected to be able to read the Bible for their own and their children's edification. How far these ideals were ever delivered on has been a matter of much scholarly debate. It may well have been more aspiration than achievement. The reality certainly seems to have been that a great many schools were underfunded and inadequately staffed, and that, even when they weren't, students were frequently kept off to work – simply to earn money or to help their parents – especially in busy seasons of the year. The consensus seems to be that, from the 18th century, whilst educational access at parish level in the Lowlands was mostly good – impressive, even – in the remoter Highlands it was patchy at very best.

Some managed better, though, and there were signs of genuine enlightenment in the cities too. The 'Ragged School' of the 19th century – offering basic education to street children – wasn't originally a Scottish idea. The first one had been opened in Portsmouth by the cobbler John Pound, in 1818. The concept fitted Scotland's charitable ethos, though, and Scots soon took up the initiative. In 1836, George Heriot's Hospital established 'free schools' in poorer parts of Edinburgh. There were 10 in all, including one in Chambers

Street and one in the Cowgate. The free school in Davie
Street (between Nicolson Street and the Pleasance) seems
to have been built as part of a later wave, but it still gives us
a vivid sense of what the originals must have looked like: as
modest as this structure is, its architectural detail unmistake-
ably echoes that of the mother foundation half a mile away
on Lauriston Place.

In Aberdeen, meanwhile, Sheriff William Watson (1796–
1887) raised a public subscription towards an 'Industrial
Feeding School', which opened in 1841. As Watson himself
described it, 'It is the place where children assemble at 7
o'clock in the morning, get breakfast, dinner and supper,
three hours instruction in reading, writing, arithmetic and
geography and are employed five hours in useful industry,
each returning to his own home at night.'

A school for girls followed in 1843; then, from 1845,
the two were mixed. In her 2012 thesis *Criminalisation of
Children in Scotland 1840–1910*, Christine Marie Kelly suggests that, especially in England, in the second half of the
century, industrial schools became 'a mechanism for chan-
nelling large numbers of children into prolonged detention
in residential industrial and reformatory schools, establishments which were penal in character'. This 'penal' dimension
had been present from the start, of course: Sheriff Watson
had been able, in his official capacity, to send children convicted in his court of begging or petty crimes to his school by
way of sentence – but few observers doubted the humanitari-
anism of his project as a whole.

Guthrie Goes to School

Most were deeply moved by Sherriff Watson's efforts, in
fact – like the novelist William Thackeray, who shed tears on
the occasion of his visit to the school, and Charles Dickens,
who became a great admirer and advocate for the Sheriff's

methods. Few, however, went so far as the Edinburgh minister the Reverend Thomas Guthrie (1803–73), who himself
became an important campaigner for the idea of Ragged
Schools. Born in Brechin (his birthplace was at the corner
of the High Street and St David Street), he grew up to study
medicine at Edinburgh University – training under Robert
'Burke & Hare' Knox (see page 163) – before deciding to
pursue a religious vocation.

After a 10-year stint as minister in the village of Arbirlot,
just outside Arbroath, he founded St John's Parish Church in
Edinburgh's Victoria Street. One of those who broke 'Free' in
the Disruption of 1843 (see page 222), Guthrie set up shop
in the Methodist Hall, Nicolson Square, for a couple of years
before building his own 'Free St John's', now St Columba's
Free Church, on Johnston Terrace, just below the Castle.
Guthrie was to be influential as a temperance campaigner.
Like John Dunlop (see page 195) before him, however, he
had come to this view comparatively late in life, and like him
too he'd been prompted to adopt what we nowadays tend
to think of as a particularly puritanical, Protestant lifestyle-
choice by a Catholic – in this case a coach-driver he'd tried
to treat to a drink during a tour in Ireland.

But it was with the campaign to extend the reach of the
'Ragged Schools' that, from 1847 on, Thomas Guthrie became
most closely identified. Walking in the streets around his
church, and especially just down the hill from the Castle in the
Grassmarket, he saw children in the utmost peril every day:

> *The sheep are near the slaughter-house, the victims are
> in the neighbourhood of the alters. The mouth of almost
> every close is filled with loungers, worse than Neopolitan
> lazzaroni, – bloated and brutal figures, ragged and
> wretched old men, bold and fierce looking old women, and
> many a half-clad mother, shivering in cold winter with
> her naked feet on the frozen pavement, and a skeleton*

> *infant in her arms. On a summer day ... careering over*
> *the open ground ... are crowds of children. Their thin*
> *faces tell how ill they are fed. Their fearful oaths tell how*
> *ill they are reared.*

Guthrie's language suggests a concern as much for the moral as for the physical dangers facing these children. Whilst many of today's readers might not necessarily share his specifically spiritual worries, nor fret too much about these urchins' 'fearful oaths', they'd recognise that these children's loss of innocence might involve the deepest and most enduring of psychological traumas, and that such defenceless souls were vulnerable to exploitation of every kind. Guthrie was, in any case, never content to offer only a Christian justification for his work: he also pointed out the tragic folly for society of raising generations of young children trained up for nothing except criminality and parasitism. The prison system, he argued, was not just cruel but abominably wasteful: 'We forget that old proverb, that an ounce of prevention is better than a pound of cure.'

Guthrie's original school, on Ramsay Lane, off Castlehill, now forms part of the museum of the next-door Outlook Tower, with its Camera Obscura, just down from the Castle Esplanade: 'Search the Scripture,' reads the inscription above the door.

Time passed, and provision for learning very gradually became more available. By the 1870s, Board Schools had made some sort of free education available to most Scottish children. In Edinburgh, Heriot's 'Hospital' became more like a modern private school from the 1880s (though it offers free places to orphan 'Foundationers' to this day). State provision continued to improve through the 20th century. At least in availability: curriculum specifics were – as they continue to be – contentious. As in the old days of the dominie, enlightened ideals weren't necessarily realised, either in 'purely' academic terms or in wider ones. For better or worse, schools were centres for the inculcation not just of the 3Rs but of social (and sectarian) attitudes. Notoriously, the question 'What school did you go to?' allowed people to be 'placed'. The few minutes' walk between them was only the very start of what separated Castlemilk High School and St Margaret Mary's, in Glasgow, say. And religious divisions were themselves often overlayered and complicated by those of class. 'Jesus Christ, one was constantly reminded, was *only* a carpenter's son,' wrote the novelist Ronald Frame (1953–) of his post-war Glasgow boyhood: 'You could never have pictured Him going to the right school...'

Self-Help

Britain's first circulating library was opened in Edinburgh's High Street by Allan Ramsay (see page 143), but its second was at Wanlockhead, Dumfries & Galloway. In 1756, 32 miners in the lead mine there clubbed together to create a library 'for our mutual improvement'. Autodidacticism has been one of Scotland's proudest intellectual traditions – and it doesn't seem too fanciful to associate this with Protestant values of personal responsibility, of individual scriptural study and spiritual development. The very notion of 'self-help' is of Scottish origin. It first appeared in 1859 as the title of a book by Samuel Smiles (1812–1904). It ultimately spawned the whole genre of self-help books that we see today, detailing how to be thinner, more energetic, more assertive ... Smiles' recipe for success was – notoriously, now – one of early-to-bed, early-to-rise industriousness, and it was founded in a naïve faith that the system would reward honest endeavour.

It's only fair to say, though, that Smiles himself was a supporter of workers' rights (as well as duties), one of Scotland's leading advocates of the Chartist cause and of the 'National Petition' calling for universal male suffrage. It's generally the case, in fact, that the ethics of puritan self-improvement and labour unionisation went together in 19th-century Scotland. That miners would come together both to buy books and to fight for fair conditions seemed natural.

Not that the establishment saw it that way. In 1838, four leading members of the Glasgow Operative Cotton Spinners Union were put on trial in Edinburgh for murder (the shooting of a blackleg) and conspiracy, including secret oaths. That the allegation of oath-taking seems to have upset Parliament and Press (and, in fairness, the general public) more than the murder is an indication of the importance given to swearing oaths back then. In those times, the unquestioning allegiance of the subject to the Crown was seen as paramount; any other sworn, secret promise would potentially undercut that loyalty. So much so that, by a strange circularity, the defendants' denials of oath-taking seem to have been taken by the court as a confirmation of the seriousness with which the oaths were taken. Did early trades unionists swear oaths of secrecy? Such pledges would have been only prudent in a political environment infested with employers' snitches and police spies. Again and again, though, in 19th-century reportage, we see wider (and, in some ways, more rational) fears of organised labour distilling themselves into fevered speculation about midnight meetings and murderous oaths.

The Barbarians Within

Such things were uncivilised, savage, it was generally agreed. Thomas Carlyle's characterisation of the 1838 case as one of 'Glasgow Thuggery' made the connection between labour activism and the 'Thuggee' – a legendary Indian group of robbers whose members inveigled their way into the confidence of groups of innocent travellers before falling on them and silently strangling them in the dead of night. But if fighting injustice was wrong, barbaric and un-British, acknowledging it was only honest, and Carlyle did so, in the most ringing terms:

> A feeling very generally exists that the condition and disposition of the Working Classes is a rather ominous matter at present; that something ought to be said, something ought to be done, in regard to it. And surely, at an epoch of history when the 'National Petition' carts itself in waggons along the streets, and is presented 'bound with iron hoops, four men bearing it', to a reformed House of Commons; and Chartism numbered by the million and half, taking nothing by its iron-hooped Petition, breaks out into brickbats, cheap pikes, and even into sputterings of conflagration, such very general feeling cannot be considered unnatural! To us individually this matter appears, and has for many years appeared, to be the most ominous of all practical matters whatever; a matter in regard to which if something be not done, something will do itself one day, and in a fashion that will please nobody.

The Irish are Coming

There were 'real barbarians' too, in the persons of the Irish. Like just about all immigrants in history, they were viewed with suspicion and fear. The 'Hanging Stanes', in the roadway outside 66 Braid Road, Morningside, in Edinburgh, mark the spot on which (in November 1814) two Irishmen, Thomas Kelly and Henry O'Neil, robbed a carter. A gibbet was subsequently erected in the same place and, the following January, Kelly and O'Neil were duly hanged in the presence of an eager crowd. Burke and Hare were both Irish too, of course – as, later in the century, would be Feargus O'Connor, the Chartist leader who threatened to turn the whole political order upside-down.

In general, though, the Protestant Irish arrived first – at the very beginning of the 19th century. Despite their Presbyterianism – and, in many cases, Scots descent – they were nevertheless distrusted because so many Ulster Protestants had participated in the United Irishmen's rebellion of 1798. (Their American- and French-inspired rebellion against monarchical authority in Britain had to some extent succeeded in bringing Catholic and Protestant Ireland together in armed resistance: it had been resolutely quelled, though not before sending a severe shockwave through British society and state.)

Despite Scots' reservations about these first, Protestant, Irish immigrants, the wave that followed the Famine of the 1840s was felt to be even worse. Not only was it much bigger, but the new arrivals were unskilled, uneducated and – above all – Roman Catholic. Again, it's important to remember how central Protestantism had been to the British self-image since 1688, an importance only underlined by the Jacobite rebellions that had happened since. As little as the average Irish peasant might have in common with the sort of aristocrat who'd supported the Stuarts, Catholicism and sedition were seen as going hand-in-hand.

The numbers were undoubtedly alarming: in the early part of 1848, over 10,000 Irish immigrants a month were arriving in Glasgow. Whilst, in 1841, a by no means insignificant 4.8 per cent of Scotland's population had been Irish-born, that figure rose fast in the years that followed. By 1851, out of a total Scottish population of a little under three million, over 200,000 had been born in Ireland – that is, 7.2 per cent of the population. They weren't all evenly dispersed: certain centres quickly came to seem more 'Irish' than others. A whopping 29 per cent of Scotland's Irish immigrants sat tight in Glasgow when they got there; in 1851, Coatbridge's population was 35.8 per cent Irish. There were fewer Irish immigrants in Dundee, and a lot fewer again in Edinburgh (by 1851, just 6.5 per cent of the city's total) – though even here there were areas of especial concentration: Cowgate had come to be known as 'Little Ireland'.

Of Apes and Irish

That the Irish met with racist prejudice isn't generally disputed. The great 'race theories' that were to blot the copybook of late-19th and early-20th-century Europe were as yet largely unformulated, but British bigots were already flexing their intellectual muscles on the Irish. Thomas Carlyle's view that the Irishman existed in a state of 'squalid apehood' was unusual only in its expressive eloquence:

> *In his rags and laughing savagery, he is there to undertake all work that can be done by mere strength of hand and back; for wages that will purchase him potatoes. He needs only salt for condiment; he lodges to his mind in any pighutch or doghutch, roosts in out houses; and wears a suit of tatters, the getting off and on of which is said to be a difficult operation, transacted only in festivals and the hightides of the calendar.*

There's no doubt – nor much to wonder at in the fact that – Ireland was exporting anger along with its emigrants. The despair of the Famine years had given way to the revolutionary anger of the Fenians (republicans dedicated to the establishment of an independent Irish state) – as small-scale and ineffective as most of their actions were. Scottish newspapers of the 1860s came out with a steady stream of scary stories about 'midnight drills' of Fenians in isolated fields outside Glasgow and Greenock. By no means was all of it nonsense.

There was anger in Scotland too, however, especially as Irish labour was drafted in to the country to take the place of Scotsmen who had departed for the Front during World War I. John Buchan's novel, *Mr Standfast* (1919; though set during the latter part of the war), articulates the feelings of the Glasgow shipyard-worker:

> *'The average man on the Clyde, like the average man in ither places, hates just three things, and that's the Germans, the profiteers, as they call them, and the Irish...'*
>
> *'The Irish!' I exclaimed in astonishment.*
>
> *'Ay, the Irish,' cried the last of the old Border radicals. 'Glasgow's stinkin' nowadays with two things, money and Irish. I mind the day when I followed Mr Gladstone's Home Rule policy, and used to threep about the noble, generous, warm-hearted sister nation held in a foreign bondage. My Goad! I'm not speakin' about Ulster, which is a dour, ill-natured den, but our own folk all the same.'*

Resentment was only boosted by the 'England's difficulty is Ireland's opportunity' calculation that was made by Irish republicans in mounting their Easter Rising, 1916. Buchan's Amos again:

But the men that will not do a hand's turn to help the war and take the chance of our necessities to set up a bawbee rebellion are hateful to Goad and man. We treated them like pet lambs and that's the thanks we get. They're coming over here in thousands to tak the jobs of the lads that are doing their duty. I was speakin' last week to a widow woman that keeps a wee dairy down the Dalmarnock Road. She has two sons, and both in the airmy, one in the Cameronians and one a prisoner in Germany. She was telling me that she could not keep goin' any more, lacking the help of the boys, though she had worked her fingers to the bone. 'Surely it's a crool job, Mr Amos,' she says, 'that the Goavernment should tak baith my laddies, and I'll maybe never see them again, and let the Irish gang free and tak the bread frae our mouth. At the gasworks across the road they took on a hundred Irish last week, and every yin o' them as young and well set up as you would ask to see. And my wee Davie, him that's in Germany, had aye a weak chest, and Jimmy was troubled wi' a bowel complaint. That's surely no justice!'

Religious Rivalries

Football has notoriously been a focus for sectarianism in Scotland, and these oppositions were established early on. Edinburgh's Hibernian was formed in 1875, Glasgow's Celtic in 1888. Both obviously advertised their ethnic allegiances in their names, and both were formed by Catholic clerics looking to channel youthful energies into wholesome athletic activities. Dundee United (formerly Dundee Hibernian) was founded in emulation, in 1909. Its players, as might have been expected, originally wore the green kit of Ireland. The on-the-face-of-it surprising switch to its present colour (though it's invariably characterised as 'tangerine', and never 'orange') came in 1969, after the team had taken part in a US tournament in tangerine and black, and it was decided that these clean and 'modern' colours should be kept.

The 'Protestant' clubs were not avowedly sectarian to start with. Glasgow's Rangers FC was founded in 1872 by athletes – a group of what were primarily rowing enthusiasts who started kicking a ball around for fun. (Clyde FC, established in 1877, had similar origins as a rowing club whose members enjoyed branching out into other sports.) That said, the religious dimension appeared as soon as the avowedly Catholic Celtic had been formed and the first 'Old Firm' game took place in 1888. Edinburgh's Hearts had been formed in 1873; Dundee in 1893 – again, their 'Protestant' identifications took shape in opposition to the newer Catholic clubs.

ORANGE DIS-ORDER

The period from the 1920s saw increasing sectarianisation in more seemingly secular areas of politics. Labour's commitment to making money available for Church schooling made them come to seem the 'natural' choice for Catholics – but led to a growing feeling that the immigrant tail was wagging what should have been a Scottish Presbyterian dog. But something of the same could be said of militant Protestantism as well: 'unionism' itself in Scotland was largely Irish in origin, its true-blue values celebrated by Protestant immigrants from Ulster. (Though the Ulster plantation policy of the 17th century had of course been undertaken largely by Presbyterian Scots: see page 98.) In the vanguard was the Orange Order, established in Loughgall,

*County Armagh, in 1795. For over two centuries now, the Order
has been at the organisational heart of Ulster Loyalism, its
meetings and parades allowing ordinary Protestants a place to
'stand up and be counted'.*

*An important ambivalence was present from the first, when
the Order was established by the loyalist winners of the 'Battle
of the Diamond'. Formed after what had been little more than a
glorified riot, the Order was solemnly dedicated to the memory
of a grander triumph, William of Orange's at the Battle of the
Boyne in 1690, hailed as the achievement that had inaugurated
the era of Protestant supremacy in Ireland. The commemoration
of this victory became the centrepiece of the Order's ceremonial
calendar, its eternal glory lending lustre to innumerable shabby
street-battles. (The English public, meanwhile, has struggled to
understand so strident, so obstreperous and even so seemingly
hostile an espousal of a 'unionist' cause which, whilst basically
accepting, it takes quietly and unexcitedly for granted.)*

*With their dignified ritual, the Order's quasi-masonic lodges
became a meeting-place for an eminently respectable (if not
necessarily very tolerant) Protestant middle class. Brought to
Scotland with Protestant immigrants, it has never really looked
back – or, for that matter, lost these contradictions. An Orange
march through Edinburgh on the eve of the 2014 Independence
Referendum, in support of the union, occasioned considerable
embarrassment to the official 'No' campaign.*

The Crofters' War

A little cottage; a plot of land (the 'croft') for growing veg-
etable crops and grass for winter hay; land for grazing held
in common by the township as a whole. The crofting lifestyle
sounds idyllic – till you factor in the Atlantic weather and the
difficulty of scratching much in the way of agricultural production from such scanty, acid seacoast soil. Most crofters
couldn't live by farming alone but had to fish as well. Even

so, it might be thought, there's a certain dignity in leading so ancient a way of life, so close to nature, in sympathy with the seasons' eternal round. Except that, in actual historic fact, crofting is more modern than the steamboat, and roughly contemporaneous with the telegraph and the electric train.

Important elements in what we call the crofting life had indeed been the same for centuries: as we saw at the beginning of this book, cultivation and grazing has taken place in the Western Highlands and Islands since prehistoric times. As, for that matter, has sea fishing. At Arnol, northwest Lewis, the traditional crofters' dwelling represented by the 'Blackhouse Museum' may date from only the 1850s, but nearby traces suggest that the same lands have been under cultivation for millennia. This blackhouse, and others like it – such as the one at the Skye Museum of Island Life in Trotternish – can't have offered much in the way of privacy, but there's no denying that they must have been very snug. Livestock and people occupied opposite ends of what was still a single continuous space: the former's breath and body heat produced a rich, warm fug in winter which was kept in by the thatched and chimneyless roof above, and by double-layered drystone walls with an insulating layer of earth inside. If the atmosphere of peat smoke must have been extremely pungent, it would also have been mildly disinfectant, suppressing germs and discouraging insect pests.

'Achieve! Achieve!'

What was new in the 19th century was the system by which tenants, organised into township communities, rented plots for cultivation from the big landlords. This arrangement had been reached in the chaos that had followed on from the Highland Clearances (see pages 180–81). Of the thousands of families who'd been turned off their traditional Highland holdings, many had been forced to emigrate, to set out for the colonies or drift into Scotland's urban slums, or to settle in some of the new, specialised fishing ports their masters founded on the Highland coast. Others, however, had been allowed to stay in their native country – albeit very much on the margins, on small plots of inferior land beside the sea. This coastal situation was crucial: if the land here was barely productive, there was at least the option of going out to fish as well. Crofting, as appealing as it may sound, never really offered more than mere subsistence – in economic terms it was a dead end.

It certainly couldn't meet the sort of rent-rises increasingly demanded by the landlords as the 19th century wore on; nor could the crofters do much meaningfully to oppose the enclosure of what had been common pasturelands by landlords, with official backing – basically, the policy of clearance continued by other means.

Geographically scattered, temperamentally independent, the crofters didn't find it easy to organise collective resistance. In 1882, however, influenced by Michael Davitt (1846–1906) and the Land League he'd founded in Ireland in 1879, Angus Sutherland formed his Highland Land League. Campaigning not just for fair rents and security of tenure but for electoral enfranchisement for crofters, this movement met with a sympathetic response from Prime Minister William Ewart Gladstone (1809–98), who'd already introduced important new safeguards for Irish tenants.

But if Ireland offered inspiration and grounds for hope for the Scottish crofters, it made for an unfortunate comparison in other ways. Whilst the crofters' organisation had shown no signs of venturing beyond minor acts of civil disobedience, like rent strikes and land invasions, the authorities were arguably much quicker to see sedition and the threat of insurrection than they need have been. Hence the violence of the 'Battle of the Braes', in 1882, when a detachment of police officers brought up from Glasgow attacked rent-striking crofters who were grazing sheep on enclosed land outside Camastianavaig, northern Skye. There was more trouble at Glendale, on the northwest coast of Skye. A navy gunboat was sent to Loch Pooltiel and a detachment of marines landed at Meanish Pier, Glendale.

The Napier Commission of 1883 listened sympathetically to the crofters' grievances, though its report the following year was not seen as helpful by either side. Francis Napier, 10th Lord Napier (1819–98) was himself a Scot – a diplomat, linguist and writer of real intellectual, as well as aristocratic, distinction, he'd been born in the family seat of Thirlestane Castle, near Lauder in the Borders. But his diplomatic magic didn't do the trick this time. The year 1884 saw the foundation of the Scottish Land Restoration League by John Murdoch (1818–1903). Born at Lynemore, Ardclach, in Nairnshire, Murdoch spent some years in Lancashire working in a factory after his family was evicted before returning to Inverness, where (in 1873) he founded his own newspaper, *The Highlander*. Its aim of restoring the rights of the Gaelic people to their native soil was in obvious accordance with Michael Davitt's principles.

By George

And with those of the American economist and social thinker Henry George (1839–97), who'd caught the imagination of progressive thinkers around the world. Early in 1884, by Murdoch's invitation, he was in Scotland. So enthused were the crofters who came to hear him speak in Portree that, when his meeting ended, they unharnessed his horses from his carriage, and pulled him halfway across Skye themselves. A few days later, on 18 February, George addressed a meeting in Glasgow City Hall. 'Man is a land animal', he told his listeners:

> *All his substance must be drawn from the land. He cannot even take the birds of the air or fish in the sea without the use of the land or materials drawn from the land. His very body is drawn from the land. Take from a man all that belongs to land, and you would have but a disembodied spirit. And as land is absolutely necessary to the life of man, and as land is the source from which all wealth is drawn, the man who commands the land, on which and from which other men live, commands those men.*

George believed that land belonged to everyone – as the air does, or the rain. Or, rather, as the rain *ought* to do. In fact, as he reminded his listeners,

> *Why, in Dundee, do you know, the people there, in order to get water, had to pay £25,000 to the Earl of Airlie for the privilege of drawing water for their use out of a certain loch. The water alone; he retains the right to the fish. The very rain as it descends from heaven is the property of the Laird of Airlie!*
>
> *Why, just think of it! You know how that the chosen people were passing through the wilderness and they thirsted, and Moses struck the rock and the water gushed forth. What good would it have done if that rock had been private property, and some Earl of Airlie had been there who would say: 'You cannot take a cupful until you pay me £25,000'?*

George didn't argue that property in land was theft: he could see the need for ownership as an incentive to enterprise and economic development. But he believed that the people should be paid for the privilege of ownership, via taxation to the state. And he didn't see why the tenant should have to pay his landlord extra in rent given that he added value to the lands through his own labours. Nor did he see how it could be fair for the landlord to sit back and watch the rental profits roll in, without actually having to do anything himself. Hence his view that the value of land for rental should be calculated on the basis of its undeveloped state. The idea that any given piece of land has an 'intrinsic' value, independent of its degree of development, is obviously problematic. Even so, 'Georgism' has the virtue of taking into account the way in which that value is enhanced by the creative efforts of those who work it, so it's easy enough to see why it would have appealed to the Scottish crofters. At the end of this Glasgow meeting, hundreds of excited people stayed behind and the Scottish Land Restoration League was brought into being there and then.

In the General Election of 1885, a special Crofters' Party put up a string of candidates on behalf of the Highland Land League – and four of these were actually elected. Not enough to make much difference by themselves, but Gladstone's victorious Liberal administration brought in a Crofters' Holding Act the following year. This introduced important concessions of security of tenure, fair rents and the right to sell. In doing so, it shot the crofter-campaigners' political fox, without doing enough to allay what had grown to be bitter discontent.

The summer of 1886 saw 250 marines being landed on the Duke of Argyll's estate on the island of Tiree from HMS *Ajax* and a supporting troopship, the *Assistance*. In 1887, a thousand crofters stormed the newly enclosed Park Deer Forest on Lewis, killed 200 deer, and cooked them on the spot. This was partly an act of desperation (things on the island were such that families were actually going seriously hungry) but it was also a demonstration, a political stunt. The crofting families sat down before an astonished audience of invited journalists and had themselves an *al fresco* feast of venison. At Clashmore, in Assynt, meanwhile, weeks of turbulence after an eviction culminated in a midnight attack on the police station by a band of local women. (And men dressed as women – a regular thing in agrarian unrest situations in the 19th century.)

Troubles rumbled on into the 20th century: in 1900, landless families from Castlebay, Barra, made a land-raid on the then-uninhabited island of Vatersay just to the south. Parties from Eriskay came across just four years later. They were joined by further squatters from Mingulay in 1907; other Mingulay 'raiders' settled on nearby Sandray that same year. Many Mingulay islanders had actually originated on this little island, but had been cleared to make way for open pastureland – as far as they were concerned, they were more or less returning home.

STEEL APPEAL

*There's no greater monument to Scotland's industrial age –
nor, perhaps, to industrialism more generally – than the Forth
Bridge, which was opened (by the future King Edward VII) in
1890. That thin line of railway running unhesitatingly straight
and true through that towering trellis of girders: it's an epic
of engineering, both in appearance and in fact. Work began in
1882 and, despite being a Scottish icon, the bridge represents the
vision of two Englishmen, Sir John Fowler (1817–98) and Sir
Benjamin Baker (1840–1907).*

*The water at this section of the Forth is well over 20m (65ft)
deep at high tide; the bridge's deck level is 45m (150ft) above
that, and its central cantilevered span is some 500m (1,640ft).
Improved metal technology had made this possible. Even modern
engineering practice hadn't been up to a challenge like this till
now: this was the first time a structure on this sort of scale had
been built with steel.*

*The need for perpetual painting has been exaggerated in
popular tradition. That it needs a great deal of painting is
certainly true, and at least in part the result of its being so
notoriously over-engineered. The Tay Bridge Disaster of 1879
had produced a near-hysterical concern for safety: the Forth
Bridge was comfortably stronger (so more massive, and more
expensive) than it had to be.*

*A well-known sight worldwide, the Forth Bridge even cropped
up miraculously on the rail route to Galloway in Hitchcock's 1935
film of John Buchan's* The Thirty-Nine Steps *(1915).*

EIGHT

RENAISSANCE
RENEWED

A Handbook of Scotland's History

LOOKING UP THE MOUND from Princes Street, just down to the left of the Castle in the heart of Edinburgh, you see a strange little cluster of cottages clinging to the crags above. They rise out of the gardens below, rearing up storey after storey like traditional Old Town tenements, though they could hardly be more different. With their red stone or creamy-finished walls, painted beams, gabled roofs and higgledy-piggledy mix of window-styles, they have the air of an English country village jammed together in montage (though there's also the odd baronial-looking cone towards the Castle end). The contrast could hardly be more striking between this perky little grouping and the dark grey masses of stone that help to frame it from either side – the Castle above, and the Assembly Hall of the Kirk below.

Ramsay Garden was built between 1890 and 1893, around what had been Ramsay Lodge, where the poet Allan Ramsay had lived in his latter years (see page 143). The development gave concrete form to the legacy of Sir Patrick Geddes (1854–1932). This Ballater-born thinker had an academic background in botany but became enthusiastically interdisciplinary in his pursuits. In the words of his contemporary, Hugh MacDiarmid, 'He knew that watertight compartments were useful only to a sinking ship, and traversed all the boundaries of the separate subjects.' Geddes' theories of urban planning reacted directly against the sort of straitjacket rationalism that the inhabitants of his Ramsay Garden development – including Geddes himself – could see from their windows, just down the hill. The New Town, with its gridiron plan, its classical symmetries and its straight facades, could be seen as the ultimate achievement of a certain kind of humanism – one which imposed reason and order upon the chaos of nature. To what extent was it actually *human*, though? In what sense did the sort of civilisation and order it proclaimed in its architecture reflect the realities of how men and women liked to live?

With Ramsay Garden, Geddes hoped to inaugurate a new and invigorating way of social living. Whilst his first spur to these projects had been the University's shortage of student and staff accommodation, he always imagined his residential complexes as homes in which mixed communities – of intellectuals and ordinary people: tradespeople, workers and their families – could live and go about their daily business close at hand.

Geddes' vision has enjoyed fresh attention as, in an age of economic globalisation, its intense localism has been rediscovered. Likewise, its recycling of old architectural heritage has sparked the interest of the sustainability movement that's risen up in recent years. There is in fact a Patrick Geddes Centre for Learning and Conservation, at Riddles Court, in the Old Town slum Geddes redeveloped as a student hall of residence. Plus you can do the Patrick Geddes Heritage Trail to get a sense of the quiet but far-reaching impact he had on the modern city.

Signs of the Times

As radical as it was, Geddes' concern to build both to a human scale and to a real-life frame of reference was very much in keeping with the spirit of his age. Thomas Carlyle had clearly prepared this ground with his rage against the 'mechanic' in modern civilisation and his promotion of the 'organic' in its place (see pages 200–1). He, in his turn, only articulated a longstanding Presbyterian dissatisfaction with what was viewed as the essentially impious overconfidence of the humanistic philosophies of the Enlightenment.

Geddes was of his time as well in his desire to make peace with the past – architectural medievalism, and specifically the 'Gothic Revival', had, paradoxically, been the defining movement of industrialising Britain. This too, in its nostalgia for an Age of Faith, could be regarded as a reaching beyond the modern and the rationalist to the deeper roots of religious belief. (Think how compelling that nostalgia must have been to enable the Elders of the Kirk to overlook the Popish associations of all those gothic pinnacles when they built their Assembly Hall in the 1850s.) In Ramsay Garden, Edinburgh living was going back to find its future. For Geddes, as for Carlyle, it was important to see the human present as being rooted in the human past; to see history not just as objective chronology but as organic growth. Yet it was growth of a profoundly paradoxical, intricately reflexive kind: suddenly the New Town seemed old hat whilst, by contrast, in the Old Town the old was the new new.

Less perversely, perhaps, Geddes' planning principles clearly accorded in many ways with the artistic values of the 'Arts and Crafts' movement, established by William Morris (1834–96) in the 1880s. We should, the Englishman had famously maintained, live our daily lives surrounded by only what we knew to be useful or believed to be beautiful. When we thought about it, weren't these ultimately the same thing? Art shouldn't be a separate sphere: a well-designed wallpaper or tablecloth could be as important to the quality of life as a beautiful painting. Morris' views stemmed in part from his socialist concern for a labour force he saw as having been left deskilled and alienated by the mechanistic ways of industrial

production. And for a generation of consumers being schooled to settle for shoddy factory goods. But his belief that art had a place (and an essential one) in every area of daily life had an appeal that extended far beyond the revolutionary left to the artists, architects and artisans of the French Art Nouveau, the German Jugendstil and the Vienna Secession – and, of course, to the artists of the 'Glasgow School'.

Work of Art

Morris' recognition that the artist was simultaneously an artisan allowed the appreciation of a new and endless range of creative possibility. His demystification of the skills of art helped erode the Romantic cult of the individual 'genius' and made it easier for egotistical artists to trade influences, to lend and borrow. He had also, as we have seen, worn away at the boundary between art-for-exhibition and art-for-use, raising the possibility of a life attended by beauty every day. The influence of this belief became evident in the sophisticated salons of Vienna, the drawing rooms of London and the halls of the Paris Métro. In Scotland, its most famous proponent was Charles Rennie Mackintosh (1868–1928), an innovator in everything from typography to architecture and furniture design. His work, like that of his wife Margaret MacDonald (1864–1932), her sister Frances MacDonald (1873–1921) and their friend Herbert MacNair (1868–1955), was as influential internationally as it was small-scale and specific in its focus.

So obvious is the creative affinity between Mackintosh and Geddes that it's no great surprise that the two became good friends. 'I am playing around with Prof Geddes at his Summer Meeting,' wrote the Glasgow artist to a friend in 1915. 'His lectures are full of interest and enthusiasm and of course they seem far away from reality – but they are really not.' For evidence of their collaboration, though, you have to go to the central arcades of the city of Lucknow, Uttar Pradesh, in India, laid out by Geddes, with architectural contributions by Mackintosh. Sure, they were doing the work of imperialism (and it's striking that Mackintosh's architecture makes no pretence of acknowledging India's own artistic tradition), yet they did make a real effort to make the place a genuinely uplifting environment in every detail.

Mackintosh's major monuments are of course to be found in his native Glasgow. (He was born at 70 Parsons Street, Townhead, close to one of his early architectural achievements, the Martyrs' School, built in the late 1890s.) Apart from the Lighthouse (the old *Herald* building, also 1890s), he also built the Glasgow School of Art (1897–1909; badly hit by a fire in 2014).

Helensburgh's Hill House was built in 1902 for Walter Blackie (1816–1906). Born into a famous Glasgow publishing family, Blackie was given Charles Rennie Mackintosh's name by Blackie & Son's art manager, who'd used him as an illustrator and designer – another example of how the new aesthetic was coming to see art as a seamless continuum, rather than a set of separate fields.

Mackintosh's example was to be an inspiration for Koloman Moser (1868–1918), Josef Hoffmann (1870–1956) and their fellow-workers of the Wiener Werkstätte to undertake wall-to-wall designs of complete domestic interiors in their quest to produce what they called the *Gesamkunstwerk* ('total work of art'). Rather as Mackintosh may be seen to have done at Sauchiehall Street's famous Willow Tearooms (1904), where he took charge of everything from the friezes on the walls to the chairs and porcelain.

Though he didn't himself design the building, the great man did indeed live with Margaret for several years in the 'Mackintosh House' (now moved physically, lock-stock-and-barrel from its original site a little further down Hillhead Street) and the couple made it artistically their own.

'Separate Territories'

Geddes didn't get to redesign the world. Nor was it possible for many people to have their homes made over by the Mackintoshes. That's hardly a big surprise. Far from rubbing along as neighbours in Geddesian communities, the different classes were being forced further apart. 'The poor you will always have with you,' Christ had said (*Mark* 14, 7), a truth only underlined by the want and squalor that had attended Scotland's decades of apparent industrial prosperity. The only question now was how far it could reasonably be said that the poor were 'with' the rich. As long ago as 1845, Friedrich Engels (1820–95), had remarked upon the existence in England of a 'separate territory' assigned to poverty, 'where, removed from the sight of the happier classes, it may struggle along as it can'. But the fact that he'd found it worthy of remark suggests that, at least at this time, for a foreign visitor, this sort of social segregation had seemed new and unexpected.

In Glasgow, however, it was becoming utterly normal: a stark division had developed between an affluent West End and an impoverished East. In the former, the Kelvingrove Art Gallery had opened in 1901; the curtain had gone up in the King's Theatre on Bath Street three years later. The East End, however, was not just another world but that state of existence which the Labour MP James Stewart (1863–1931) described as the 'earth's nearest suburb to hell'. This tendency towards geographic segregation reflected the political polarisation now emerging in a Scottish society increasingly racked by class conflict.

Keir Hardie's Covenant

The Independent Labour Party was established in 1893 in Bradford, but its founding fathers included several Scots. The most enduringly famous of these, James Keir Hardie (1856–1915), had been born in Legbrannock, outside Holytown, Lanarkshire (you can still see the cottage where he was born). The family moved to Glasgow for a time before returning to Lanarkshire, where James' father managed to get taken on at the Quarter Iron Works. At the age of 10, James himself found work: as a 'trapper' at a local colliery, it was his responsibility to operate the trapdoor that regulated the air supply in the mine.

Though now a working 'man', he'd missed so much of his early schooling that he was still illiterate, so his mother Mary taught him reading and writing each day after work. In a similar spirit of self-improvement, he embraced the temperance culture of his time and place – and the Evangelical Christianity that went with it. Drawing inspiration from his attendance at churches, first in South Parks Road, Hamilton, and then in Cumnock, Keir Hardie was to become a lay preacher of the Evangelical Union Church.

A retrograde step, it might be thought, for an icon of left history, and one taken in opposition to the atheism of James' parents – though it's actually a truism that Britain's Labour Party has owed more to Methodism than to Marx. Despite the 'bolshy' stroppiness and aggressive entitlement the right-wing media has traditionally liked to attribute to trade unionism, the movement has, for most of its history, been marked by this same spirit of sober self-improvement. Samuel Smiles' early involvement with Keir Hardie's Chartist precursors (see page 231) is a reminder of just how vital this particular element has been in the Labour Party's past.

Another way of looking at it, moreover, might be that Marx was the original 'history man' and that Scotland's history of political struggle had long been inflected with religious aspects. Though certainly no materialist, Keir Hardie does seem to have seen things this way to some extent, identifying strongly with earlier Scottish fighters for faith and freedom. As a young trades unionist, he invited striking miners to a meeting on Airds Moss – a convenient open space, but also the site of a battle that saw the slaying of Covenanters in 1680. 'I thought,' he was subsequently to recall, 'they were like the Covenanting armies of yore, gathering their strength to fight for freedom and justice and a new Covenant among working men.'

It's well nigh impossible to keep a comprehensive track of Keir Hardie's movements over the years, between the vicissitudes of his childhood and his (inevitably) peripatetic political career. In his early years repeatedly sacked for his activities and forced to move on, he was to remain nomadic in his mission: in 1892 he was to win the London parliamentary seat of West Ham South; he later lost this, but became MP for Merthyr Tydfil till his death. Suffice it to say that there are official Keir Hardie Trails in Lanarkshire and in Ayrshire – and others could very easily be devised.

Organised Labour

It would be nice to be able to say that Keir Hardie's true legacy has been the Labour Party. And he'd no doubt be happy to have his share of the credit for the NHS. Much of modern Labour historiography, however, amounts to an attempt at an assessment of just how fast he's spinning in his Cumnock grave. As for the study of the specific contributions he made to the development of the party in his own time, that's a surprisingly exacting area of scholarship. Not least because the 'Scottish Labour' party he founded in 1888 with Robert Cunninghame Graham (see page 296) was not the same as either the Independent Labour Party he was to form in 1893, or the 'Labour Party' (an amalgamation of the ILP and other progressive movements of the time), which he was finally to help launch in 1900.

Among Keir Hardie's co-founders of the ILP was John Bruce Glasier (1859–1920): he lived largely in Glasgow, but had taken an early and eager interest in rural landholding, joining John Murdoch's Scottish Land Restoration League (see page 242) on its foundation in 1884. Arthur Henderson (1863–1935) had been born at 10 Paterson St, Anderston, Glasgow (now nestling in the shadow of the M74), in 1863 – though he moved to Newcastle at the age of 12. James Ramsay MacDonald (1866–1937) was born in Gregory Place, Lossiemouth, Moray. You can follow a 'Ramsay MacDonald

Trail' around his native town. Ramsay MacDonald's place in history is secure as the United Kingdom's first Labour Prime Minister (for a few months in 1924 and then from 1929 to 1935). In the Labour Party's annals, of course, he was to become something of a hate-figure after what was seen as his sell-out over the 1931 National Government, a coalition with the Conservatives and Liberals, which committed itself to (what might now be termed) a programme of 'austerity'. MacDonald's well-publicised friendships with figures associated with the British Establishment and 'High Society' didn't do anything to endear him to the Labour rank and file.

Sisters in Struggle

Scotland, as we've seen (page 228, above), had been comparatively advanced in providing schooling for girls – even if its reasons had been religious, rather than what might now be regarded as 'progressive'. Whatever the motive, though, the reality was that Scottish women were ahead of the historical curve when it came to education.

This meant that, at the very least, Scotland was well-placed to take advantage when, towards the end of the 19th century, the idea of women's education for its own sake began to be taken up more widely. When Cambridge's Girton College opened in 1869, its first students included the Aberdonian Louisa Lumsden (1840–1935); she went on to be its lecturer in Classics. And she went on from that to found St Leonard's School, St Andrews (1877). In the following decades, the school became something of a hub, not just for girls' education but also for feminist consciousness. Its alumnae include (Elizabeth's daughter) Louisa Garrett Anderson (1873–1943), who played a role in the Women's Social and Political Union (WSPU), set up in 1903 to fight for electoral enfranchisement. Catherine Marshall (1880–1961) was a St Leonard's-educated Suffragette. Their fellow Leonardista, Eunice Guthrie Murray (1878–1960), of Moore Park, Cardross, was a member of the more moderate Women's Freedom League, so is conventionally referred to as a 'suffragist'.

But the Women's Suffrage movement had already been under way when St Leonard's was first founded. Rochdale-born Priscilla Bright McLaren (1815–1906) was the sister of Anti-Corn Law campaigner John Bright (1811–99). She came to Edinburgh after she married the Presbyterian clergyman and Liberal politician Duncan McLaren (1800–86), and lived in Newington House, Blacket Avenue. Both for them and for their daughters, Helen (1851–1934) and Agnes (1837–1913), women's education and emancipation seemed a natural fit with other issues with which they'd been involved – like the abolition of slavery and the advancement of public health. Whilst Helen McLaren was active as a philanthropist, she seems to have shied away from more open political engagement; Agnes, a doctor, campaigned vociferously on both women's rights and women's health.

Born about 1834 in Glasgow, Eliza Scott Kirkland had been campaigning for women's suffrage since the 1870s. She lived in Edinburgh for a time, at 13 Raeburn Place. A similarly early start was made by Sarah Siddons Mair (1846–1941), the founder in 1867 of an 'Edinburgh Ladies Education Association' and, in 1869, an 'Edinburgh Ladies' Debating Society'.

As, from 1909, the WSPU campaign gathered momentum, demonstrations were held at Edinburgh's Tron Church, at St Giles' High Kirk and on the Meadows. Ann Macbeth (1875–1948), who was head of embroidery at Rennie Mackintosh's Glasgow School of Art – and in this capacity made herself useful preparing some of political history's most artistically distinguished protest banners – was also an activist in her own right. So much so that, in 1912, she suffered force-feeding while on hunger strike in prison. The daughter of an

Edinburgh wine merchant, Agnes Syme MacDonald (1882–1966) was born at 23 Dublin Street in the city; in 1912 she was arrested for breaking the window of a London police station. A chemist's daughters, the Gorrie sisters – Belle (1883–1954), Mary (1886–1959) and Beth (1891–1973) – were born and brought up in Edinburgh (largely in Newington's Cameron Park) and grew up to play their part in the suffragist struggle.

Nurse and suffragette Edith Hudson was born around 1872 – as for when she died, that's still a mystery: she went on the run and disappeared after being temporarily discharged from prison where she was serving a sentence for arson. (She and a couple of fellow-conspirators had attempted to set fire to a stand at Kelso Racecourse.) What was known as the 'Cat and Mouse Act' had been introduced in 1913 specifically to enable the government to take the sting out of suffragette hunger strikes: the legislation allowed the authorities to release prisoners whose health gave cause for concern and then to re-arrest them subsequently when they seemed recovered.

Ethel Moorhead (1869–1955) was another victim of the Act. Born in Kent but brought up in Dundee and later in Edinburgh, she'd been gaoled for an attack on an exhibit at the Wallace Monument, in Stirling; she'd also thrown an egg at Winston Churchill. Held in Calton Gaol, she was taken to the more comfortable surroundings of Morningside's Royal Edinburgh (mental) Hospital to be brutally force-fed. Moorhead is also believed to have been the mysterious accomplice to Fanny Parker (1875–1924) in her bid to set fire to Burns' Cottage in Alloway, in 1914. Notoriously a niece of Earl Kitchener, so a suffragette at the very heart of the British Establishment, Fanny had previously (in 1912) broken into the Music Hall, in Aberdeen, where she had hoped to disrupt an appearance by then Chancellor, David Lloyd George.

How far the suffragettes could claim success for their struggle is still heatedly contested. Some maintain that, rather than bowing to feminist protests, a stern patriarchy was moved to softness by the sacrifices Britain's women had made on the Home Front (and in the field of battle as nurses) in World War I. Whatever the decisive factors, though, votes for women over 30 – in Scotland, as elsewhere in Britain – were introduced in 1918; full equality in voting came 10 years later.

ELSIE INGLIS AND WOMEN'S MEDICINE

Women had always been involved in less formal medical practices – which had been the only kind available for many centuries. Housewives' kitchen can-do flair made them the obvious providers of herbal cures, whilst they self-evidently had relevant understanding and experience to equip them for midwifery.

Even if it was never articulated quite this way, however, the advent of 'modernity' meant the marginalisation of earlier 'folk' understandings and practices. In so far as the witch hunts of the 17th century were anything more than a spree of misogynistic violence, they may perhaps be seen as early evidence of this shift in attitudes. Scotland was an early adopter of Enlightenment values, which included the increased professionalisation – and, consequently, masculinisation – of medicine.

It became a big struggle for women to get back in, its difficulties exemplified by those faced by the famous 'Edinburgh Seven', a group of young women who applied to study medicine at Edinburgh University in 1869: Sophia Jex-Blake (1840–1912), Isabel Thorne (1834–1910), Edith Pechey (1845–1908), Matilda Chaplin (approximately 1846–1933), Helen Evans (approximately 1833–1903) and Mary Anderson (1837–1910). Emily Bovell (1840–85) applied a couple of years later. Only Anderson was Scottish-born (in Bondie, Banffshire); the others had been drawn to Edinburgh by its reputation as a centre for medical study. Whilst they won influential supporters, including Midwifery Professor Sir James Young Simpson, they were fiercely resisted by the medical establishment at large.

Even when she'd finished her studies, Sophia Jex-Blake was frozen out by Edinburgh's Royal Infirmary: she got more help from Leith Hospital, however. Back in the city after a spell in London, she turned her home on Bruntsfield's Whitehouse Loan into her own 'Provident Dispensary for Women and Children'. Enlarged and made official as the Bruntsfield Hospital for Women, this became an important centre: Elsie Inglis (1864–1917) – most famous for her wartime service in Serbia – both trained and consulted there. Now, like so many other once-distinguished health facilities, this hospital has been converted into flats.

Though most of her work was done in her native New England, Dorothea Dix (1802–87) campaigned in Edinburgh against the terrible conditions she found in facilities for the mentally ill. Thanks to her efforts, the private (and largely unregulated) establishments in use till then were closed to make way for better and (on the whole) more humane state-run facilities. There's a plaque to her on the wall outside the Royal Edinburgh Hospital in Tipperlinn Road. The novelist Naomi Mitchison (1897–1999) was an important campaigner for reproductive rights in the 1930s. Despite her later literary fame, she was a science graduate – and daughter of J.B.S. Haldane (1892–1964), the distinguished Scots physiologist.

James Young Simpson (1811–70) was something of a history-maker himself. He was the first to use anaesthetic (chloroform)

*as a treatment during labour. Though he has his statue in
Princes Street Gardens, his chief memorial has been the shining
faces of generation after generation of Edinburgh children. The
city's main maternity facility, the Simpson Memorial Pavilion,
was named in his honour, though when the Royal Edinburgh
Infirmary moved out to Little France, outside the city, it was
downgraded to the status of the 'Simpson Maternity Ward'. His
New Town home at 52 Queen Street is a now counselling centre
for drugs and alcohol problems.*

The Workers United

Along with industrialisation had come the whole vexed question of 'industrial relations', complicating the age-old clash
of 'high' and 'low', of rich and poor. Modern mines, foundries and factories functioned very differently from the farms,
estates and craft-workshops that had previously provided
the economic focus in the Scottish Lowlands, as elsewhere
in Britain. And not just in the negatives (the 'alienation' –
see page 200), but in important positives as well. Industrial
labour illustrated every day the disproportionate results that
could be achieved by workers when the machinery was right
– and what was attainable when individuals worked together
as a team.

There was also a growing appreciation of the collective
power possessed by those with a productive capacity that
could be withdrawn. The costs of keeping a major industrial
enterprise standing idle put the worker and employer on
something much more like an equal footing than ever before.
It meant that 'class conflict' could be something more than
sullen resentment punctuated by the occasional outburst
of violent rage. Scottish history hadn't been short of popular flare-ups of this kind (see pages 223–24 and 242), but,
beyond the exciting adrenalin rush they afforded, these bouts
of burning and looting had for the most part been politically

VOTE FOR

Home Rule.

Democratic Government.

Justice to Labour

No Monopoly.

No Landlordism

Temperance Reform.

Healthy Homes.

Fair Rents.

Eight-Hour Day.

Work for the Unemployed.

KEIR HARDIE.

futile – when they hadn't actually been self-destructive.

Unity could now be a source of real strength. Paradoxically, the consciousness of exploitation and oppression not only resulted in anger, but also collective spirit and even pride. The ultimate expression of workerist power was, of course, to be the Bolshevik Revolution of 1917, but this was only the culmination of a rise of left-wing activism that had already erupted into violence in Russia by 1905. Workers in the British Isles hadn't lagged too far behind. A General Transport Strike brought the port of Liverpool to a standstill in 1911; in 1913 came the Dublin Lockout, which was the employers' angry reaction to the formation of Jim Larkin's Irish Transport and General Workers' Union.

But the outbreak of war in the summer of 1914 caused both the workers' and the women's suffrage struggles to be reined back. A radical fringe apart, people did not want to appear to be taking unseemly advantage of what was clearly a national emergency, whatever they may have thought of the conflict's rights or wrongs. However, as we shall see, the fires were by no means completely extinguished by war.

The Dalmuir Dreadnoughts

However shocking the assassination of Archduke Franz Ferdinand was; however diplomatically disorientating the 'July Crisis' of 1914, no one could claim that World War 1 was unexpected. An arms race between Britain and Germany had been ratcheting up for a decade now, and whilst HMS *Dreadnought* herself (the first of a new generation of technologically advanced battleships) had been built and launched in Portsmouth in 1906, the shipyards of the Clyde had also done their bit. William Beardmore's yard at Dalmuir built the dreadnoughts HMS *Conqueror* (launched 1911), *Benbow* (1913) and *Ramillies* (1916). (The Golden Jubilee National Hospital now occupies much of the site where these great ships were made; on the remainder stands the Beardmore Hotel.) The dreadnoughts promised to revolutionise war at sea, with their speed, their range, the size and accuracy of their guns. Almost as extraordinary, though, was the speed with which they could be built by modern shipbuilders like those along the Clyde. Britain's naval strength was growing by the month.

William Beardmore and Company were in fact a one-stop-shop for almost anything a nation on the brink of war might need: aircraft, armour and heavy guns were also manufactured there. Ammunition was for the most part made elsewhere, though. A Tesco Metro now stands on the site of Alfred Nobel's Regent Factory in Linlithgow: this was built in 1902 to serve the mining industry, but converted to war-work in 1914. HM Factory Gretna, opened in 1915, was a gigantic self-contained munitions complex, 12 miles across and employing 20,000 workers (mainly women). The Devil's Porridge Museum at Eastriggs takes its name from Sir Arthur Conan Doyle's bleakly facetious description of what the factory's high-explosive product looked like when it had been combined with gun cotton ready to be packed into shell-casing. The museum gives a vivid sense of the kind of work that went on there.

A Strategic Shift

It had also been in the expectation of war that the Royal Navy had switched its focus further to the north, from the English Channel to the North Sea. Though still important, Portsmouth was beginning to be rivalled in significance by new naval ports like Rosyth on the Firth of Forth. In 1914, indeed, Scapa Flow became the base for the Grand Fleet: mines and onshore fortifications were installed to defend this haven in the heart of the Orkney Islands. The Forth islands, like Inchgarvie, were fortified as well – you can still see these defences from the railway bridge.

War was also to be transformed by the advent of aviation – though the implications for Scotland itself were as yet unclear. In so far as there was any evidence, indeed, the reality seemed rather bathetic. Whilst in September 1915 an air station was opened at East Fortune, near North Berwick, to help guard against German attacks from the North Sea, the only such raid to materialise – when, on the night of 2 April 1916, two zeppelins appeared over Edinburgh, the fighter scrambled to respond completely failed to find them. As if that weren't enough, the Avro 504C crashed on its return to base: fortunately its pilot, though badly hurt, survived.

Numbers Game

That this was about the only bit of direct action Scotland saw directly does not of course for a moment mean that the country wasn't impacted – massively and tragically – by World War I. Of the 700,000 Scots who joined up, almost 150,000 were eventually to give their lives according to official figures, though some (eminently respectable) historians have suggested that this number's far too high. Such statistics should be a matter of simple fact, it might be thought: the reality is, though, that in the fog of wartime record-keeping a great many records have been lost – whilst, on the other hand, contemporary and subsequent estimates for casualties may well have been exaggerated.

Where no clear certainty exists, an element of interpretation becomes necessary – which almost inevitably means ideology is not far behind. Hence, the claims and counter-claims (all, on the face of it, supported by 'the evidence') over the 'disproportionate' casualties suffered by Scottish troops. The vulgar version – that brave young Scots were deliberately used as cannon-fodder by a cynical England – may be the next best thing to nonsense; that Scots were 'overrepresented' (in the less moral, more purely statistical sense) among those killed is less obviously absurd (though still by no means certain). The long tradition of military service, in which so many Scots had taken such pride, was real – even if it could be dismissed as a romantic rationalisation of a trend that had always arguably been driven by poverty. The tradition certainly existed, though, and a great many Scots felt fiercely patriotic – even as economic factors undoubtedly appealed as well (especially after the government promised continuing support for the families of anyone who fell).

The celebrated 'Pals' Battalions' were mostly an English thing, though there were exceptions. The 15th Highland Light Infantry, for example, was drawn mainly from the employees of Glasgow's Tramways Department; the 16th Highland Light Infantry from former officers and members of the Boys' Brigade. Abashed by public criticism and stoked by the media, pretty much the whole Hearts FC team signed up with the 16th Royal Scots (see Jack Alexander's fascinating *McCrae's Battalion*, Mainstream, 2004).

SKIRLING OFF TO WAR

Kilted pipers famously led Scottish and other troops into action at the Somme and other battles of World War I, and they were also important in 'selling' the conflict back in Britain. If the national recruitment drive was famously spearheaded by the pointing finger of Earl Kitchener, much of the mood-music was whipped up by 'Highland Bands'. (That the most celebrated of these bore the name of the Portobello-born entertainer Harry Lauder underlines how vague prevailing perceptions of Scotland's cultural geography really were.)

*Historian James Taylor (*Your Country Needs You*, Saraband, 2013) records the stir – if not the mania – these bands caused in English country towns: 'What other band could sound the slogan in the world war but a band of pipers?' asked one Private Joseph Quigley. Like proto-Bay City Rollers, the 'Scotties' took England pretty much by storm. 'Numerous girls pleaded for small pieces of tartan kilt as a keepsake,' Quigley recalls. 'At the end of the tour, the inside folds of several kilts had shrunk considerably.'*

Whilst army modernisers had for some time been pressing for this antiquated gear to be replaced with something a bit more practical, its glamour could not sensibly be ignored. Tartan was certainly à la military mode ('Someone had said he'd look a god in kilts,' reflects the wheelchair-bound veteran in Wilfred Owen's bitterly ironic poem 'Disabled'), and just as the girls of England flocked to see the Highland Bands, their brothers and boyfriends signed up for Scottish regiments in their thousands. Something was certainly needed to inject a little romance into the recruitment programme for a war in which the prevailing tone had so far been set on the muddy, cratered ground in France by mass slaughter, mustard gas, the machine gun and barbed wire.

Scotland at War

Whatever the disagreements, no one disputes that a great many tens of thousands of Scots were killed – and many more wounded, some left with lifelong disabilities or health problems. Families and communities – and, arguably, Scotland as a whole –were scarred. It seems invidious to single out specific regiments or battles, though the King's Own Scottish Borderers were to be among the first off the mark in experiencing the horrifying realities of modern warfare at the Battle of Mons (late August, 1914). Though scholars warn of the amount of myth-making associated with the idea of that first winter's 'Christmas Truce' of 1914, an Argyll and Sutherland Highlanders 11 does feature (indeed, it apparently won 4–1) in one of the most famous No Man's Land football match stories. Scots regiments were well to the fore at the Battle of Loos (in October 1915) as they were at the Battle of the Somme, the following June. In just one day's fighting at the Somme, the 17th Highland Light Infantry alone lost over 450 men as well as over 20 officers.

The officer class was in some ways harder hit than the lower ranks: 17 per cent of the British Army's officers were killed; as against 12 per cent of its other ranks. Those figures were reflected in the casualty lists of Scotland's posher schools. Some 3,100-odd former pupils of George Watson's in Edinburgh signed up for duty, of whom just under 20 per cent were killed; almost a quarter of the 1,375 Glasgow Academicals who served went west. War memorials can be seen to this day at a great many Scottish schools – and in all sorts of other seemingly random places: big banks, railway depots ... – all parts of the country, and walks of life, are represented. Where old buildings have been cleared or radically redesignated, memorials have often been moved: the one from the old Younger's Brewery at the bottom of Edinburgh's Royal Mile has been placed on the outside wall of the Canongate Kirk, along with several more from other demolished buildings.

It's worth remembering too that those who 'survived' weren't necessarily ever the same again. Edinburgh's Craiglockhart War Hospital became a centre for the treatment of 'neurasthenia' or 'shell shock' – or, as we'd now call it, Post-Traumatic Stress Disorder. A former hydro hotel, and now a part of the Napier University Campus, Colinton Road, Craiglockhart was for much of 1917 home to (among many others) the subsequently-celebrated 'War Poets' Wilfred Owen and Siegfried Sassoon. The latter had actually been given his diagnosis on the grounds that he'd refused to return to what he now saw as an immoral war. They seem to have worked on their poetry together there. Owen also ventured out to do some English teaching at Tynecastle High School – not, obviously, in the new building opened in 2012 but in another one a bit further down McLeod Street. A success story, of sorts, for Craiglockhart, Wilfred Owen recovered sufficiently to return to the Front in 1918 – only to be killed there just a week before the Armistice.

Others came to Scotland a little less willingly. Beside the old station sidings at Stobs, New Mill, south of Hawick, is the site of a camp in which, from 1914, anything up to 6,000 German prisoners were held. They were set to work on building projects and helping out on nearby farms. Prisoners were also held in the illustrious but uncomfortable surroundings of Edinburgh Castle, and in old miners' cottages on Raasay (where they dug for iron ore in a nearby open-cast mine).

Donkey in Chief?

One of military history's greatest commanders, or its biggest buffoon (or even worse)? Few reputations have been as hotly contested as that of Douglas, the 1st Earl Haig. He had his ancestral home at Bemesyde House, in the Borders, though he'd been born in Edinburgh's Charlotte Square. Buried amidst the ruins of Dryburgh Abbey, not far from

Sir Walter Scott, he was laid to earth (in 1928) a national hero – but has hardly been allowed to rest in peace. Since the Seventies, especially, the whispered criticism has grown to a clamour. He's widely been condemned for his incompetence as commander-in-chief of a British Army on the Western Front whose unfortunate soldiers were so many 'Lions Led by Donkeys'.

And not just for his incompetence, but for what might be characterised (or caricatured?) as a quite preposterous complacency. His diary doesn't make reassuring reading – that's for sure. On 2 July 1916, the second day of the Battle of the Somme, its entry reads: 'The total casualties are estimated at over 40,000 to date. This cannot be considered severe in view of the numbers engaged, and the situation is much more favourable than when we started today.' A contemptible ability to keep a stiff upper lip about other people's suffering, or just a calmly realistic appraisal of the way things were?

Is the criticism of Haig's generalship warranted? In hindsight, almost certainly, up to a point, and yet maybe not so self-evidently in the context of his time. There does seem to be a degree of scholarly consensus on the dogged (not to say 'donkey'-ish) unimaginativeness of his tactical instincts. That said, with his forces literally bogged down in France for so many months, and an enemy entrenched in such strength and depth; with both sides hammering the other's positions round the clock with heavy artillery and cutting down one other's advances with machine-gun fire, it's hard to see what scope there really was for flair.

And what of Haig's alleged callousness? His bullying style? He certainly couldn't be accused of having shown an exaggerated concern for the safety of his men – but then just how solicitous was he seriously to be in a field of war? And if it seems beyond distasteful now that he should have had over 300 so-called 'cowards' executed *pour encourager les autres*, few in the military or public life appear to have thought this untoward. (Indeed, it wasn't to be until 2006 that the campaign for these men to be posthumously pardoned finally prevailed.) Uniquely among the War's participating armies, Britain's had no mutinies to speak of – a tribute, perhaps, to Haig's care in keeping up morale behind the scenes. Not so much in soft words, perhaps, as in actions: improvements in catering and in the sourcing of rations; and a military mail service that, despite the demands of the censor, could get a letter or parcel from Scotland to the Front in just a couple of days.

The War of Words

For his confirmed admirers, Haig has been posthumously martyred to an increasingly popular view of World War I as a murderous fiasco. The centenary saw a renewed offensive across a wider front by academic forces reluctant to accept that the Great War was really one of the Great British Disasters. Even Michael Gove, then the Conservative government's Education Secretary, weighed in, arguing that the war was a 'just' one fought for a 'noble cause' by men prepared to give their lives for the 'western liberal order'. In his eagerness to defend the dead against the attacks of modern 'left-wing academics', he obviously overlooked the contribution of conservative scholars to the 'misbegotten shambles' view of World War I (not least that of the sometime Tory minister Alan Clark, who'd actually coined the 'Lions Led by Donkeys' phrase himself – though he attributed it to a German commander).

For better – or, much more generally, for worse – Haig has become emblematic for many people of World War I itself.

More than that, through the foundation of the Poppy Fund (which until the 1990s actually bore his name) he became emblematic of the War's posterity – and that of other conflicts. Inevitably, that's made him a controversial figure, though the severest criticisms may be harsh, and the vast majority of them are arguably anachronistic.

Much the same might be said for another great military man, for whom World War I came at the very end of an already distinguished (if, again, controversial) life. The public figurehead for Britain's patriotic effort, the First Earl Kitchener could be seen as having been emblematic too – in his case representing the folly of fighting a modern European war with a military mindset formed in colonial conflicts in South Africa and the Sudan. Again, the objection would appear anachronistic. It certainly doesn't seem to have occurred to his contemporaries. When, in 1916, he was lost at sea off Marwick Head, Orkney, his ship having hit a mine and sunk, the local community raised the money for a (recently refurbished) memorial to him on the headland.

Watery Graves

The War at sea had a definite Scottish flavour: certainly its climactic engagement did. The Battle of Jutland was fought 31 May–1 June, 1916. Admiral John Jellicoe (1859–1935) and Vice-Admiral Sir David Beatty (1871–1936) were the two most senior commanders in the Royal Navy. Whilst the former's fleet was kept at anchor in Scapa Flow, Orkney, the latter's 1st Battlecruiser Squadron remained at Rosyth. Beatty was uncomfortable there, feeling that the Firth of Forth could too easily be blocked in by enemy mines – or, worse still, that the Forth Bridge might be brought down by bombing to form a barrier that would confine his ships semi-permanently to port. Both, however, were able to make it out to sea when the moment came.

The battle, off the Danish coast, didn't produce a clear outcome really, but Britain's commanders had less reason to be gloomy than Vice-Admiral Reinhard Scheer (1836–1928). He had felt he could all but obliterate the British fleet in this single action – and in that objective he clearly failed. The British took some serious casualties, though, losing no fewer than 14 ships (far more – and with almost twice the tonnage – than the Germans did). Over 6,000 British crew were lost; many of the wounded were brought back to South Queensferry for treatment.

At the bottom of Scapa Flow lie the wrecks of the captured German fleet. After the Armistice, having first been paraded in the Firth of Forth, the ships were escorted there and left at anchor but then scuttled by their German crews in a final act of defiance. Seeing what was happening, British crews were able to board and bring 20 ships to shore, but they were unable to prevent a further 52 from going down. Over the years that followed, most of these vessels were salvaged – to be sold for scrap, but also to clear safe ways for shipping. Seven still remain: the battleships SMS *König*, *Kronprinz* and *Markgraf* and the light cruisers SMS *Dresden*, *Karlsruhe*, *Brummer* and *Cöln*. These days they comprise both a historical monument and a playground for scuba divers.

Landlord and Tenant

Life hadn't stopped in Scotland while its sons went off to fight, its daughters to work in munitions plants; others farmed, fished, cooked, cleaned and generally carried on with life. The same old romantic and family dramas went on – heightened, if anything, by the fear of separation and bereavement; as did the same social problems – often exacerbated by the stresses and strains of wartime service. As powerful as the call of patriotism was – and there's no doubt that it did, to some extent, dampen down political unrest and help quell radicalism – it couldn't completely suppress the sullen anger many felt. From time to time, inevitably, it flared up.

The left, of course, liked to make the point that the workers' cause transcended national boundaries – that, indeed, nationalism was a myth that helped keep working people in servitude. As early as 1894, standing as a socialist candidate in Edinburgh's St Giles' ward, the future Irish rebel leader James Connolly (1868–1916) had argued in his manifesto that:

> *The Irish worker, who starves in an Irish cabin, and the Scottish worker who is prisoned in an Edinburgh garret are brothers with one hope and destiny. The landlord who grinds Irish peasants on a Connemara estate and the landlord who rack-rents them in a Cowgate slum are brethren in fact and deed.*

The landlord class could see that they were 'brethren', with common interests, so, for Connolly, working people of all kinds and in all countries had to do the same. Activists worked hard to drive home the idea that a Düsseldorf factory hand and a Fife miner had a great deal more in common with each other – and a great many more shared interests – than the former with a German *junker* or the latter with a Scottish lord.

Nor was it only in Connemara that there were 'peasants' being 'ground' by landlords: in the islands, the Highland Land League was to be re-formed in 1909, with a renewed programme of land raids taking place in the years following World War I. Urban landlords weren't necessarily any better – but they too could be resisted, as 'Mrs Barbour's Army' found when they held their first rent strikes in Govan in the spring of 1915. Mary Barbour (1875–1958) and her supporters were reacting to what they saw as an unacceptable double-whammy of rent hikes along with neglected repairs.

Tenants organised themselves to keep sheriff's officers from entering homes to confiscate possessions in lieu of overdue rent and to prevent evictions, and on 17 November they staged a mass march on the Sheriff's Court. Their campaign has to be adjudged at least a partial success: the government was forced to rush through the Rent Restriction Act, capping rents for the remainder of the War.

Five years later, Mary Barbour was to become the first female Labour councillor in Glasgow's history. Her birthplace, at 37 New Street, Kilbarchan, Renfrewshire, has been demolished; as have her homes in Govan's Macleod Street (which no longer exists at all) and in Ure Street, which has since been renamed Uist Street.

Crisis on the Clyde

October 1917 brought revolution to a war-ravaged Russia; the following November it was Germany's turn. Tough times, then, for the imperial monarchies of Europe. These examples must have been uppermost in official minds when, on 31 January 1919, anything up to 90,000 workers turned out for a trades union demonstration in the very heart of Glasgow. Thankfully, there were no fatalities, though at what became known as the 'Battle of George Square' (or 'Bloody Friday'), there was serious fighting and the red flag was raised – a red rag to the bull of the British state.

The authorities' paranoia was heightened even as their scope for action was severely circumscribed by signs of restiveness in those very forces on which they relied to reaffirm their power. At Maryhill Barracks, troops actually had to be locked in, lest they join the crowds streaming through the city-centre streets in what amounted to open rebellion. Among those arrested in the aftermath was Emmanuel 'Manny' Shinwell (1884–1986), a future Labour minister (and, eventually, national treasure), but at this time held in deep suspicion as an official of the seaman's union. As one of the protest's supposed ringleaders, he served five months for incitement.

No single moment made what is now referred to as 'Red Clydeside'. That chaotically complex and drawn-out episode coalesces into clarity only in retrospect (and most notably in a really gripping narrative history like Maggie Craig's *When the Clyde Ran Red* (Mainstream, 2011).) Social and political pressures had been building in Glasgow's working-class districts for years before men and women at the world's biggest sewing-machine factory – Singer's, in Kilbowie Road, Clydebank – walked out to support 11 women staff who'd been sacked for striking. But if the Singer Strike and other subsequent actions undertaken by an emboldened trades union movement were important in boosting working-class confidence and pride, there were also the Glasgow rent strikes – still ongoing throughout World War I.

That conflict itself had impacted on the Home Front in ways that didn't necessarily accord with the officially sanctioned spirit of cheerful co-operation. Left-wing campaigners like James Maxton (1885–1946) and his Marxist comrade John Maclean (1879–1923) argued that, the ethics of killing apart, there was no working class interest to be served by a contest for supremacy between imperialist powers. A bayonet, the socialist slogan went, was a weapon with a worker at each end. As if to underline its truth, HM Government in 1915 passed the Munitions of War Act, suspending workers' rights and making trades union activity illegal.

A minister's wife in the Gorbals district, Helen Crawfurd (1877–1954), embodied the continuity between the fights for fair rent and women's rights: she helped lead rent strikes in the Gorbals and campaigned vociferously for women's suffrage. And, perhaps, violently – though it isn't clear whether she was really responsible for the 1914 bomb attack on Glasgow's Botanic Gardens for which she was locked up in

'NO SURRENDER – God help the sheriff officer who enters here.'

the city's Duke Street Prison (now replaced by the Ladywell Housing Scheme). Like her friend and fellow rent-strike organiser, Agnes Dollan (1887–1966), Crawfurd was also a fierce campaigner against the War, establishing the Women's Crusade for Peace in 1916. Whilst, rightly or wrongly, the wider women's suffrage movement had seen fit to suspend its open struggle for patriotism's sake, working-class socialists were much slower to see the sufferings of the poor in war as worthwhile 'sacrifices'; and were quicker to see the political opportunity.

Deepest Red

Both Maxton and Maclean had been born in Pollokshaws, and both were schoolteachers, but whereas the former's parents had themselves been teachers, the latter's had been working-class incomers from the Highlands. John Maclean was to follow James Connolly in seeing a community of interest between the rural and the urban worker.

Whilst Connolly's campaigning work had eventually found its focus in the urban working class of Edinburgh and

Dublin, Maclean remained an influential supporter of the activities of the Highland Land League. He also found his way indirectly into a left-wing version of what we'd now see as a nationalist argument, concluding that a Scottish workers' state could be achieved only with independence from England. But he never lost sight of the local issues, backing Mary Barbour and her rent strike. On 23 August 1920, rent protestors made common cause with trades unionists who'd called a city-wide general strike: Notices of (rent) Increase were ceremonially burned at a mass demonstration on Glasgow Green.

The Clydeside spirit flowed into the Labour mainstream, to some extent, when the 1922 General Election saw several leaders returned to Parliament. These included Manny Shinwell, James Maxton (who sought to 'make the English-ridden, capitalist-ridden, landowner-ridden Scotland into a free Scottish Socialist Commonwealth'), Neil Maclean (1875–1953) and George Buchanan (1890–1955).

The memory of Red Clydeside remains inspirational on the Scottish left, though critics say it's been romanticised, even idealised – which is no doubt true. But given that the 20th century panned out as some way short of utopian for many Scots, it's hardly surprising that there should be some nostalgia for this time.

It wasn't just the Clyde that ran red, of course. There may have been a degree of wishful thinking in the Aberdeen Communist William Leslie's view that, proportionately, his home city was 'more red than Glasgow', but there's no doubt that working people were organising and fighting for their rights across the whole of urban Scotland. His fellow Aberdonian, Mary Brooksbank (1897–1978), moved to Dundee at the age of eight and started working in a jute mill just four years later. A tireless labour activist, she joined John Maclean in calls for an independent 'Scottish Workers' Republic'.

The Late, Great Lafayette

Despite all the unrest, it would be wrong to think of early 20th-century urban Scotland as being all about class war. There'd been a theatre on the present Festival Theatre site on Edinburgh's Nicolson Street since the 1820s, and the Lumiere Brothers demonstrated cinema there in 1896. On the night of 9 May 1911, however, the illusionist the Great Lafayette, and his dog Beauty (a present given to him by Harry Houdini) were killed when fire tore through the backstage area of what was at that time called the Empire Palace Theatre. Ten others were killed as well, though all the audience were successfully led to safety. A quarter of a million people turned out for Lafayette's funeral. He and Beauty were laid to rest together, as they surely would both have wished, in an impressive-looking grave at Piershill Cemetery, northeast of the city.

Like many another Scottish theatre, the Empire Palace became a bingo hall in 1963 – though it was to buck this trend by resuming its status as a theatre in 1994. The Glasgow Empire, on Sauchiehall Street, was only metaphorically and stereotypically a 'grave' for unfortunate comedians, but it's been deceased itself since 1963. The Britannia Panopticon music hall, Trongate, Glasgow, opened its doors for the first time in 1857. Stan Laurel (1890–1965) made his stage debut there in 1906. Though it was closed for good in 1938, the building still survives and is currently being restored.

The Scotia Music Hall, originally built in the 1870s, was refurbished in 1899 and renamed the Metropole Theatre. Situated on the western side of Stockwell Street, just north of the River Clyde, it was often host to the singing star (and later 'Sir') Harry Lauder (1870–1950) in the early days of his career (though he'd made his professional debut in Larkhall, South Lanarkshire, where he'd been working as a miner). Burned down in 1961, the Metropole has since made way for housing.

'ZAINAB'

'When I reply that I come from the far North, they conclude that it is Turkey: their minds cannot visualise a land farther North than that.' The first British-born (at 13 Great Stuart Street, Edinburgh) Muslim woman to perform the Hajj, Lady Evelyn Cobbold (1867–1963) had indeed come a long way from her native Scotland – not just geographically but intellectually. And spiritually most of all, perhaps. If she had joined a long and distinguished line of British lady travellers to the Arab world, she had broken even with that tradition by actually embracing Islam. She did so strictly on her own terms, an indomitable aristo to the last, but that doesn't mean she didn't do it with all her heart and soul. She published her first memoir of her travels in Arabia and North Africa in 1912 and from 1921 spent a decade in Britain, dividing her time between her family's town house in London and its Glencarron Estate, in Wester Ross. But it was not until 1933 that she made her pilgrimage to Mecca, at the age of 65.

Flourishing Forests

There's a widespread assumption that Britain was in ancient times completely covered with thick forests, which were then relentlessly hacked away by hundreds of generations of human settlers. T.C. Smout (in *People and Woods in Scotland*, Edinburgh University Press, 2002) makes the point that, in Scotland at least, this was never really so. The receding Ice Age left behind it endless expanses of open tundra, which was only slowly colonised by birches and other trees. Vast as it was, the predominantly pine Caledonian Forest (which is still to be seen in pockets at, for example, Rothiemurchus, Aviemore and Loch Maree) covered no more than 20 per cent of what we now know as Scotland.

Tree-planting was, however, essential to the Improvement movement of the 18th century. In the 1730s, for example, the Earl of Haddington carried out a major programme at Tyninghame House, outside Dunbar, East Lothian. The Earl of Atholl introduced the larch – of which he planted almost 10 million. At the suggestion of the visiting artist Alexander Nasmyth, he fired off cannon loaded with seeds, so as to plant trees on inaccessible crags in the grounds of his family seat at Blair Castle, Perthshire. The great tree collector David Douglas, returning from his travels in North America in the 1820s, brought back specimens of lodgepole pine and Sitka spruce – and, of course, of Douglas fir. Born in Scone, he'd worked in the grounds of the Palace as a boy. Later on, he found a patron in Sir John Murray Naesmith, the laird of Dawyck House (built at the beginning of the 19th century on the site of the 13th-century Dawyck Castle). Sir John, who sponsored some of Douglas' expeditions, planted lots of the trees he brought back in the Arboretum at Dawyck, near Broughton. Now it's in the care of Edinburgh's Royal Botanic Garden.

Despite the efforts of such luminaries, Scotland was comparatively sparsely wooded by the start of World War I; the UK as a whole was quite badly short of timber. This hadn't seemed to matter, all the softwood needed for construction being readily shipped in from Scandinavia. Now, though, with U-boats prowling up and down the North Sea, that source was effectively cut off. Such forests as Britain did have had to be raided for wood. By the time the war was over, it was clear that the domestic supply had to be restored somehow – not just to replace what had been cleared, but to build up a reserve for future crises. Hence the foundation of the Forestry Commission in 1919.

Its early sponsors had more ambitious aims than simply replenishing the country's trees, however. In Scotland, Lord Lovat and Sir John Stirling-Maxwell saw large-scale reafforestation as a way of resettling the Highlands and bringing what had been essentially empty, 'barren' areas into production. The first area to be planted was what is now the Argyll Forest Park, the land having been leased from the entertainer Sir Harry Lauder in 1921. A few years later, the village of Glenbranter was built for the workers and their families. The Highlands were being sown with people, as well as trees, and Glenbranter was only the first of many such communities created in what had been virtually abandoned parts of Scotland. With agriculture in the doldrums long before the official 'Great Depression' of the Thirties had descended, the Commission was able to buy large tracts of land at little cost. By 1940, it was to have over 71,000 ha (1.75 million acres) under timber across Scotland, approximately half of that in the Highlands and the Islands.

As time went on, however, and as mechanisation crept in – even into what might have seemed the most unpromising of industries – it became clear that forestry wasn't really going to repopulate the glens. Self-sufficiency in timber might be nice, but the Scottish product still had to compete in price with foreign imports and, when the going got tough, inevitably, jobs were shed. All in all, indeed, the whole Forestry Commission project has been of dubious success. The environmental benefits of tree-planting were taken for granted for quite some years – even if many lovers of the countryside took aesthetic exception to the regimented stands of conifers that seemed invariably to result. As time went on, however, and eco-awareness gradually increased, the desirability of these forests was called increasingly into question.

The one man who might have had the vision to reimagine Scotland as a country in which woodland environments could build beauty and enhance the life of all had been lost to America half a century before. John Muir (1838–1914), whose Dunbar birthplace is now a museum and study centre, emigrated to the United States with his family when he

was ten. Growing up in rural Wisconsin, in a strict Presbyterian household, he himself was drawn increasingly to science – specifically botany. But there was a well-nigh religious fervour to the way he pursued his studies. And to the way in which, in later life, having jacked in work to walk among the mountains and forests of the American West, he began to preach the values of what we'd now see as 'environmentalism'. As successful as he was in championing the protection of the giant sequoia trees and the preservation of Yosemite as president of the 'Sierra Club', his full significance is perhaps only now being recognised.

The 'Scottish Renaissance'

A small-'r' renaissance in the Scottish arts had been ushered in by Charles Rennie Mackintosh and other practitioners of the 'Glasgow Style' in the early years of the 20th century, as we've seen. The focus shifted east to Edinburgh in the years that followed with the advent of the 'Scottish Colourists': painters like Samuel Peploe (1871–1935), John Duncan Fergusson (1874–1911), Leslie Hunter (1877–1931) and Francis Cadell (1883–1937). Why 'Colourists'? A glance at any of their paintings makes that clear: the boldness and the vividness of their colours is exhilarating.

If, in the Bluffer's Guide version, the 'Colourists' could be said to have pursued a post-Impressionist style influenced by that of continental artists like Cézanne, Matisse and Van Gogh, their successors in the 'Edinburgh School' tracked French progress on into more assertively modern movements such as Cubism. Those enrolled in the Edinburgh School (and, confusingly, many had literally studied together at the Edinburgh College of Art on Lady Lawson Street) included

Renaissance Renewed

William Crozier (1893–1930), William Geissler (1894–1963), Anne Redpath (1895–1965) and William MacTaggart (1903–81; his grandfather and near-namesake William McTaggart (1835–1910) had also been a distinguished painter).

What is more officially known as the 'Scottish Renaissance' was a campaigning modernist movement, primarily in literature, and led by the poet Hugh MacDiarmid (real name Christopher Murray Grieve, 1892–1978). There's a little museum in Brownsbank Cottage, outside Biggar in South Lanarkshire, where he spent the last couple of decades of his life. Born (at 17 Arkinholm Terrace) in Langholm, Dumfries & Galloway, MacDiarmid was educated at the old academy in the town. He then went up to Edinburgh to train as a teacher at the Broughton Junior Student Centre (later to be Broughton High School) on McDonald Road, off Leith Walk. A postman's son, and strongly radical in his views, MacDiarmid started out as a journalist on left-wing papers before enlisting in the Royal Army Medical Corps for World War I.

Back in Montrose after the Armistice, he set about the poetic output that was going to make him one of the acknowledged giants of Scottish literature. Written in his own, hand-crafted form of Lallans (southern and central Scottish dialect) – what he himself called a 'Synthetic Scots' – it represented an ambitious attempt to forge a new and unapologetically Scottish language in which a new and unapologetically Scottish consciousness could be expressed. Not content with creating his own language, MacDiarmid arguably introduced the whole idea that this was a 'Scottish Renaissance' – he'd certainly predicted that some sort of 'renascence' was coming in Scottish culture. But rival claims can be made on behalf of his friend, the Edinburgh artist William Johnstone (1897–1981), and Johnstone's cousin the composer Francis George Scott (1880–1958), both of whom had looked forward to 'a splendid revival, a Scottish Renaissance of the arts'.

There's little dispute, though, that MacDiarmid produced the era's epic work. Published in 1926 to simultaneous excitement and bemusement, *A Drunk Man Looks at the Thistle* looked at Scotland, its history, its culture and its place in the modern world. Like Ireland's James Joyce, MacDiarmid saw his supposed duty to be Scotland's bardic saviour as an irksome if not overwhelming responsibility:

A Scottish poet maun assume
The burden o' his people's doom,
And dee to brak' their livin' tomb.

At the same time – again like Joyce – he embraced that role with apparent enthusiasm.

He certainly succeeded in inspiring other writers. Or in inspiringly alienating them: the greatest figures of the 'Scottish Renaissance' that followed him aren't so much imitators of MacDiarmid's style as emulators of his ambition. Even his friend and sometime student William Soutar (1898–1943) differed from his mentor in the function he saw for Scots. The language question was crucial for this generation's poets: 'should' Scottish literature be written in Scots, or did that make it parochial? Did works of international stature have to be written in an international language? It was never really to be resolved, of course. Any more than the other great crux that confronted the generally socialist writers of the 'Scottish Renaissance': how were their nationalist feelings and their internationalist principles to be reconciled?

Renaissance Renewed

'Now I Can Be a Poet'

Few writers can claim to have had so precisely identifiable an epiphany as Soutar, who recalled in his journal the day in 1924 when he stopped in an Edinburgh street and was able to say to himself, 'Now I can be a poet.' Sadly, this moment had been brought on by his doctor's revelation that the spinal inflammation that had already afflicted him with well-nigh unbearable pain for much of his adulthood was going to remain with him and worsen, ruling out more active ways of life. (The house in which he stayed from this time on – 'Inglelowe', at 27 Wilson Street, in Perth – may still be seen, though the collection there was badly damaged by a flood in 2010.)

Other young Scots were meanwhile coming to the realisation that they could be poets too. MacDiarmid did seem to have given Scotland back its literary pride. Edwin Muir (1887–1959) was expelled from his Orkney 'Eden' as a young teenager after his father's death and his family's removal, where a life of dead-end jobs apparently awaited. Made by his marriage to the Montrose-born translator and future novelist Willa Muir (née Wilhelmina Johnston Anderson, 1890–1970), he moved to Prague and thence to a succession of central European cities, which gave him a distinctly cosmopolitan perspective on his Scottish home. Linguistically, as well as geographically, he took his own route to a Scottish Modernism, rejecting MacDiarmid's Lallans to write in English. By contrast, Edwin Morgan (1920–2010) barely left his native Glasgow, except to serve during World War II. He too, however, showed a cosmopolitan cast of mind – translating poetry from several different tongues – and had omnivorous artistic tastes, referencing other media, such as cinema and music, in his work.

Whilst poetry was probably the flagship genre, the 'Scottish Renaissance' brought important achievements in prose fiction too: of these the novels of Lewis Grassic Gibbon (1901–35) are probably the best known. *Sunset Song* (1932;

made into a Terence Davies film with Agyness Deyn in 2015) kicked off a trilogy that, with *Cloud Howe* (1933) and *Grey Granite* (1934), has since been known collectively as *A Scots Quair*. A tale of rural life in the Kincardine Mearns, it's rich not only in local colour and Doric dialect (the language of northeastern Scotland) but also in narrative techniques like those to be found in the work of international modernists like James Joyce, Virginia Woolf, William Faulkner and Gertrude Stein. And like Grassic Gibbon, Nan (Anna) Shepherd (1893–1981) found inspiration in the landscape and rural communities for her novels and other writing.

Neil M. Gunn, from Dunbeath in Caithness, used what might seem the most parochial of Highland settings as his jumping-off point to explore some of the most painful chapters in Scottish history, some of the wildest extravagances of Scottish myth – and, by exploring those – to address the challenges and tragedies of the modern world.

Along with Willa Muir, the most important woman novelist of the Scottish Renaissance, Catherine Carswell (1879–1946), was till more recently more famous for her controversial biography of Robert Burns. What to the customary keepers of the Ploughman Poet's reputation seemed like gratuitous scurrility now reads more like the kind of bid for an 'honest' and 'grown-up' perspective you'd expect from a friend, fan and future biographer of D.H. Lawrence. By the same token, the accompanying scandal might be seen with hindsight as an important coming-of-age for a Scottish literary consciousness readying itself to relinquish some of the cosy complacency of former, perhaps politer times.

A GAELIC RENAISSANCE?

'Four there are to whom I gave love,/to four a service of varying effect:/the great cause and poetry,/the lovely Island and the red-haired girl.' The cause is Communism; the island Skye; the red-haired girl a composite … and, as for the poetry, well, the work of Sorley MacLean (1911–96), speaks for itself. Or does it? MacLean's exhilarating verses, though written in Gaelic, were always more widely read in English: was he an unwitting Ossian for his time? With so small a 'natural' readership, has his Gaelic text been an 'empty vessel' for anglophone readers to fill with their fantasies of a Celtic creativity that is 'close to nature'?

And how are we to take seriously a body of work built on the assumption that what the Highlands and Islands chiefly needed was immediate annexation to the Soviet Union? The challenges we meet in MacLean's poetry can be seen as a distillation of the key dilemmas faced by the Scottish Renaissance in general: First, how precise and local can a poet's vision be before it becomes parochial? Second, how is a writer to articulate his or her Scottish preoccupations for a wider audience without leaving the language and the culture that gave rise to them behind?

However successful he's judged to have been (or not to have been) in resolving these issues, there's no disputing that MacLean dedicated his whole life to the attempt, both as a poet and, less directly, as an educator. Born on Raasay, at Osgaig, a tailor's son, he was educated at the island's primary school, and then at (what's now) Portree High. He then studied at Edinburgh University, and took a teaching qualification at the city's Moray House, before going back to Skye to teach in his old school. After a spell in Tobermory, he spent much of the 1930s teaching at Boroughmuir High School, Viewforth, Edinburgh; he joined the regular writers' gatherings at the Abbotsford Bar in Rose Street. He returned to Boroughmuir after his service in World War II. From 1956 he was headmaster of Plockton School, in Wester Ross.

Pictured on the previous page: Portree Harbour.

NINE

RAILPLANES,
RAZORS AND
REALITY

'SWIFT, SAFE, SURE,' said the slogan on the poster for the Bennie Railplane, built – at least in prototype – in Milngavie, northwest of Glasgow, in 1929–30. In 1956, the gantries and the girders of a line that had never actually run was finally dismantled and the whole thing carted off for scrap. From the perspective of today, the Railplane contrives to look simultaneously futuristic and impossibly antiquated: suspended from a monorail above, with guides below, it was driven by propellor.

Like an aeroplane without wings, in other words. And about as useful, the investors of the 1930s thought: despite a seemingly successful test-run with 50 passengers, carried in comfort down a 130m (426ft) track at Burnbrae, no one ever did turn up to sign the bottom line. Auldhouse-born George Bennie (1892–1957) never lost his own faith in an invention he claimed was capable of average speeds of over 190kmh (120mph), making Glasgow to Edinburgh a 20-minute trip, but he did lose all his money; his vision and belief had set him on a fast-track to bankruptcy.

Where did it all go wrong? Why didn't Bennie become another addition to Scotland's glittering technological and entrepreneurial hall of fame? How, more generally, indeed, did Scottish Renaissance sink into Scottish Slump? It didn't, in the strictly narrative sense: rather, the two coincided, the dampening pall descending over the Caledonian economy even as MacDiarmid & Co were setting the cultural Clyde on fire.

From Roar to Whimper

The Twenties didn't roar for long at all; the initial burst of optimism over, an economy founded in heavy industry sank into steady and steep decline. With hindsight, indeed, it already seemed as though World War I had only given a temporary (if extremely welcome) reprieve to a sector already subsiding into stagnation. Between 1921 and 1923, the tonnage of ships built annually along the Clyde fell from 710,000 to 170,000. Locomotive construction fell by two thirds by 1930. From fishing to textiles and from coal and jute to agriculture, production was falling pretty much across the board.

Unemployment soared. Over the course of the 1920s, 90 per cent of shipbuilding jobs were lost along the Clyde; unemployment in Motherwell rose from 2,000 to 12,000. Over half a million Scots – a fifth of the total working population – emigrated by 1930, bound for Canada, New Zealand, Australia and South Africa – or just for England. If unemployment was the stick, the Empire Settlement Act of 1922 was the accompanying carrot, offering assistance with passages, plots of land and start-up loans. All this before the 'Great Depression' of the 1930s had officially even started. (Indeed, in the worsening global situation, Scotland started to look less comparatively unattractive, and a slow but steady trickle of emigrants started heading home.)

Popular anger at these conditions was starting to outstrip the audacity of the politicians and trades union officials who nominally 'led' the working class movement. The Trades Union Congress (TUC) and Labour Party were themselves alarmed at what seemed a resurgence in 'revolutionary' feeling. They were more or less dragged along in the workers' wake when, on 3 May 1926, a General Strike – which was supposed to be confined to selected sectors in transport, steelmaking and printing – prompted a walkout of over 1,750,000 workers from a range of industries across the whole UK. It felt like something more than a strike.

Derailment and Crash

Indeed, the derailment of a London-bound *Flying Scotsman* by striking miners at Cramlington, Northumberland, sounds like something out of the Mexican Revolution (Margaret Hutcherson has provided the classic account in *Let No Wheels Turn*, TUPS, 2004). The men's target was apparently a coal train, and it was a miracle that nobody was killed. Hysterical passengers spurned the help of the miners' wives trying to rescue them, Hutcherson reports: such was their shock – and such were the vitriolic feelings of the time.

The Wall Street Crash in 1929 was a shock for the whole world and the Great Depression hardly helped, in either George Bennie's Railplane's case or Scotland's. But Bennie's increasingly frantic rounds of the London financial houses only brought home to him realities that had already been made painfully clear to other Scots.

It wasn't just the Great Depression that did for the Railplane in the end, of course – Bennie's best friends would have admitted his lack of clear-sightedness about costs. But he still seems somehow emblematic of a 20th-century Scotland in which inventive ingenuity, entrepreneurial dash and daring get-up-and-go were no longer going to cut it as apparently once they had.

Mutiny!

In the absence of a Scottish Eisenstein, the Invergordon Mutiny has been largely forgotten, though it sent a shockwave through the Britain of its time. In 1931, this was a nation for which naval power was still enormously important in real terms – and in imaginative ones perhaps more vital still. The Royal Navy wasn't just a military force but a national talisman of sorts. Britannia had ruled the waves since the 18th century and its sailors' 'hearts of oak' were essential to its image. That, like any other workers in any other sector, they should simply down tools and go on strike struck a major blow to Britons' sense of who they were.

Yet that was exactly what a thousand or so sailors did on 15–16 September on the vessels of the Atlantic Fleet moored at Invergordon, in the Cromarty Firth. In the interests of national budget-balancing, the National Government of

Ramsay MacDonald had just announced that wages were being cut by 10 per cent at least, and by as much as 25 per cent for some. The measure might have been more cheerfully accepted had the Navy hierarchy taken more care with their communications, explaining what was happening, and why it was felt to be necessary: instead, the ratings read about it in the press.

Ignoring the (increasingly heated) orders of their officers, men milled about on deck, chanting and singing; Royal Marines, sent in to restore order, joined the protest. However, the demonstrations were all good-humoured and a compromise was quickly reached over wages. In the end, some 200 'troublemakers' were discharged and a few 'ringleaders' gaoled, so it was hardly an epic confrontation. But the 'Mutiny' had sent a shiver through the London Stock Market and prompted a run on the English banks, driving Britain to leave the Gold Standard just a few days later.

ST KILDA

This little island group is farther from Lewis than Lewis is from the Scottish Mainland. It is something of a world apart, with its own distinct subspecies: the St Kilda woodmouse and St Kilda wren. Ancient sheep breeds like the Boreray and Soay can still be seen on the island today, though they are now feral after the people evacuated together in 1930. Should St Kilda's stone-age sheep be seen as bellwethers, pointing the way to the future for human communities out in the Atlantic? Certainly, they make a telling symbol for the traditional Highlands-and-Islands way of life, which was to find the 20th century a considerable challenge.

By the late 1920s, emigration along with World War I, crop failure and flu, meant that St Kilda's dwindling (and disproportionately ageing and infirm) population had no real option but to give up the struggle to keep going. With only 36 St Kildans left in place, it wasn't difficult to transport them all

together for resettlement on mainland Scotland's Morvern peninsula.

Conventionally mourned – and understandably enough, perhaps, for those of us who never actually had to live there – St Kilda was cruelly demystified by the late Donald John Gillies. His autobiographical exposé, The Truth About St Kilda, *was written in the 1980s but edited by John Randall and republished (Birlinn, 2014). Gillies recalled a relentlessly bone-wearying working routine revolving around crofting, fishing and fowling – broken only by the interminable idleness of the Sabbath. Hunger was an ever-present threat, especially as a declining population made agriculture unviable; storms kept food-deliveries and help for the sick at bay. 'I don't wish to remember anything about the life I lived on the island of St Kilda,' he concludes: an odd thing for a memoirist to say, but you see his point.*

And yet, the archipelago's mystique endures: it's a rather melancholy place, with its abandoned cottages and the ruins of earlier medieval and prehistoric constructions. The island is now owned by the Scottish National Trust, which organises regular work-party visits there – or you can take a bouncy-but-exhilarating boat trip there from Leverburgh, Harris, in the summer months.

From Renaissance to Razors

Unemployment, poverty and hardship obviously brought suffering on a fearful scale for those involved, but they also afforded entertainment of a lurid kind. In 1935 Depression-hit Glasgow was recharacterised as *No Mean City* in the best-selling novel by H. Kingsley Long and Alexander McArthur. Novel? Well, up to a point, but the story of Johnnie Stark, young 'Razor King' of the Gorbals, came complete with a breathlessly excited, authenticating 'Appendix', including everything from overcrowding statistics and infant mortality rates to press reports of gang-fights and dance-hall violence.

The narrative itself describes 'sick children who wail' and 'half-drunken men who snore and mutter', and it condemns the slum-dweller to an existence at the mercy of battles, sex and drink. For better or worse, the world of *No Mean City* defined Glasgow and its image for generations. The Gorbals district in particular came to represent a sort of gold standard in urban deprivation, with the razor-wielding thug being the iconic Everyglaswegian. (As, conversely, the fur-coated figure of the Morningside Lady, refined and prudish, embodied Edinburgh until Irvine Welsh came along. A Kelvinside equivalent existed, of course, but didn't seem to define the city in quite the same way.) This image of a basically barbaric Glasgow, an urban jungle in whose remotest reaches strange tribes warred, was carried through into the post-war period. Eddie Linden's long poem 'City of Razors' was written in the early Seventies, though it recalled his childhood in the late Forties and early Fifties, when Glasgow's streets were 'littered with broken milk bottles'.

Johnnie Stark had a rural counterpart in Andy Walker, the protagonist of John McNeillie's *The Wigtown Ploughman: Part of His Life* (1939). To read this (woefully neglected) novel now is to feel a real sense of cognitive dissonance. On the one hand, its loving, lyrical descriptions of the Machars countryside make it a marvellous contribution to British literature's longstanding 'nature tradition'; on the other, it's genuinely shocking in its representation of poverty and violence.

Scots were shown a much more reassuring picture of themselves and of Scottish life in the *Sunday Post* newspaper. This concoction of cosy folksiness and heartwarming human interest had been founded in 1914, though the comic strips which came to epitomise its view of Scotland – *Oor Wullie* and *The Broons* – weren't actually launched till 1936.

The Idea of Independence

In 1934, the Scottish National Party (SNP) came into being as a result of the merger of the National Party of Scotland (itself an alliance of more or less left-wing groups) and the (broadly posher, more conservative) Scottish Party, formed a couple of years earlier. So broad a spectrum of backgrounds, attitudes and opinions probably couldn't have been successfully held together without the charisma of the party's first president, Robert Cunninghame Graham (1852–1936). An extremely colourful figure, he was famous as a travel writer and adventurer before he embarked on his political career. He was an ideological traveller too, his trajectory having taken him first through liberalism to a (strongly paternalistic) socialism. He had been one of the founders of the Independent Labour Party in 1893.

For its first few decades, the SNP got nowhere: neither the Great Depression nor World War II were ever really likely to foster separatist fervour. Most Scots regarded it with bemusement at best. Its marginal status seemed destined to make it a perpetual political underdog, which strengthened the hand of the romantically nationalist – and (moderately) right wing – ex-Scottish Party element. 'Natural' supporters of the NPS among the urban working class saw no point in voting for the 'Tartan Tories'.

THE GAUCHO LAIRD

Robert Cunninghame Graham had no need of 'conventional achievements', said G.K. Chesterton: he was too taken up with 'the adventure of being Cunninghame Graham'. Though made in admiration, the suggestion is unjust: it isn't everyone who helps found not only the Labour Party but also the Scottish Nationalists. He wrote highly-regarded books, was a horseman of astounding skill and an explorer of real significance. It's true, though: simply being Cunninghame Graham really does seem to

Railplanes, Razors and Reality

*have been quite an adventure in itself. From the Pampas to Pall
Mall; from the Matchgirls' Strike to the Moroccan mountains,
his life bestrode continents, cut across class divisions and took in
some of the crucial conflicts of its age.*

*Having passed much of his boyhood on the ancestral estate
of Gartmore, Perthshire, Cunninghame Graham clearly felt an
exhilarating sense of liberation as a teenager in his transportation
to the estancia his family owned in Argentina. Hence his styling
as the 'Gaucho Laird' (or 'Cowboy Lord'), which was always
more than a raffish pose. Caught up by accident in Argentina's
civil turmoils, he rode with a band of desperadoes raiding
ranches and villages. Then, when peace came, he became a
working gaucho, driving cattle for hire across the Pampas. The
horsemanship he'd acquired as a gentlemanly accomplishment
was perfected by months in the saddle, equipping him for the
more formal expeditions he was to undertake thereafter. The first
major one, up the Paraná into deepest Paraguay, brought him
into contact with a 'Vanished Arcadia': his account became the
basis for Roland Joffé's film, The Mission (1986).*

*The late 1870s saw him in Paris, on an adventure of a
different sort: he married the young actress Gabrielle de la
Balmondière after a whirlwind courtship. There was more to this
exotic Chilean-descended Spanish-French beauty than met the
eye (not least the fact that she actually hailed from Yorkshire).
The couple made pioneering treks together in the North
American West.*

*Back in Britain in the 1880s, though, his interests turned
towards politics: he stood as Liberal candidate for Northwest
Lanarkshire at the 1886 General Election and entered
Parliament. He considered himself a socialist and was a
friend of Keir Hardie – ideologically, though, he seems to have
travelled light. His concern for the common man appears a tad
paternalistic in hindsight, and it's hard to avoid a suspicion that
his main motivations may have been a taste for drama and a
romantic attachment to the idea of revolution.*

Political history may see these things as flaws, but they at least guaranteed Cunninghame Graham a colourful career. By 1887 he had been suspended from the Commons for making a 'disrespectful' remark about the House of Lords. Prosecuted for his role in the protests that brought London to a standstill in November 1887, he spent six weeks in prison. Parliament finally tired of his insurrectionary spirit and he was pushed out in 1892; literary ventures took up more of his time from that point on. So too did his growing friendships with writers like Hardy, Galsworthy, Shaw, Madox Ford and Bennett – and most of all with Joseph Conrad, who took him as his model for Nostromo. 'When I think of Cunninghame Graham,' the great seafaring novelist said, 'I feel as though I have lived all my life in a dark hole without seeing or knowing anything.'

Morningside's Long Hot Summer

Glasgow is notorious for its history of sectarian violence, but anti-Catholic feeling existed far and wide. Even, it seems, in the sleepiest, most comfortable corners of Edinburgh's Morningside district – a byword for quiet respectability then, still more than now. In 1935, the area was home to John Cormack, founder and leader of the Protestant Action Society. Its members campaigned against what they claimed was the preferential hiring of Roman Catholic workers by the city's council, and at the awarding of civic honours to Catholic officials.

The skilled-manual, white-collar workers and small tradesmen who made up the Society for the most part were recognisably the demographic who elsewhere in Europe had been gravitating towards fascism. Sir Oswald Mosley packed out Edinburgh's Usher Hall for one meeting in 1934. Such warm support notwithstanding, Mosley's British Union of Fascists (BUF) felt off-limits to a great many Scots Protestants. Despite the anti-immigrant feeling of so many of his grass-roots members in England, Mosley identified romantically with Irish nationalism and had issued a stream of sympathetic statements during the 'Troubles' of the early Twenties. Whilst some Scots were prepared to embrace the label (like the followers of William Weir Gilbert's Scottish Democratic Fascist Party, for the most part in the west of Scotland), the sectarian question was a sticking point – even if it arguably masked a more immediately racist, anti-Irish feeling. (Hence in part, perhaps – along with an obviously understandable loyalty to the mother country – why Scots-Italian railway-punctuality enthusiasts in Leith launched their own local brand of *fascismo*, black shirts and all.)

Cormack lived in Springvalley Gardens, just a stone's throw away across the Morningside Road from St Andrew's Priory (now the site of St Peter's RC Primary School). In June 1935, this Catholic foundation held a 'Eucharistic Congress' and was besieged by over 20,000 Cormack supporters from Protestant Action – shouting, jostling, spitting and (depending whose testimony you believe) stone-throwing and worse. There were unholy scenes at 'Holy Corner' (the junction of Morningside and Colinton Roads, so called because there are four churches at this intersection – none of them, ironically, Roman Catholic) and in the city centre, at Waverley Market and elsewhere.

An unseemly episode, then, with Cormack's cronies very much the aggressors – though the question of quite *how* aggressive they'd really been raised a riot of words in the Scottish media in the weeks that followed. To hear Cormack & Co tell it, they'd pretty much simply stood there in dignified protest; for the Catholic hierarchy, it'd been little short of an anti-papist pogrom.

CAUTION MONEY PAID

Edinburgh Councillor Released from Saughton Prison

TWENTY-FOUR hours after he had been taken to Saughton Prison, Edinburgh, Councillor John Cormack, the Protestant Action society leader, was released on Saturday night.

The £20 necessary to secure his liberation had been deposited by a friend whose identity has not been disclosed.

Councillor Cormack was arrested in consequence of alleged failure to pay £20 caution money which was ordered by the Sheriff as a deposit for his good behaviour following a conviction over a month ago in connection with a sectarian disturbance in the City.

JEWISH SCOTLAND

Not much is known about the Scottish Jewish community (if there even was such a thing) prior to 1691, when an Edinburgh Council Minute shows an application by one David Brown for a licence to live and trade in the city. By 1816, there were known to be 20 Jewish families in the capital. That same year this little community opened its own cemetery in Newington's Sciennes House Place. It's still there, though only tiny (with just 29 gravestones in total), having been preserved since it was closed in the 1870s. The synagogue round the corner in Salisbury Road was opened in 1932.

If the Morningside incident of 1935 is indicative of the tensions that have existed between Scotland's different religious communities, then it's no surprise to learn that Jews were also victims of prejudice. Take the 19th–century historian William Skene, for example, writing in his East Neuk Chronicles *(published posthumously in 1905), which includes this all-too-recognisable portrait of the German-born Lazarus Myres, a supposedly familiar figure in the Aberdeen of Skene's 1880s youth:*

> I can fancy I see him yet – wizened, round face and stubble beard, keen eyes looking through spectacles, and everlasting blue cloak, with brass chain at the neck, ... by all accounts ever I heard he found money-lending, etc., profitable. And like his great prototype 'Shylock,' he always secured his pound of flesh when it was obtainable by possible means.

Nathan Abrams, in Caledonian Jews *(McFarland, 2009) points out that there's no record of any such character having existed in the Aberdeen census of the time. He does find records of a (Russian) Isaac Myres and a (Polish) Lazarus Lubon – but, then, Myres/Lubon, Lazarus/Isaac, Germany/Russia/Poland: when you're indulging in a bit of casual anti-Semitism, what's the difference?*

It certainly seems that Scots were just as quick as other nations to see Jewish immigrants as essentially the same as each other – and, naturally, the same as their 'great prototype', Shakespeare's grasping and sadistic Shylock. By the 1890s, though, despite the widely-held assumption that they'd enriched themselves at the expense of their Christian neighbours, Aberdeen's Jews seem still to have been among the poorest people in the city. And among the most diffident: their synagogue being basically a pair of rented rooms on the first floor of a house at 34 Marischal Street, just a stone's throw from Trinity Quay. (It smelled strongly, a later visitor complained, of fish.) Even so, in 1900, they clubbed together to buy six shares in Theodor Herzl's Jewish Colonial Trust, investing in the future formation of a Jewish State.

Though generally seen as the capital of Jewish Scotland, Glasgow's community was established comparatively late. Some German and Dutch Jewish merchants were to be found there from the start of the 19th century. Most of Glasgow's Jews, however, were refugees from the Russian pogroms who, passing through on their way to the United States, ran out of money or momentum before they could make the Atlantic crossing. Accidental arrivals, then, but they mounted up: Glasgow's Jewish community is believed to have been about 10,000-strong by 1914. Again, despite the anti-Semitic rhetoric, very few were even remotely rich: most lived in the Gorbals, already notorious for its slums. But if the construction of a brand new synagogue in 1879, represented a sort of coming-of-age for the community, its address, on Hill Street, Garnethill, did suggest a degree of upward mobility for at least some of the city's Jews.

World War II was of course to bring renewed and redoubled persecution in central Europe. A lucky few children were brought to safety on the Kindertransport. *For example, in 1939, 20 children from Austria, Germany and Czechoslovakia arrived in Selkirk, in the Borders. They were put up in the Priory Children's Home, in Ettrick Road, which later became a hotel before being partially demolished and remodelled to make 'The Priory', a residential development, in the 1990s.*

Scotland and Spain

The enmities that ran deep in Scottish society during the early 20th century were to inform the Scottish people's response to the next big crisis on the wider European stage. The rise of the Far Right was signalled as early as 1922, when Mussolini and his Blackshirts marched on Rome. *Il Duce* became Italy's dictator three years later. Hitler's ascent was slower: he became Germany's *Führer* in 1934. Mounting tension tipped over into full-blown geopolitical emergency two years later with General Francisco Franco's military uprising against the Republican government in Spain. Notoriously, the nasty little civil war that followed ended up dragging much of Europe into diplomatic crisis – or, in the case of Fascist Italy and Communist Russia – direct military involvement.

Individuals became involved as well: most famously the writers, artists and intellectuals who flocked to enlist in the International Brigades on the Republican side. Alongside the Audens, Orwells and Hemingways, though, were thousands of ordinary trades unionists, teachers and other young idealists alarmed at the prospect of fascism finding a foothold in Spain from which to spread across Western Europe. If most men went as soldiers, others offered service as engineers or medics; women went too, in nursing, interpreting and other roles. Others, though still in Scotland, campaigned, held fundraising fêtes and bring-and-buys, collected clothes and welcomed refugees. This fascinating chapter in Scotland's modern history is described a great deal more fully in *Homage to Caledonia: Scotland and the Spanish Civil War*, by Daniel Gray (Luath Press, 2008). Gray gives us a panoramic sense of a Scottish anti-Franco front extending all the way from Teruel and Jarama to Cowdenbeath and Hawick.

In Scotland, as in England, reactions to the Spanish conflict were to some degree shaped by feeling on the slower-burning question of appeasement towards Hitler and his as yet still quiet but prospectively much more frightening Nazi

state. Advocates of a soft, concilia-
tory line towards Germany weren't all
crypto-fascists, by any means. Ramsay
MacDonald, for one, could hardly have
been accused of being a Nazi sym-
pathiser. Like many thoughtful individuals of his generation, across the
parties, he dreaded a repetition of the
carnage of World War I above all else,
and saw almost any compromise that
might help secure that as worthwhile.

'Country House Nazism' did exist, however, even if its
significance owed more to the prominence of its supporters
than to their number. One such in Scotland, the Conservative
MP for Peebles, Captain Archibald Maule Ramsay, a viru-
lent anti-Semite and member of the 'Council of the Nordic
League', was to be interned after hostilities started in World
War II. There was also some support in Scotland for Franco's
Fascist cause – it was certainly unusual, but not unheard
of. Francoism was openly and triumphantly pro-Catholic;
his forces, the *Generalissimo* claimed, were embarked on a
'Crusade'. Rome reciprocated his feelings in full, seeing him
as 'saviour' to a Spain in the grip of godless communism,
socialism, anarchism, feminism, loose-living liberalism ...
you name it. This was the sort of language that upper class
Catholics in Scotland could understand – men like (the
writer's great-great-grandson) Sir Walter Maxwell-Scott, at
Abbotsford, and Colonel Rupert Dawson, who had a house
at Braco, Perth and Kinross.

The loyalties of working class Catholics – the vast majority, of course – were more divided. Their socio-economic and
spiritual situations were at odds. Whilst, on the one hand,
they had much in common with the workers fighting for the
Republic in Spain, on the other, the Catholic establishment
was firmly against the Republicans.

BRODIE'S NOTES

Born at 160 Bruntsfield Place and educated at the nearby James Gillespie's School, the novelist Muriel Spark (née Camberg; 1918–2006) was very much a product of 1930s Edinburgh. Her memoir, Curriculum Vitae *(1992), paints a brief but vivid portrait of the Edinburgh of that time. As, more notoriously, does her novel,* The Prime of Miss Jean Brodie *(1961). Miss Jean Brodie's model, Spark's sometime teacher Christina Kay (1878–1951), lived in Grindlay Street (by the Lyceum Theatre). Herself a Gillespie's alumna, she was also, more controversially, an intense admirer of Mussolini and Hitler.*

Developments on the Continent provide a colourful if distant backdrop to Spark's story – including one unfortunate student's enlistment (and death) in the Spanish Civil War. Yet the tension at the novel's heart could hardly be more Scottish. Seemingly aspiring to be 'the God of Calvin', Miss Jean Brodie gathers about her an arbitrarily chosen 'elect' – the 'Brodie Set'; the crème de la crème *as she famously calls them – and tries to dictate their emotions, manage their destinies.*

The complete archive of Muriel Spark's papers are now held at the National Library of Scotland, on George IV Bridge. A PhD student, working on Spark before he turned to crime writing with his Inspector Rebus novels, Ian Rankin (1960–) led the campaign to have them made available to public view.

War Footing

As the 1930s wore on, the threat of war with Germany loomed ever larger, but for the majority of Scots life carried on much as before. It was difficult, in other words – these were the years of the Great Depression – and global con-flict wasn't at the forefront of people's minds. Despite dire warnings from Winston Churchill, the sometime (1908–22) MP for Dundee, Neville Chamberlain's policy of appease-ment still held sway. But if Britain was still speaking softly, in Teddy Roosevelt's terms, there were at least signs of its getting some kind of big stick ready: rearmament was already under way – welcome news for the shipbuilders of the Clyde.

The government was also, with increasing urgency, attempting to waken the wider population to the danger of a war that was beginning to seem inevitable, however long it might be diplomatically postponed. The authorities started taking steps to set up a system of civil defence, and the first Air Raid Wardens were enrolled as early as 1937.

The introduction of 'Blackout' regulations from the first day of the War appears to have been a conscious effort to instil in the population a sense that these were, indeed, extraordinary times. It's not generally believed that the darkening of Scotland's cities can really have been any great hindrance to Hitler's bombers, but it did drive home the need for people to rally round. The organisation of air-raid patrols; the installation of sirens; the building of shelters; the practising of drills were of course ultimately to have an important role in saving lives, but their immediate effect was to mobilise and motivate ordinary people, for whom the War still seemed a distant thing.

Most of the associated structures were swept away with considerable relief when the hostilities were finally done, but there are still air-raid shelters like the one tucked away behind Walker Road, in Aberdeen. The ruined 'starfish' bunker at Lang Craig, Dumbarton, was built to house the command centre for a 'decoy city' whose lights, it was hoped, would draw attacking bombers away from the genuine urban centres. And in Ardrossan Road, Saltcoats, Ayrshire, little plates in the pavement were removed to allow lengths of girder to be fitted as upright obstacles for tanks.

Invasion seemed more likely from the east, of course. Traces of the once-elaborate fortification systems all the way down this coast are still to be seen in – for instance – the cuboidal concrete tank-traps on the beach outside Longniddry, East Lothian, or at Balmedie, Aberdeen.

War Breaks Out – Or Does It?

So much for the preparations. Actual hostilities between Britain and Germany broke out on 1 September 1939 – though even then there were to be several months of 'Phony War'. For some Scots, however, it started to seem real enough just a few weeks in, on 14 October, when HMS *Royal Oak* was sunk in Scapa Flow, Orkney. Of the 833 sailors who were lost when the *Revenge*-class battleship was sent to the bottom by a torpedo from a lurking U-boat, 120 were under-18. A further 189 men went down with the E-class destroyer HMS *Exmouth* the following January, torpedoed while escorting a cargo ship some miles off Wick.

A few weeks later, on 16 March, James Isbister of Brig o' Waithe, just east of Stromness, became Britain's first civilian casualty of World War II when he was caught by bombs being offloaded by German Junkers 88 dive-bombers on their way back from a raid on Scapa Flow.

The main theatres of war being in Europe, North Africa, the Pacific and elsewhere, Scotland's role was largely a backstage one, with its industry being particularly vital. Of course, its volunteers were heroic – though, for the most part, they played their part far from home. The country did find itself on the front line on occasion, though. The 'Battle of Britain' was the best part of a year away when, on 16 October 1939 (so just two days after the *Royal Oak* sinking), the first shots were fired in Britain's air war with Germany. Scotland was caught napping, its air warning system utterly inert, its air defences unready (or, rather, they were actually engaged in a drill with dummy ammunition, and had to switch to the real thing) when bombers were suddenly sighted heading for the naval shipyard at Rosyth. They had hastily to be intercepted by fighters from Turnhouse (now Edinburgh Airport) and Drem, East Lothian. Three Heinkel He111s were shot down in the ensuing action.

The losses from the *Royal Oak* and *Exmouth* apart, though, the events of the conflict did still seem quite remote at this early stage: the scramble in the Firth of Forth had been something of a farce. The War still had a phony feel, in other words, and people didn't yet quite know what they should make of it or how they should react. Even as things hotted up, the sense we now have of the War as some sort of moral and pivotal moment in the history of the 20th century had yet to take form. Having been in a degree of denial about the evil and capabilities of the Nazis for so long, people weren't yet in a position to see its full extent (an extent which it had of course not yet nearly reached – the Final Solution was only formally decided upon in 1942). And whilst Scots men and women might be at war, Scotland itself didn't really seem to be.

The Blitz Begins

This state of affairs went on for many months, right through the 'Battle of Britain' (July–October, 1940). Minds were soon to be concentrated, though, as the conflict deepened and the air raids on Scotland began in earnest. About 400 German bombers took part in the Blitz on Clydebank (13–14 March 1941). Its shipyards made it an obvious target (as did the Rolls Royce factory on the southern bank), but their work-forces lived nearby: 4,000 homes were destroyed and over the two nights more than 500 civilians were killed. (Leading a desperate defence were the crew of the Polish destroyer ORP *Piorun*, which happened to be in John Brown's shipyard for repairs. Its guns were in perfect working order, and it kept up a furious barrage of ack-ack fire. This may indeed have helped protect the yard, which wasn't too badly bombed.)

Two months later, on the nights of 6–7 May, it was Greenock's turn; only 50 bombers made the trip this time, but they left over 2,000 dead behind, and hundreds of homes destroyed – ironically, again, the city's shipyards emerged unscathed.

Materiel Well-Being

Scottish industry was rising to the challenge. Though HM's vast Factory at Gretna had been demoted to depot status, arms were being manufactured elsewhere in Scotland. The old Argyll Motor Works at Alexandria, Dumbartonshire – pressed into service making shells and torpedoes during World War I but since abandoned – was brought back into use for the exclusive production of torpedoes. At a new Royal Ordnance Factory at Bishopton, Renfrewshire, extending over more than 800 ha (2,000 acres), 20,000 men and women made the explosive propellant that was required for shells and bullets. This facility survived long enough to be privatised in 1984, albeit with a much-reduced workforce. (It's still there, indeed, though it's owned by BAE Systems and is little more than a laboratory these days.)

From 1940, the iconic Rolls Royce Merlin engine for the even-more-iconic Spitfire fighter was made at a specially built factory at Hillington, on the western outskirts of Glasgow. Or, rather, discount knock-offs were made, for this was one of several 'shadow factories' in which copying was officially sanctioned for the sake of the war effort. Some 10,000 women were employed at this enormously important plant, which, by 1943, was turning out 400 engines a week. So well did they do in mocking up Rolls Royce engines that the company took the place over itself after the War. (Indeed, it didn't finally close till 2005.) Further south, on the Ayrshire coast, Prestwick became important as a centre for Spitfire repair – as well as a depot for aircraft being brought in from the United States. For military supplies being brought by sea, a new 'secret port' was opened beside the Gare Loch, Argyll and Bute – Faslane is now famous (or notorious) as the base for Britain's Trident nuclear submarines.

All this industrial production was powered by electricity supplied by a new 'National Grid', whose maiden pylon had gone up at Bonnybridge, not far from Falkirk, in 1928. Tory Prime Minister Stanley Baldwin was later to be roundly (and not altogether unjustly) chastised for his support of appeasement, but if he hadn't driven through this massively ambitious and expensive government programme (26,000 pylons were constructed over five years), the nation would have been woefully unprepared for waging war.

New Model Armies

Industrial technology was changing the nature of battle. In February 1940, in Palestine, where they were attempting to enforce the League of Nations Mandate, the Royal Scots Greys made their last ever cavalry-charge – against a crowd of Arab rioters. By the end of the following year, they would be galloping around in tanks. That summer, members of the 1st Royal Scots and the 51st Highland Division were among those left behind by the La Bassée Canal after the British Expeditionary Force had been cut off by Rommel's panzers in their lightning dash across northern France. Needed to hold off the advancing Germans, they weren't able to avail themselves of the celebrated Dunkirk evacuation.

Other innovations in fighting were meanwhile being introduced at Scalloway, Shetland, where the first SIS (Secret Intelligence Service)/SOE (Special Operations Executive) operations were in preparation – the hope was to help Norwegian Resistance fighters.

Commando training was meanwhile taking place at Spean Bridge and Inveraray. Standing over 5m (17ft) in height, the trio of figures atop the Commando Memorial at Spean Bridge certainly don't seem to be making any effort at stealth, towering magnificently above the Lochaber landscape. One of the pioneers of what were eventually to become known as 'special operations' (and widely held to have been a possible model for Ian Fleming's James Bond), Sir Fitzroy MacLean (1911–96) was a Scot. Though born in colonial Cairo, his family's ancestral seat was at Duart Castle (see page 48). After loyal – if highly irregular – service around the world from Soviet Central Asia to the Sahara, he spent the last years of his life at Strachur House, Argyll.

The art of war was changing by the week, it must have seemed. And Scotland was making an important contribution. Loch Linnhe was home to HMS *Western Isles* and, in turn, to the 'Terror of Tobermory', Commodore (later Vice-Admiral) Gilbert Stephenson (1878–1972), who was developing his own new and utterly unconventional ways of waging anti-submarine warfare.

And, as Allied fortunes changed for the better and Churchill's end-of-the-beginning at last gave way to the beginning-of-the-end, rehearsals for the D-Day landings began to take place at selected locations round the Scottish coast. Understandably, attention has tended to focus on the ill-fated Operation Tiger (28 April 1944) off Devon's Slapton Sands, in which one such rehearsal cost 800 American lives. Earlier, though, practice landings on the shores of the Tarbat Peninsula of Easter Ross had fared rather better. Rehearsals went on for several months – under conditions of such strict secrecy that the populations of several local villages had to be moved to nearby towns for the duration. Similar exercises took place around the shores of Western Islands like Arran, Eigg and Rùm and at mainland beaches on Loch Fyne and the Moray Firth.

The military history of World War II has of course been covered in extravagant detail. As with World War I it seems invidious to pick out this or that individual exploit or regimental achievement in engagements in which generally an array of different Scottish – as well as English, Welsh and other Commonwealth – units fought. Not to mention those of the other Allies. Suffice it to say that Scottish servicemen and -women played their full part across the world from the Firth of Clyde to Burma and from Yugoslavia to the Cape.

Out of Sight...

Scotland was to see some strange and striking scenes when the War came to an end as well. In *The Grey Wolves of Eriboll* (Whittles, 2010), David Hird describes how, amidst the utmost secrecy, 33 U-boats gathered to surrender in the quiet waters of this remote Sutherland loch. More of the German submarines – such a scourge to British shipping in the months before – came ashore at Loch Ryan, outside Stranraer.

That extreme tip of southwest Scotland was, perhaps, the end of the earth as far as Whitehall was concerned: mandarins certainly saw fit to use Beaufort's Dyke, the deepest part of the North Channel between Britain and Northern Ireland, as a weapons dump. Huge quantities of armaments were committed to the sea there in the months and years after World War II – and, it seems, since (including low-level radioactive waste in concrete). Some incendiaries, washed up on the Galloway coast in the 1990s, served as nasty little reminders of this episode.

OUT OF THE BLUE

The abrupt appearance of Rudolf Hess (1894–1987) in Scotland, on 10 May 1941, is among the odder events of World War II. Hitler's Deputy Führer *hoped to meet his fellow-aviator Douglas Douglas-Hamilton, the 14th Duke of Hamilton (1903–73). The entire enterprise was quirkily unaccountable, but Hess appears to have believed that, if they could only meet and discuss this whole European-conflagration thing over a drink like gentlemen, it might all be sorted out and common sense again prevail. In the event, all it achieved was capture and lifelong captivity for Hess himself – and an extremely uncomfortable few weeks for the 14th Duke.*

Douglas-Hamilton had attended the Berlin Olympics in 1936 and (with a great many other British visitors) met Nazi officials. He could never have been accused of being left wing in his views. How much he knew of Hess' intentions isn't clear, however: he denied any knowledge, and whilst that seems to strain credulity, there's no real evidence of his having been actively involved.

Expected or not, Hess crash-landed his Messerschmidt near Waterfoot, Eaglesham, south of Glasgow. Whilst the plane came down at Bonnyton Farm, Hess, who'd baled out, landed on nearby Floors Farm and was arrested by David MacLean,

a worker there. Douglas-Hamilton's role was investigated but – whether it's a tribute to his truthfulness, to the British establishment's magnanimity or, on the other hand, cover-up capacity – Douglas-Hamilton was quickly and completely cleared of blame.

Wattage from Water

Both during World War II and in its aftermath, hydroelectric power increasingly came to be looked upon as vital in helping the nation meet its energy needs. Scotland, of course, has never been exactly in short supply of water, and it has therefore naturally been hugely important in the development of hydroelectricity in the UK. But the industry's beginnings go way back before World War II. Though an Englishman, Sir William Armstrong (1810–1900), had been quickest off the mark with a scheme at his home at Cragside in Northumberland as early as 1878, Scotland hadn't trailed too far behind. In the Great Glen, at Fort Augustus Abbey, in 1891, the monks had developed their own generating system to power not just their own foundation but the nearby village.

Hydroelectricity has long been associated with aluminium smelting, and it was first used for this purpose in 1895, when a project was launched at the Falls of Foyers above Loch Ness. The British Aluminium Company's power station and smelter at Kinlochleven followed in 1909 – its sudden opening in what had been crofting country a jarring cultural shock. Next, in 1929, came the Galloway Hydro Electric Scheme: a series of dams and power stations working in conjunction.

To this day, the dam at Clatteringshaws Loch's worth seeing; there's a visitor centre at Tongland Turbine Station. Like the other power stations built under the scheme, Tongland is of interest for its modernist design by Broughty Ferry-born engineer-architect (and Telford biographer) Sir Alexander Gibb (1872–1958). Hydroelectic power was seemingly the future, and History itself had symbolically to make way, the ruins of the 13th-century castle of the Earls of Carrick being moved to higher ground to allow the enlargement of Loch Doon.

Churchill's Wartime administration embraced hydroelectrity, and the North of Scotland Hydro-Electric Board was founded in 1943. The electrification of the glens became an

Building Sloy Dam, on Loch Lomond (begun in 1945).

important aspect of the socialist vision of sometime Scottish Secretary Tom Johnston (1881–1965), who in 1945 became Chairman of the Hydro-Board. And, whilst it may have pre-dated them all, it seemed a natural fit with all the other great programmes of the Attlee government: the nationalisation of the 'commanding heights' of the economy – railways, coal, steel … – and, of course, the launch of the National Health Service (NHS).

Further important projects followed, notably the pumped-storage power station at Cruachan, Argyll and Bute. Given the difficulty of storing generated power during times of low demand, this plant used it to pump water back from below the dam to the reservoir above, so constant power would be available when the need was great. Construction having been commenced in 1959, the plant was operational by 1965.

However promising this early history, hydroelectricity's development in Scotland has seemed to stall as its position in the whole energy-vs-ecology debate has become increasingly ambiguous. On the one hand, it's the ultimate renewable, to all intents and purposes carbon-free. On the other, those people who have been most concerned for the well-being of the natural environment and the local communities have been least tolerant of seeing entire valleys and villages drowned. Whilst no scheme in Britain has ever even come remotely close to causing the sort of damage and disruption created in recent years by those of more gung-ho governments like Turkey's (the Ilisu Dam in Kurdish country) or China's (the Three Gorges Dam on the Yangtze), such examples have helped give the hydroelectric industry a bad name.

OPERATION SEAGULL

Whilst Britain's big cities burned under the onslaught of the Blitz, the Highlands of Scotland seemed a world away from the commotion and shock of war. But these wilds were to have their fleeting front-line moment. Far off in the midst of the mountains, newly-made lochs glistened behind bare concrete dams: among these was Loch Laggan in Lochaber. Water was piped from there to Loch Treig and thence via a specially built tunnel 24km (15 miles) long and 4.5m (15ft) in diameter to drive the turbines of a power station at Fort William. The development and expansion of the scheme had taken place in parallel with that of aluminium smelters at nearby Inverlochy, and Kinlochleven further south around the coast.

Aluminium is prized in aircraft construction because it couples strength with lightness. But its processing, in out-of-the-way places like this, made it a tempting target for sabotage. 'Operation Seagull', an attack masterminded by Kurt Haller of Germany's all-service undercover-operations outfit Abwehr II, was conceived with precisely this in mind.

Sifting through the PoWs being held in Brandenburg's Friesack Camp, Haller had picked out a small group of Irish nationals and recruited them into the service of the Reich. His hope now was that one of them might easily be parachuted in somewhere around Glasgow, among whose Irish community he had agents. They would then head for the Highlands and strike at the Kinlochleven smelter and Fort William power scheme.

Not for the first time, an Abwehr II operation ended not with the bang of high explosives but with a whimper. The Seagull's flight was cut short before it could quite get airborne. The chosen agent, Tipperary-born Andrew Walsh, was just about to leave for Norway, preparatory to his final insertion into Scotland, when he was rushed back to Berlin and arrested by the Gestapo. He had apparently told a comrade that he had no interest in serving the Germans and planned to give himself up to the authorities on arrival in Great Britain.

TEN

DREAMS
AND SCHEMES

FOR MANY THOUSANDS AROUND THE WORLD, the idea of Edinburgh is inseparable from that of its Festival – and it's certainly been a fixture of the post-war scene. It was the idea of Rudolf Bing, who ran the Glyndebourne Opera Festival, and who in 1946 had the idea of an arts extravaganza that would be both local and international. As difficult as it may be to imagine now, he had the idea pretty much in the abstract: there was absolutely no inevitability about it being an *Edinburgh* festival, as such. And there was an extraordinary bloodlessness about the way in which the British Council's Scotland head, Henry Harvey Wood, would later describe the criteria by which the place was to be chosen:

> *Certain preconditions were obviously required of such a centre. It should be a town of reasonable size, capable of absorbing and entertaining anything between 50,000 and 150,000 visitors over a period of three weeks to a month. It should, like Salzburg, have considerable scenic and picturesque appeal and it should be set in a country likely to be attractive to tourists and foreign visitors. It should have sufficient number of theatres, concert halls and open spaces for the adequate staging of a programme of an ambitious and varied character.*

The first Edinburgh International Festival took place in August and September 1947. And the rest is history: it's happened every August since. The Royal Edinburgh Military Tattoo, with its pipers, its drummers, its dances and drill displays – and of course its fireworks – didn't follow until 1950. A celebration of military tradition, it was quickly established as a tradition in its own right. The Fringe is as old as the Festival itself. It started spontaneously when, in 1947, several performing groups turned up in Edinburgh uninvited, planning to piggyback on the publicity for the official event. Gradually, over the years, it's grown.

And yet, in some strange and confusing way, it all has nothing much to do with Edinburgh – and still less Scotland. Like some travelling circus (albeit one that doesn't actually go anywhere else), it blows into town each summer, stays a few weeks, then blows out again. This sense of the Festival as something that's at once utterly of Edinburgh and external – even alien – is an important ingredient in its worldwide appeal, perhaps. The 'international' dimension, as vital as it is, is just one aspect of its emphasis on variety: whether it's an Australian stand-up, an American symphony orchestra, a troupe of tap-dancing Oxford undergraduates or a Kiev company offering Ukrainian-language Shakespeare, the visitor can find a world of entertainment on offer there.

And it mainly is the visitor. For, whilst Edinbourgeois hostility to the Festival and Fringe is easily exaggerated, there's no doubt that a certain amount of grumbling goes on. Maybe that resistance is the grit the artistic oyster needs. Certainly, there can be intriguing counterpoints between performances and setting: the spacious elegance of the New Town, the anarchic nooks and crannies of the Old, the sobriety of the suburbs, with their Victorian church halls; they all 'frame' concerts, plays, revues and other shows in different ways. Then, for Edinburgh itself, there's that dull sense of returning to reality once the whole thing ends – however unwelcome it may have felt while it was there. It doesn't help that the end of the Festival more or less dead-heats with the end of summer, heralding umpteen months of darkness, damp and cold.

Housing Horror

It must have been a bit like that for Scotland as a whole in 1945. Not that there'd been anything especially festive about the War. But the sense of exhilaration at its ending, as shown by the impromptu parties in Glasgow's George

Square on VE Day (8 May), and the relief at having simply survived and of knowing that loved ones had, soon gave way to a reality of a rather grimmer sort. Not just the continuing fighting in the Pacific (victory over Japan didn't come till 15 August); nor the mourning for those who hadn't come back; nor even the continuation of rationing, which went on till 1954. The War being won, the pressure was on to 'win the peace'.

That looked like being a tall order. In the aftermath of World War I, Prime Minister David Lloyd George (1863–1945) had famously promised 'homes fit for heroes' (more precisely, if less snappily, he'd promised 'habitations fit for the heroes who have won the war'). All too many of Scotland's homes weren't fit for the vermin with which returning soldiers and their families had to share them. These slums would have to be cleared before they could be replaced with something better.

At the start of the century, a quarter of Glaswegian families had been forced to live in 'single ends' – homes with only a single room (that room typically about 4.25m (14ft) x 3.5m (11ft)). Almost half of the city's families did better, with two rooms at their disposal (though they often had to fund that luxury by taking lodgers). Altogether, this still meant more than two-thirds of the population living in cramped and overcrowded conditions. As of 1913, of Glasgow's 44,000-plus one-room homes, 93 per cent had to share a WC.

Edinburgh had only 7,000-odd single-room homes, though 93 per cent of these had to share WC facilities – and, unlike in Glasgow, almost half had even to share a sink. Infant mortality reflected these conditions: almost a third (32 per cent) of Glaswegian children who died before the age of five came from single ends, as compared with two per cent from homes with five rooms. In the Gorbals, approximately one in five children died in infancy.

To look at it from another perspective, that of average density: in 1911, 72 per cent of Dundee's population crowded into their homes at a rate of more than two people per available room, as against 32 per cent of London's people. Thankfully, the availability of at very least basic sanitation and clean water meant that the cholera and typhus epidemics of the 19th century had gone. That still left plenty of other problems: of the city's schoolchildren, 44 per cent had hearing difficulties and 48 per cent had eyesight deficiencies; the list of other problems – low birthweight, rickets, TB ... – went on and on.

Building the Future

It was to be in Dundee, indeed, that Scotland's first local authority scheme was built. Logie went up between 1919 and 1920. Its dwellings constructed firmly on low-rise, low-density principles, it was conceived with a collective, communitarian spirit, which extended to the installation of a district-heating system (though this was to be discontinued in the 1970s). Care was taken to have greenery – gardens, allotments, avenues of trees. These were thought to be healthy, restorative, life affirming – and why not? Torry, Aberdeen, is another Garden Suburb from this time.

But this sort of improvement was only scratching the surface. Council housing was still scarce, and whilst it was new and comfortable, it was comparatively expensive, so overcrowding continued for the vast majority in the private-rental sector. The housing problem of Scotland had been many decades in the making and was going to take great determination to resolve. Certainly, strenuous efforts were made. In the decades after World War II, vast schemes were built around the periphery of Glasgow, from Drumchapel to Coatbridge; and round Edinburgh from Wester Hailes to Pilton and Craigmillar. Dundee had Downfield, Fintry and Kirkton.

It wasn't just the major centres. Schemes were also built in smaller cities: Stirling (which, by the early 20th century, had overtaken Glasgow in its death rate) had the Raploch and the (pre-War) Riverside; Kirkcaldy had Torbain. And, whilst rural housing was to run short in the longer term, at this time there were efforts to provide it: drive through even the smallest Scottish settlement and you'll probably see a little cluster of council homes. Soon Scotland had the highest proportion of public housing in Western Europe. By 1979, on the eve of the Thatcher government's introduction of the 'right to buy' for council tenants, 54 per cent of Scottish housing was local authority-owned. Only 35 per cent of the country's housing was owner-occupied, as against 63 per cent in southeast England, outside London.

Complete 'new towns' were built: places like East Kilbride, begun in 1947; Glenrothes (1948); Cumbernauld (1955); Livingston (1962) and Irvine (1965). Whilst a generation's prayers for decency and dignity in their immediate living conditions were answered by such schemes, less tangible yearnings of just about every kind went unaddressed. A dreary appearance and lack of community spirit seemed to have been built in to these undeniably ambitious but ultimately unimaginative new projects. Amenities lagged far behind housebuilding both as conceptual priority and constructed fact. That was true in the big-city schemes as well, but at least there you weren't marooned in open country, where there was nothing much to do apart from sit at home and go to work.

Which itself became a problem when the single big employer around which these towns had generally been conceived hit difficulties. East Kilbride's whole *raison d être* was the Rolls Royce factory – which, after years of contraction, closed down in 2015; Glenrothes' was the Rothes Colliery 'superpit', which proved unviable and had to be axed in 1965.

HIGH RISE AND FALL

The 1960s was the heroic age of the tower block; just about ever since it's been a story of decline. Scotland's high-rises haven't been unique in their fall from grace, but, having invested so enthusiastically in public housing, the country's been hit particularly hard. Glasgow's Red Road Flats have been pretty much emblematic. Built between 1964 and 1969, these eight blocks comprised a mini-Manhattan northeast of the city centre: almost 5,000 people lived in towers, which at their highest rose to 30 storeys (89m or 290ft).

What's there to say that hasn't been rehearsed practically to death over decades now? By the beginning of the Seventies it was all unravelling. What worked on affluent Fifth Avenue, backed up by top-dollar maintenance and round-the-clock security, didn't seem such a winning formula for poor and unemployed Glaswegians waiting weeks for council workmen to come and unjam the rubbish chute or fix the lift. Bored teenagers made mischief; drunks used stairs and landings as a latrine; those who had the option moved out – leaving a spiral of decline. 'Nothing in his life became him like the leaving of it,' says Malcolm of the late King Duncan in Shakespeare's Scottish play, and it was a little bit like that with the Red Road

Flats. Brought down by explosives between 2010 and 2015, their demolition became a popular public spectacle. (Indeed, it seems to have come close to being the centrepiece attraction of the opening of the 2014 Commonwealth Games in Glasgow until some sense of civic self-preservation finally intervened.)

Building the Blight

By the 1970s you couldn't pick up a local paper anywhere in Scotland without seeing complaints about 'The Planners'. If the designation was unhelpfully simplistic – and did an injustice to decent officials doing their best with the challenges they faced with the resources they had – it did in its impersonality reflect an approach to urban policy that didn't seem to have too much of a human face.

And it wasn't just in housing, or for that matter in the public sector, that the blight was spreading, but in unsightly shopping malls and office complexes. Cumbernauld, for example, had been built around what was within a few years being derided as Britain's most hideous shopping mall. Irony loses the will to live when confronted with the fact that the Cumbernauld Development Corporation, which presided over this whole project, headquartered itself in the splendour of William Adam's post-Palladian Cumbernauld House (1731).

Glasgow's Anderston Cross Commercial Centre, completed in 1972, offered a blend of retail and residential properties. Only its architect could love the overall result. Edinburgh's St James' Centre brought together shops and local government offices. These schemes, controversial to begin with, only grew more so when the years went by and (for the most part) the promised regeneration didn't happen and the areas had to be re-regenerated. (In the case of the St James Centre, it seems, with a new meta-mall to be constructed more or less around the original.) And, often as not, rebranded – hence the Anderston Centre's now being officially titled 'Cadogan Square'.

Far from feeling inhibited by their consciousness of their Enlightenment inheritance, Edinburgh University felt so okay about having demolished half of Georgian George Square to make way for a pair of glass-and-concrete towers that they actually named the uglier of the two (which housed the humanities) after David Hume. Sir Edward Appleton (1892–1965), the former University Vice Principal who gave his name to the nearby science building, was being honoured in spirit, if not (in the view of most) aesthetically.

A Road Runs Through It

But then 'Brutalism' was the norm now, in everything from academic institutions through office blocks to roadbuilding projects. The flyovers and underpasses that looked so effortlessly graceful in the artists' impressions and architects' models always seemed that much more massive and ungainly once they were actually realised in grubby concrete.

But only eco-fundamentalists would reject the roadbuilding programme of the post-war period entirely. And it would be churlish to deny the elegance of a Forth Road Bridge whose central span, at 1,006m (3,300ft), was the longest outside the United States at the time it opened in 1964. Or the excitement its construction occasioned throughout Britain as a whole: 'Like a moon-landing for Scotland,' it's been said.

There's a generous dash of hindsight in the perception that's gradually prevailed that this crossing is, in engineering terms, a poor relation to the Forth Bridge proper – the rail bridge. A more valid criticism might be that it's emblematic of an age that placed too much trust in the transformative powers of infrastructural improvements – whilst simultaneously underestimating the transformation they'd help bring about. Within a few years of its opening, daily traffic levels were several times the absolute maximum the bridge had been designed for – whilst the political climate was begrudging funds for inspections and repairs. The ultimate ignominy came towards the end of 2015 when – with the proposed 'Third Crossing' still quite some time away – the Road Bridge was forced to close completely for several weeks.

Maybe, in fairness, the Road Bridge bore the brunt of a more generalised disaffection with the whole post-war Optimism Thing. Again, 'The Planners' were in the firing line. Slum clearance and traffic management came together in what would ultimately be seen as an unholy alliance, 'tearing the heart' (as the objectors invariably had it) out of Glasgow's Charing Cross, Dundee's riverside and innumerable other urban scenes. That this 'heart' had generally been a site of semi-dereliction dampened the critics' case, perhaps, but it didn't make these new highway schemes any more appealing. Charing Cross, notoriously, was for years the site of the 'Bridge to Nowhere', an empty podium over the M8, upon which the Tay House office block was eventually built.

The controversy continues: current critics of the proposed new western bypass around Aberdeen point to the American-style sprawl that prevails already along the southern approaches to the city.

The Stone of Scone

Last seen flaring up briefly in the colourful career of Cunninghame Graham (see page 296), Scottish Nationalism more or less languished after World War II. For a heady few months from April 1945, Robert McIntyre (1913–1958) was elected MP for Motherwell in a by-election, though he was to be swept away by the Labour Landslide that July. (The SNP wasn't to have another MP at Westminster till Winnie Ewing (1929–) took Hamilton in 1967.) To many Scots, Nationalism still seemed more a romantic cause than a seriously political one – a view its supporters' conduct didn't do too much to counter. Take this incident from 1950, for example…

At that time, an ordinary-looking block of sandstone was kept at Westminster Abbey in London. Some believed it to be the very pillow that Jacob, in the Book of Genesis (28, 12), rested his head upon when he dreamed of a ladder reaching up to heaven. It was certainly the stone over which successive Scottish kings had been seated for their coronations (at Scone Abbey, Perthshire) through an early-medieval period in which the value of holy relics was taken as read. It was at very least a powerful talisman – hence the sense of Scottish dismay and English triumph when it was captured and carried off by Edward I. He installed it in Westminster Abbey, where it remained for the next six and a half centuries.

Then, on Christmas Day, 1950, a group of Scottish Nationalist students broke in and took it – breaking off a corner as they did so. The two pieces were briefly separated but reunited back in Scotland by its abductors, who managed to elude the authorities long enough to place the stone on the altar of Arbroath Abbey.

The impossibility of imagining any of Scottish Nationalism's current or recent leadership taking any interest in an escapade like this tells us how much – for better or for worse – the movement's changed. Besides, they didn't have to, having (they might not unreasonably suggest) achieved a great deal more through political pressure. In 1996, the Stone of Destiny was brought back north with the rest of Scotland's Crown Jewels for permanent display in Edinburgh Castle.

Cold War Caledonia

A tourist attraction since 1994 – so arguably as much an aspect of Scotland's historical 'heritage' as St Andrews Castle, just a few kilometres up the road – the Secret Bunker at Troywood had a serious strategic importance in the 1980s. It did in theory, anyway: the Cold War that followed immediately on from the defeat of Nazi Germany in 1945 was peculiar in that, so long as the fear of Mutually-Assured Destruction (MAD) succeeded in deterring attack, then nothing much had to happen.

It's all a bit unfathomable now. A stand-off that, for a whole generation, defined reality – not just military, but political, economic and cultural – makes less sense to us with every passing decade. That's one reason for the difficulty we have today in deciphering a place like Troywood, in making sense of it as we might a medieval castle or a man-of-war. But it was hard to make sense of the conflict then as well. The concentration of undreamt-of destructive power in the hands of a tiny political leadership in Communist East and Capitalist West had transformed the whole experience of enmity. The threat overhanging the human race was quite genuinely without any precedent, but few felt much actual disquiet day by day; the sense of personal involvement was in inverse proportion to the stakes. As a citizen, you could see it optimistically as the protection of the 'nuclear umbrella' or, more pessimistically, as the 'shadow of the bomb'. Either way, such action as there was appeared to be taking place at one remove, and the threat – as terrible as it was – seemed unreal somehow.

From a vantage point in Scotland – and several decades into the future – the conflict can be seen as having involved a lot of shadow-boxing on both sides. Some said at the time that the Communist threat was deliberately exaggerated by Western politicians in thrall to the 'military-industrial complex'. Left-wing critics of Britain's Cold War strategy mostly objected to the resources being ploughed into military development, and the attacks on labour activism and popular protest being licensed by a government-fostered fear. It wasn't that they liked or supported the Soviet leadership, they argued, but that the Russian 'threat' was being distorted and exploited to establishment ends.

Real or imaginary, that threat was the mainstay of post-war defence policy in Britain as in other Western countries. Troywood was first built as a headquarters for civil defence in eastern Fife; it was rebuilt and expanded in 1978 as a command centre. Today we have the luxury of looking at it as a glorified setting for some science-fiction dystopia: had the balloon gone up, Scotland would have been run from there. Another bunker (since demolished), deep beneath Pitreavie Castle, outside Dunfermline, would have co-ordinated all NATO (North Atlantic Treaty Organisation) naval forces between the North Sea and the Arctic. It follows, perhaps, from the peculiar character of the Cold War, that it produced such profoundly unimpressive monuments. Though they could hardly be less interesting to look at, the government offices at Saughton House, in Edinburgh's Broomhouse Drive are of historic significance: they're believed to have been built as a military hospital in case of nuclear war.

Protest and Survive?

In Scotland, as in England, opposition to Britain's nuclear defence policy came together in the Campaign for Nuclear Disarmament (CND). Founded in 1957, a few years after Britain became a nuclear power by detonating its first atomic bomb, this was a loose alliance of left-wingers and those with religious-based objections – most notably the Quakers (the Society of Friends). Many were Labour Party members, albeit disillusioned with the leadership's espousal of 'Atlanticism' – basically, NATO membership and enthusiastic (slavish?) alliance with the United States.

When, in 1960, Westminster agreed with the Americans that they could base their Polaris submarines on Holy Loch, this was inevitably viewed as a provocation. A protest camp was quickly established outside the base on the Firth of Clyde, whilst there were demonstrations in Scottish cities such as Glasgow. The ethics of nuclear war aside, there was an obvious nationalist dimension to the quarrel: Scotland was being made both an accessory in nuclear annihilation and a target.

Boat-borne protestors tried unsuccessfully to prevent the arrival of the first submarine, but it docked safely on 3 March 1961. One way and another, the Polaris submarines were to remain at Holy Loch all the way through to the end of the Cold War in 1991. Faslane, not far away, was an important nuclear base for the Royal Navy. A similar peace camp was established there, and a series of demonstrations mounted over the years (including one, in 2013, at which 47 people were arrested).

Kinloss, on the Moray Firth, became a base for nuclear-armed Vulcan bombers, kept in readiness round the clock until 1968, when missile-armed Polaris submarines took over their role. Nimrod maritime patrols were carried out from Kinloss until 2010. Hardened Aircraft Shelters were built there to protect planes and other hardware against attack. Further Vulcans were based at RAF Machrihanish, in Kintyre, which also boasted one of the longest runways in the world. (The military airfield is now a business park, though the adjacent Campbeltown Airport still functions.) Tornado GR4/F3 Fighter Interceptors from Lossiemouth (Moray) and Leuchars (near St Andrews, Fife) protected UK airspace from Russian bombers; the RAF base at Leuchars was closed in 2014 and handed over to the Army.

The New Scots

Italian immigrants had been trickling into Scotland since the end of the 19th century, the number significantly increasing after World War I. The Great Depression had come early to an Italy left disappointed after the Versailles Conference, and that same despair, which helped drive so many into the arms of Mussolini and his emergent Fascist party, impelled others to leave their country (especially its impoverished south) in enormous numbers. Most, of course, went to the United States, or Argentina and Uruguay, but Britain was to have its share of immigrants as well.

Quite how welcome they were made must be doubtful, given that they were unceremoniously interned during World War II (at which time, of course, *Il Duce*'s Italy was an Axis ally of Nazi Germany). Some of these Italian Scots were shipped to Canada: on 29 June, 1940, 470 were lost, as well as 300-odd victims of other nationalities, including captured German merchant seamen, when the *Arandora Star* was torpedoed in the Atlantic.

A new wave of Italian immigrants arrived as PoWs. Many of these were sent north, to Orkney, where they were kept busy building the 'Churchill Barriers' (causeways connecting Mainland and other islands, like Burray/South Ronaldsay and Glimps Holm). Lamb Holm's Italian Chapel – a couple of Nissen huts transformed into an extraordinarily ornate church – is a quirkily magnificent monument to this episode. But Scotland's Italian heritage is to be seen in just about every corner of the country: stereotypically, in restaurants, cafés, ice cream bars and chip shops. And in all the important artists, musicians, journalists and other public personalities to be found in every walk of Scottish life.

Since 1945, Scotland has generally proven less of an economic draw than the English southeast (and, at least for a while, the northern English textile towns). Immigration through this period was accordingly quite low. Throughout the country, people of Pakistani origin make up 0.93 per cent of the population, as against 1.86 per cent of the UK population as a whole. (That overall figure irons out significant local variations, of course: in London, those of Pakistani descent make up 2.4 per cent of the population; in Yorkshire 4.28 per cent – whilst in Bradford it's more like 20 per cent.) Even so, there was a significant flow of migrants from the South Asian subcontinent into Scotland's major towns and cities. Further waves of immigrants came – during World War II, and again after the 1990s – from Poland.

The New Non-Persons

The 21st century has seen the arrival of significant (and very varied) communities of asylum seekers. In 2013, there were 10,000 foreign 'refugees' in Glasgow alone, their presence (and their work in the black economy) often resented by the existing local poor. Their refugee status is officially disputed, of course: those deemed not to have a justifiable fear of persecution in their home countries, and consequently refused 'political asylum', aren't allowed to work – or entitled to any sort of state support. They accordingly exist in a sort of shadowland, their presence not really recognised by the authorities, who won't discuss their cases with the charitable bodies that try to help them.

Whilst refugees in Scotland's cities have had all too many stories of hostility and persecution to relate, the country's claims to have been more enlightened in its attitudes than England don't seem totally unfounded. There have been good pragmatic grounds for this, hence the SNP's insistence, early in 2014, that immigration had to be encouraged to help offset the problems posed by an ageing population. Claims that Scots are more tolerant of immigrants have been supported by a British Social Attitudes Survey (also 2014), but not so much as some commentators had supposed. In Scotland, 69 per cent of those questioned believed that the number of immigrants should be reduced, against 78 per cent in England – there was no 'come one, come all' Caledonian welcome, then.

THE 'BLACK PRINCE OF PERTHSHIRE'

In 1746, Castle Menzies, near Weem, Aberfeldy, was graced by the presence of Bonnie Prince Charlie, who stayed for a couple of nights before Culloden. Later, however, it was to provide a longer-term home for another foreign royal: Duleep Singh (1838–93), the last Maharajah of the Sikh Empire.

His mother and regent, Jind Kaur, was deposed and imprisoned by the British after the First Anglo-Sikh War of 1846, and Duleep was brought up well away from what the imperial authorities regarded as her bad influence. Taken to Britain, with Sir John Spencer Login and Lady Login as his guardians, the boy grew up a popular pet of Queen Victoria and of the aristocracy. He lived at Castle Menzies from 1855, when it was leased for him by his guardians as an appropriately grand – and sequestered – home. Three years later, when the lease expired, the young Maharajah moved a short distance to the mansion house at Auchlyne before going to England in 1860. Most of Scotland's Sikh community arrived in rather different circumstances, of course, from the 1920s – and especially in the post-war period.

Muslims in Scotland

Bashir Maan has suggested (in *The Thistle and the Crescent*, Argyll Publishing, 2008) that officials from the court of the Caliph Abd al-Rahman II may have visited Scotland in the mid-9th century. They were on a diplomatic mission in the wake of the Viking raids that had been afflicting al-Andalus – Muslim Spain. If this theory has in colour what it may lack in corroborating evidence, it's certainly true that contact with the Islamic world will have started a great deal earlier than we may generally assume.

That most of that contact was uncomfortable is somewhat beside the point. War is one way in which different societies interact. Whilst early Western pilgrims who made their way to Jerusalem would have made more or less peaceful connections with Muslims in the Middle East, the Crusaders who (from 1096) went out to 'protect' them and 'take back' the Christian Holy Places were also taking part in a form of cultural outreach. As, arguably, were the Barbary Pirates who, setting out from the ports of North Africa as late as the 17th century, mounted slave-raids on Christian countries much further north. They're known to have attacked sites in England, along the Bristol Channel, and in the southwest of Ireland. Could they have ventured as far as Scotland or its offshore isles? Scottish seafarers in the Mediterranean and the Bay of Biscay were definitely taken: in 1677, the Privy Council for Scotland agreed to pay a ransom for several crewmen of the *Issobell*, Montrose, taken that September by pirates off Algiers.

From the 19th century, the story of Scotland's encounter with Islam was a more familiar one of British imperial expansion in Mughal India, the Malay Archipelago, the Arab Middle East, the East African littoral (or Swahili Coast) and elsewhere. The flow of Muslim immigrants into Scotland took place mainly from the 1950s, and originated especially in Pakistan and Bangladesh.

Like earlier waves of immigrants, Scotland's Muslims worked hard to establish themselves, and raise emblems of arrival: Glasgow got an impressive Central Mosque in 1983. Edinburgh's wasn't completed until 15 years later. In 1997, Mohammed Sarwar (1952–) established a different kind of landmark by becoming Britain's first Muslim MP, representing Govan (and subsequently Glasgow Central) till 2010. By that time, of course, the Muslim community's existing problems of old-fashioned racism had been compounded by post-9/11 suspicions of Islam.

'Ninety-Minute Bigots'?

Older intolerances continued, meanwhile, throughout the post-war period – not only unabated but inflamed anew by Northern Ireland's problems. The Old Firm rivalry persisted, with support for Celtic and Rangers a focus for existing, historic sectarianism. That said, it has to be acknowledged that at certain periods – during much of the 1970s, for example

– football hooliganism became a serious problem in non-sectarian England too. Moreover, fans were blameless in some of modern football's most horrific moments. Both of the 'Ibrox Disasters' seem to have stemmed from the difficulty of managing large numbers of supporters in limited space. The first, in 1902 (which killed 25 and left over 500 injured) doesn't seem so different from the Bradford City fire of 1985; the second, in 1971 (which killed 66 and injured about 200) in some ways prefigured Hillsborough.

In 1989, after years of pressure, a reformed Rangers made history by signing its first Catholic player, Maurice 'Mo' Johnston (1963–). Ten years later, Bari-born Lorenzo Amoruso became team captain. But the impact of such steps on the terraces was limited. And, if all-seater stadiums and stricter stewarding helped reduce actual violence in the grounds, it didn't do anything to prevent fighting on the streets outside. (Or, some suggested, in the home: findings that rates of domestic violence in Glasgow doubled in the 24 hours during and after an Old Firm game led to calls for the fixture to be completely banned.)

Nor did it quell the chants calling for copious quantities of Fenian Blood to flow. Whether the Boys of the Old Brigade so lustily celebrated by the Parkhead crowd were really in any way preferable to the Billy Boys of Ibrox must be questionable. That said, as a general rule, Celtic's status as the team of the immigrant minority militated against out-and-out racism as such. Where its supporters have offended against good taste and decency, it's generally been in the celebration of IRA atrocities, and the overseas misfortunes of British forces.

Some would argue that the situation hasn't been helped by a more light-hearted, tongue-in-cheek tribalism on the part of comparatively privileged personalities who 'should know better'. In 1999, the former footballer and Scotland manager Craig Brown (1940–) was recorded singing a sectarian song; leading advocate and public figure Donald Findlay QC

(1951–) has made something of a habit of being caught this way. And, for many participants on either side, it may just be a more-than-usually-charged form of male bonding. (Hence the notorious – but not necessarily self-evidently stupid – suggestion by a Rangers official that there was 'such a thing as a 90-minute bigot'.) Given that government measures had largely eliminated the sort of overtly discriminatory practices that undoubtedly had disadvantaged Catholics in the pre-war period (and given that, as of 1998, peace of a sort had come to Northern Ireland) couldn't this all be filed under 'colourful tradition'?

It seems unlikely that Mark Scott would have agreed. The young Celtic supporter was stabbed to death after an Old Firm game in 1999, prompting a group of his friends to found the anti-sectarianism campaign Nil by Mouth a few years later. Nor, presumably, would thousands of other victims of the violence and intimidation – that still goes on. So too does the inability of establishment bodies to find a coherent response. In February 2015, former footballer Stan Collymore was dropped as a BT Sport correspondent for saying that Rangers shouldn't be televised if their fans wouldn't stop their sectarian chanting.

Pumping Prosperity

The North Sea's oil and gas reserves can be seen as a continuation of the same field first prospected on the Scottish mainland by James Young in the West Lothian oil shales (see page 205). Modern exploration started in the 1960s and the *Sea Gem* rig struck gas in 1965 (though it sank, with the loss of 13 lives, soon after). With further finds, gas production quickly soared, and 'natural gas' from the North Sea soon replaced 'town gas' (made out of coal).

Oil wasn't found till a little later, starting with the Ekofisk field (towards the end of 1969), followed by the Forties field

(1970); Brent (1971) and Piper (1973). As global prices rose, following the international oil crises of 1973 and 1979, the sudden surge in income seemed to hold out the prospect of a real transformation in the economic fortunes (and expectations) of the UK and Scotland. Scotland certainly experienced a surge in prosperity in key centres such as Aberdeen (the oil port *par excellence*) and Peterhead (an important base for support vessels). Sullom Voe in Shetland became one of Europe's biggest oil terminals.

A big and complex infrastructure sprang up on the Scottish mainland to serve this new industry. The St Fergus Gas Terminal, north of Peterhead, became the main centre for gas to be brought ashore and for its methane content to be separated out, the remaining liquid being piped south to Mossmorran (near Cowdenbeath, in Fife) for 'fractionation'. The resulting products were then moved through further pipelines to the tanker terminal at Braefoot Bay, on the northern shore of the Firth of Forth near Aberdour, to be shipped out to markets around the world. Some propane and butane was also carried away by road. (From 2012, the 'T in the Park' music festival had to be moved from Fife to the grounds of Strathallan Castle, Perthshire, since the gas pipeline ran beneath the old Balado airfield where it had been held, and there were fears of leaks.) Oil is carried via the Forties Pipeline system, first to shore at Cruden Bay, north of Aberdeen, and from there on down to Grangemouth for refining.

Not that there wasn't a downside too, in environmental damage – and not just the obvious ones of pollution, ecological disruption and unsightly installations. There have been complaints that, after half a century of drilling, the North Sea has been left littered with debris and other hazards, making commercial fishing difficult. Fishing boats have already arguably been driven out of Aberdeen harbour. There have been hazards for the workers in the industry as well: the crash of a Chinook helicopter at Sumburgh, Shetland, in 1986, killed

44. Two years later, 167 were to lose their lives in the Piper Alpha disaster. Casualties have generally been high, given the deep waters and stormy conditions to be contended with in the North Sea oil- and gas-fields. This rich resource is to be secured only at great human cost.

Rumours of North Sea Oil's imminent exhaustion are exaggerated: an estimated 20-odd billion barrels still remain. Nevertheless, it is a finite resource that will run out in the (only too foreseeable) future. And, with the last reserves expected to be that much more inaccessible and consequently difficult and dangerous to extract, the long-term viability of the industry must be under question. (Part of the problem is that what we loosely describe as 'North Sea Oil' is less likely to come from the North Sea proper than it was before: the focus for exploration has gradually shifted around the coast to the 'West of Shetland Basin' and Atlantic. Extraction in these much deeper waters depends on the use of floating platforms rather than fixed rigs: it's all more complicated, and a great deal more expensive.)

The industry's difficulties have been compounded by the fact that global oil prices began to fall from the second half of 2014. Just as rising prices had played to Scotland's advantage in the 1970s, this fall in price was obviously a threat. (So much so that it cast a retrospective shadow over that year's Independence Referendum, prompting accusations that the 'Yes' campaign had been counting its oil-revenue chickens irresponsibly, promising a Scottish Shangri-La founded on imaginary oil wealth.) Aberdeen certainly started to feel the pinch. And whilst, on the one hand, its significance as a centre of expertise for the worldwide offshore extraction industry should have given it some protection, the fact that the downturn was global didn't help.

'We're on the March...'

It's one of the great imponderables of modern Scottish history whether the national football team's ignominious showing at Argentina '78 (apart from Archie Gemmill's goal, too late to make a difference) established an inescapable mood of defeatism before the Devolution Referendum the following year. There's no doubt that, in the run-up to the World Cup, Scottish excitement had been heightened by the knowledge that England had failed to qualify. The disappointment that followed had been crushing.

So too, though, was the small print on the referendum paper once you read it. The terms and conditions were strict – indefensibly so, some argued. For even limited devolution to be introduced, the 'majority' opting for it was going to have to be of all those eligible to vote, not just of those who did. Anyone who stayed in bed was going to be assumed to have voted 'No'.

On the one hand, it might be felt that this made sense for what (at least at the time) seemed a radical re-think of Scotland's status. Voters should have actively to choose if they wanted their relationship with Britain to change. On the other, it demanded a higher democratic standard than was required in any other area of public life. And all this for a poll that was supposedly being held to rubber-stamp plans for an assembly which had already been promised in legislation by Jim Callaghan's Labour government.

The 'No' campaign was launched at a public meeting in the Golden Lion Hotel, in King Street, Stirling. A Conservative Party that had, till 1965, actually called itself the 'Unionist Party' was in little doubt as to where its loyalties lay. Labour, though nominally pro-'Yes', was badly divided both within itself, and externally against its ostensible allies in the 'Yes' campaign: the breakaway Scottish Socialists and SNP. In the event, Scots voted for devolution in sufficient numbers to secure a majority (51.6 per cent) of those who polled, but only 32.9 per cent of the electorate as a whole. (No more than 64 per cent of eligible voters had turned out.) If there'd been no pro-devolutionary landslide, there'd certainly been no sign of real enthusiasm for a status quo, whose all too technical 'triumph' was only to bring dissatisfaction and disillusion.

The Scottish Nationalists had been moving to the left since the start of the Seventies – and into more urban areas, exploiting working-class disaffection with complacent local Labour administrations. The cynical way that aspirations to devolution had been undercut – by the same Labour government that had promised an assembly in the first place – only underlined the disillusionment of many Scots. When former Labour lefty Jim Sillars (1937–) won Glasgow Govan for the SNP at a 1980 by-election, it showed how deep the resentment had become.

Post-Industrial

The extent to which a country celebrated for its scenic wildernesses had become the quintessential industrialised nation was perhaps not completely clear until it all went downhill. The last few decades of the 20th century were marked by industrial unrest and industrial decline – ideological opponents argue about which preceded which.

Upper Clyde Shipbuilders (UCS) wouldn't have existed had the whole shipbuilding industry not been in trouble. Underwritten by the Labour government, it was formed in 1968 by the merger of five yards that hadn't appeared viable on their own. Ted Heath's Tories pulled the plug in 1971, but, surprisingly, the yard's unions managed to make the whole thing a good-news story. Rather than call a strike, with all the disruption and general negativity that would entail, they organised an upbeat-sounding 'work-in', to keep the shipyard in production.

Shop steward Jimmy Reid (1932–2010) shot to fame: he and his comrades insisted on dignity and discipline among their rank and file; their protest won support – and generous donations – from around the world. So much so that the liquidated company was saved. It was arguably a pyrrhic victory, though, only postponing the inevitable. (It may even have given Mrs Thatcher's Conservative government the warning it needed to get the gloves off for future struggles.)

If the shutting down of the shipyards of the Clyde through the 1960s and 1970s spelled the end to a century or so's industrial history, that of the Linwood car factory in 1981 was in some ways more alarming. This plant had only opened (with considerable fanfare) in 1961, to build the Hillman Imp. This kind of place had been supposed to represent the country's future. When its gates closed after just 20 years' production, 4,800 jobs in the factory itself were lost, as well as an estimated 6,000 or so indirectly. Unemployment rates in the locality were to soar well into the 1990s. The town has to some extent reinvented itself in the last few years with leisure centres and retail parks – and if well-paid industrial jobs have been replaced by low-wage positions in the service sector, few feel in any position to complain.

Miners' Strike

The National Coal Board (NCB) announced a programme of pit closures across all its coalfields on 6 March 1984. The National Union of Mineworkers (NUM) called for nationwide industrial action and Polmaise, in Fallin, outside Stirling, was the first Scottish colliery to come out on strike (in fact, its miners were already out due to an earlier dispute). The strike in Scotland was mainly solid, so there wasn't the widespread trouble seen further south, where support was divided and nerves and tempers correspondingly frayed. Flying pickets did, however, turn up at Bilston Glen near Loanhead, south of Edinburgh: this colliery hadn't been marked for closure, and was working on, amidst increasingly angry scenes. There was trouble, too, at Ravenscraig, Motherwell, where hoped-for sympathy action from steelworkers wasn't materialising, driving anxious striking miners to a fury.

The miners and steelworkers had traditionally been the 'aristocrats of labour' – though this wasn't the sort of social hierarchy for which Mrs Thatcher had much respect. Nor were voters in the Tory heartlands wild about the heavy subsidies needed to keep the industry even remotely viable. The counter-argument – that it was strategically important for the UK to maintain its access to this resource – did not convince. In fact, many believed that the government's plan all along was to smash the NUM – and hence intimidate the trades union movement as a whole.

The strike ended in exhaustion on 5 March 1985. No deep mines are now left working in Scotland. Fallin is now a dormitory town for commuters to Stirling, Glasgow, and Edinburgh (though there's a little colliery museum there). Bilston Glen, which had ignored the strike-call, was quickly demolished and replaced by an industrial estate – you'd never know there had been a colliery there. Despite such regeneration projects, there's still a residue of un- and under-employment across Scotland's old coalfields (as, of course, there is in those of England).

TREETOP VIGIL

The scene of some decidedly ill-tempered stand-offs during the Miners' Strike, Bilston later (from 2000) became the focus for a very different kind of dispute when environmental protestors set up a complex of tree-houses there. Their hope was to prevent a bypass being forced through a wood that was both a famous beauty spot and a designated Site of Special Scientific Interest. In the end they made history, not just by thwarting the roadbuilders' plans but by becoming the occupants of the world's longest-landing 'treesit protest'. For many of the activists, their campaign (of 15 years and counting) hasn't just been about stopping the bypass scheme but about developing new earth- and people-friendly ways of living.

'Subsidy Junkies'

Despite an eight-week occupation by its predominantly female workforce, Bathgate lost Plessey Capacitors in 1982. That left 160 workers – mostly women – redundant, to add to the 2,000 Plessey employees already shed at the plant since 1973. Leyland's Bathgate truck plant followed in 1986, this time with the loss of 1,800 jobs. Shipyards were continuing to close along the Clyde: Scott Lithgow would seemingly be 'saved' by its Trafalgar House takeover of 1986, but 1,500 jobs still went, as unemployment across the west of Scotland soared.

The privatisation of what had been state-owned industries opened the way to rationalisation of a kind that generally ended up meaning 'slimming down'. British Steel was one of the biggest companies to undergo this treatment. In 1990, the Trade and Industry Secretary, Nicholas Ridley, announced that the hot strip mill at Ravenscraig, outside Motherwell, was to be closed down early the following year. Even Scottish

Tories were uncomfortable, and Malcolm Rifkind openly questioned the decision. The Scots, said London's *Evening Standard*, were 'subsidy junkies'.

The strip mill closed on schedule; the rest of the plant in 1992. Whilst 770 jobs were lost at Ravenscraig itself, getting on for 10,000 are believed to have followed indirectly. Attempts to redevelop a site that became an embarrassment for the government were complicated by the difficulty of decontaminating soils left toxic by so many decades of heavy industrial use. Central Scotland was starting to look like a semi-derelict 'rust belt'.

Real Junkies

A good many Scots were looking semi-derelict too. Strathclyde had lost 37 per cent of its manufacturing jobs between 1971 and 1981; 30 per cent of positions in the textiles sector. Overall, by the mid-1980s, one in five of the workforce in the Strathclyde region was without a job; things weren't too much better in the Central region or in Fife. Sobering as they are, such averages masked the extremes of local variation: Edinburgh's better-than-Scottish-average unemployment rate of 13 per cent concealed the distinction between leafy Cramond, with four per cent of its eligible workers unemployed, and Craigmillar, with over 30 per cent.

Increasingly, moreover, unemployment had an air of permanence: 45 per cent of Strathclyde's unemployed had been out of work more than a year. And for a new generation of teenage school-leavers, what should have been a time of hope and excitement was one of apathy at best. By 1986, in Edinburgh's Muirhouse scheme, youth unemployment (16–24-year-olds) stood at 45 per cent. There was no realistic prospect of a working life for many – no prospect of adulthood as traditionally envisaged.

Though still conventionally associated with the moneyed Bohemian New York of lofts, Lou Reed and the Velvet Underground, heroin had come a long way by the 1980s. Specifically, it had come into some of Britain's poorest neighbourhoods; it sat like a blight upon many of Scotland's council schemes. Those of Glasgow most obviously: it was at this time that Easterhouse became known as 'Smack City'. But Dundee, Edinburgh and Aberdeen certainly weren't spared. Nor were smaller towns like Peterhead or Fraserburgh. You didn't have to be a user to have a drug problem in the Scotland of this time. As local gangs grew rich and ruthless; as the relentless demands of addiction drove a wave of daily, petty crime; and as families failed under the accompanying stress, life became pretty much miserable all round.

As if all this weren't enough, the heroin problem brought AIDS (Acquired Immune Deficiency Syndrome) in its wake. This condition, still new and effectively untreatable, was barely known about in the Scotland of the early Eighties. It too was conventionally associated with the moneyed Bohemian New York of lofts and so forth. Widely described as a 'gay plague', it wasn't seen as threatening to a working-class Scotland in which it seemed axiomatic that homosexuality did not exist.

And it's true that, for what it's worth, gay sex was not to be the main vehicle for the spread of the syndrome in the country. Edinburgh's emergence, by the late-1980s, as the 'AIDS capital of Europe' has to be attributed to heroin use and, more specifically, to the problem of needle-sharing. In 1983, the first HIV+ diagnosis was identified in Edinburgh's heroin-using community; within six months, it was believed that 60 per cent of the city's heroin users had been affected. Effectively green-lighted by the Scottish Committee's 'McLelland Report' of 1986, the city's first needle exchange was opened in 1987. By now, though, the problem had grown considerably: as of June 1988, there were 1,500-odd reported cases of HIV/AIDS in Edinburgh and Lothian – seven times the UK average. In a quarter of these cases, infection was believed to have been by heterosexual sex.

The result was a macabre sort of celebrity for the city. Edinburgh, wrote Francis X. Clines in the *New York Times* (4 January 1987), 'is experiencing a grinding combination of public bewilderment and press sensationalism. Camera crews arrive looking for deathbed tableaux ... Neighborhood workers complain that at least one addict has been paid by television journalists to allow filming of his heroin injecting.'

The laureate of this Edinburgh is of course the Leith-born novelist Irvine Welsh (1958–), whose instant classic, *Trainspotting*, came out in 1993. Leith Central Station, which in its derelict (since the Seventies) state plays a memorable role in the novel's action, was at the bottom of Leith Walk. It became the site of a council leisure centre/swimming pool, and is now – ironically, perhaps – a toddlers' softplay centre.

Community Values

Anyone who imagines that 'politically correct' euphemism is the preserve of the political left need look no further than the name Mrs Thatcher gave to her replacement for the Council Rates. Put very crudely, this 'Community Charge' replaced a graduated system based on the value of property each household owned with one that asked everybody for the same set tax. Fair, as far as she was concerned, because it refused to penalise the better-off and recognised the choices they made to use private services. But, to others, it looked like a way of pampering Tory voters whilst clobbering the poor.

The social ethics aside, Thatcherite true-believers seem to have been slow to appreciate the paradigm shift this transformation of local government finance was going to involve for the voting public, or how little sympathy it was likely to command, even among many of its beneficiaries. Indeed, taking a leaf out of left-liberalism's book, Maggie's supporters seemed in some cases consciously to be 'reappropriating' the abuse being hurled at them. Nicholas Ridley didn't seem so much to be admitting as boasting when he declared that 'a duke would pay the same as a dustman' under the charge.

Its introduction to Scotland in 1989, a year ahead of its roll-out across England and Wales, must have seemed a good idea at the time – a chance to assess the implications, iron out little difficulties, over a limited area. No one wants to be a guinea pig, though, and certainly not for a policy that is already enormously unpopular. Scotland's use as a test-bed for the tax gave a nationalist dimension to an ideological alienation that had already been there before, and had been underlined by events during the Miners' Strike.

Scotland's recent history – and specifically its labour history; its tradition of highly-unionised heavy-industrial work; its high proportion of public-sector employment through the post-war era; its comparatively high ratio of council tenants to owner-occupiers … All these things set Scotland at odds with the southeast England in which Mrs Thatcher had her electoral stronghold. Maggie's charisma didn't really reach this far north.

The Prophet Motive

There was certainly very little excitement in Scotland about the attitudes and ideas that had made Mrs Thatcher revered in her heartlands – the whole individualism, popular-capitalism thing. She chose the Church of Scotland's Assembly Hall in Edinburgh as the venue for an eloquent and impassioned articulation of her Christian creed, and the 'Sermon on the Mound' (as it was waggishly dubbed by the media) spelled out the importance of individual responsibility, hard work and thrift and personal betterment along with a belief in consumer choice that shadowed the spiritual doctrine of free will. The listening clergy managed only minimally polite applause.

That was a good deal better than the reception she got in the rest of Scotland. Her flagship policy, the Poll Tax was resented from the start. While most paid up reluctantly, a large-scale programme of refusal was led by local Anti-Poll Tax Unions (the first of these had been set up as early as 1987 in Maryhill, Glasgow), which ultimately came together under the auspices of the All-Britain Anti-Poll Tax Federation. Things got ugly. And not just in the moral sense: there was a hideous theatricality about the procedures used to enforce payment. Backed up by policemen, sheriff's officers were sent in to flats and houses to 'poind' non-payers' property – basically, place a price on items that could be removed for re-sale at public 'warrant sales'. Noisy confrontations between distressed householders, angry protestors and embarrassed officials were just about inevitable. Arrests were made: Federation leader Tommy Sheridan (1964–) spent six months in gaol.

In the end, the problem went away because the Charge went down so badly in England (provoking major riots in 1990). But that didn't do anything to allay Scottish resentments: Westminster had been happy to ride out the public protests north of the border. The mood was summed up in the 1991 Tennents advert that, against a soundtrack of Frankie Miller's cover of Dougie MacLean's 1978 song 'Caledonia', showed an unhappy young man in an anonymous, crowded, jostling, uncaring, rat-race-running London. Hearing Scotland calling him, he went home to welcoming back-slaps and pints of lager.

They were never really to be honoured in their homeland, but the great prophets of New Labour were both Scottish-born, of course. For the market-minded social democrat, what could possibly be more moving than a pilgrimage to 5 Paisley Terrace, in Edinburgh's eastern suburb of Willowbrae, where the infant Tony Blair (1953–) spent his first 18 months or so? Or to see St Brycedale's, Kirkcaldy, Fife, where Blair's successor, Gordon Brown (1951–), was son of the manse?

System Crash

Named in jokey reference, obviously, to California's Silicon Valley, 'Silicon Glen' is more an idea than a geographical location. Some might suggest, indeed, that it's actually a slightly desperate rationalisation, an attempt to put a positive spin on the downsizing of Central Scotland's industry through the 1980s and early 1990s. Silicon Glen was, in fact, never more than a collection of assembly lines.

The electronics industry had been in Scotland since the 1940s, when Ferranti had opened an important plant in Edinburgh. IBM had followed at Greenock (and, in fairness, they're still there), leading the move towards what came to be known as IT. The impact on Central Scotland was significant, of course – the more so because it came at a time of contraction in traditional heavy industries. Plants of one sort or another opened at Dundee, Glenrothes, Linlithgow, Livingstone and East Kilbride, in the Borders at Selkirk and Galashiels – and even (taking the fullest possible advantage of government assistance to the Highlands and Islands region) in the improbable setting of the Isle of Bute.

For a while, the techno-optimism didn't seem misplaced. With the new millennium, however, came another round of closures. The 60-hectare (150-acre) Hyundai semiconductor plant beside the M90 outside Dunfermline was to become emblematic. Built in 1997, it was never to be used; instead it sat empty for 13 years before being sold for demolition and redevelopment.

CAPITAL OF THE HIGHLANDS

A city since 2001, Inverness has been an important centre since Pictish times and there's been a castle on the hill since the 11th century. But its strategic importance has long since gone; as, really, has the significance of its situation at the lowest bridging-point for the River Ness.

It's conventional in this kind of 'city-sketch' to point to the advantages of the site. However, for the firms and individuals who've helped make Inverness not just Scotland's, but one of Western Europe's, fastest growing cities, it could arguably be pretty much anywhere. The new high-tech enterprises that have set up shop do all the important things online – so why not find the place that best combines great communications with quality of life? Inverness scores consistently high in a sort of assessment that no one even thought to make till recently: that of the happiness of its inhabitants.

Miles Better

'Rebranding' was a buzzword (a buzzword in itself) by the 1980s. Scotland arguably had more than its fair share to do. Glasgow in particular: it was frustrating for officials and entrepreneurs (not to mention ordinary citizens) that external perceptions seemed to begin and end with sectarian violence and social squalor. Work on building a different and more favourable set of associations was under way by 1983, with the 'Glasgow's Miles Better' campaign. Though much derided, this was an attempt to offset the enduring image of poverty, dirt and drunken violence, and conjure up a new one of style, culture, affluence.

Swanky shops and smart cafés might seem shallow things to aspire to, but they beat old stereotypes of the Gorbals and the 'Glasgow Kiss'. At least they offered the suggestion of some sort of civic and commercial life in place of the sort of high-noon-for-hardmen that seemed permanently to prevail in popular representations of what William McIlvanney (1936–2015; 'Scotland's Camus') characterised as 'the city of the stare'.

Scottish writers were mostly sceptical (at best) about all the new 'regeneration', gentrification and the rest of it, but there's no doubt that they were doing their bit towards a general heightening of self-confidence and soft-nationalist pride from the Eighties onward. Alasdair Gray's *Lanark* (1981) was acclaimed for a scope and technical ambition that cleared the way for the emergence of younger writers like the poet Tom Leonard (1944–) and the novelist James Kelman (1946–). Neither man showed any obvious interest in 'rebranding' the working-class language and culture (and the conflicts) of the west of Scotland; but both showed how they could become the basis of real literary art, as did poet Liz Lochhead (1957–).

After them came a range of innovative authors like Iain Banks (1954–2013), Janice Galloway (1955–), Jackie Kay (1961–) and A.L. Kennedy (1965–). Meanwhile, the films of Bill Forsyth (1946–) had put Scotland on the cinematic map: *Gregory's Girl* (1981) and *Local Hero* (1983) charmed the world. Elizabeth Blackadder (1931–) set the UK purring with her watercolour cat-stamp series for the Royal Mail (1995). Add the innovatory genius of younger artists like John Bellany (1942–2013) and Peter Howson (1958–) and you have something of a Scottish mini-Renaissance.

Lockerbie's Long Shadow

'Sister Scotland' to the propagandists of Irish Republicanism, and a world away from the conflicts of the Middle East, this country was for the most part spared the attentions of the 20th century's terrorists. It seems to have been by a random chance that, on the night of 21 December 1988, the bomb that brought down Pan Am Flight 103 (en route from Frankfurt to Detroit) did so over the little town of Lockerbie in the Borders. In addition to the 259 passengers and crew on board the Boeing 747, 11 people were killed when burning debris ploughed a devastating furrow through a residential area round Sherwood Crescent, just south of the centre of the town.

It was a terrible tragedy for the victims and a fearful crime: that much was clear. But just about nothing else about the 'Lockerbie Bombing' was. Conspiracy theories flourished: stories of cover-ups at the crash scene; conspiracies of official silence in the weeks and months that followed; and persistent suggestions that the finger of suspicion very publicly being pointed at Colonel Gaddafi's Libya was being quite consciously and calculatedly misdirected by shadowy denizens of that deep and sinister twilight zone of official conduct in which backdoor diplomacy meets downright dirty tricks.

The man eventually charged with the bombing, Libyan security official Abdelbaset al-Megrahi (1952–2012), always stoutly maintained his guiltlessness of this crime. Nor, many felt, did the evidence really support his conviction – which, however, came in 2001. Even then, though, the story wasn't over: a first appeal having been rejected, by 2009 a second seemed more likely to be successful, if rumoured evidence of official skulduggery were really to emerge. Ministers denied that any embarrassment at this prospect played any part in the decision to release Megrahi – by now suffering terminal cancer – and send him back to Libya before this second appeal could be heard. In a final twist, the 'dying man' took what some cynics felt was too long to reach his end, not finally passing on until late May 2012.

Referendum Revisited

From atop its own acropolis on Calton Hill, the Old Royal High School building looks down on Edinburgh like a Scottish Parthenon: for many, it's the Parliament that never was. Built between 1826 and 1829, it ceased to be a school in the late-1960s when the Royal High relocated to new buildings in Barnton, northwest of the city. Made ready for the 1979 Assembly, it was then left without a function when that vote failed to make the majority required. It accordingly became a symbol of Scottish nationalism's unfinished business – and, with its strongly Athenian appearance, an ironic one of democratic deficit. The potency of that symbolism is suggested by the (unconfirmed but persistent) rumours that Labour Scottish Secretary Donald Dewar (1937–2000) committed to the construction of the present Parliament at the bottom of the Royal Mile specifically to avoid using this now-iconic building.

The establishment of this Scottish Parliament was green-lighted by a referendum of 1997 on devolution, with a supplementary question (also answered in the affirmative) as to whether a new Scottish Parliament should have tax-raising powers. The democratic dramas of 2014 have arguably occluded our view of what this vote achieved, but it brought Scotland more political autonomy than it had had since the Act of Union.

Psychologically, too, it was significant – profoundly so, giving Scots a whole new perspective on a nationalism debate that had, for so many years, been haunted by the let-down of 1979. However justified the complaint may be, the complainer's role is never really dignified: recrimination always feels like a loser's game. Gradually, over the years, though, small-n nationalists had been clawing back the ground they'd lost – the very concession of this new referendum showed how much progress had been made. Support for devolution did not of course necessarily mean support for independence and the capital-N Nationalism of the SNP, but the party's leader, Alex Salmond (1954–), could justifiably feel that things were starting to turn his way.

Those for whom the idea of a Scottish Parliament still seemed an outrageous folly could point to the post-modern premises built across from Holyrood under the direction of Enric Miralles. The Catalan architect died in 2000, during the construction of a building whose cost-overruns (at £414 million, 10 times or more the initial estimate) threatened to upstage the devolution debate itself – at least till they were matched (and maybe surpassed) by those of the new Edinburgh trams.

ELEVEN

THE NEW
MILLENNIUM

YESTERDAY'S NEWS MAY INDEED BE 'tomorrow's fish-and-chip papers'. The day after that, though, it's liable to be uncrumpled, smoothed out flat and returned to afresh as the 'first draft of history'. Here we go then: the events of the first few years of the millennium, undoubtedly, were the 9/11 attacks on America and the subsequent 'War on Terror'. Scotland wasn't to escape entirely, the main passenger entrance to Glasgow Airport becoming a target in a 2007 attack. Baghandler John Smeaton (1976–) made headlines as a have-a-go-hero for tackling the terrorists, who'd driven a Jeep Cherokee, laden with explosives, at the terminal entrance. Both of the would-be bombers, badly burned, were arrested at the scene, and two further suspects subsequently stopped on the M6 motorway in Cheshire, England. Islamic radicalism was in the news – and Scottish Muslims under scrutiny.

All sorts of other things happened, though. It was in 2002 that Conservative leader Iain 'Quiet Man' Duncan Smith had his Easterhouse Epiphany and saw that the poor would be helped by having their benefits slashed. That same year, fire tore through Edinburgh's Cowgate and environs, tearing a ragged hole in the capital's medieval heart. In 2004, an explosion at Stockline Plastics, in Grovepark Mills, Maryhill, Glasgow, killed nine people and left more than 30 injured. Ten people died in 2013 when a helicopter came down on top of the Clutha Vaults bar in the city centre.

In the meantime, evidence was mounting that, whether or not they aspired to independence, ordinary Scots were increasingly comfortable with (or, at least, decreasingly spooked by) the SNP. By 2007, indeed, Alex Salmond was First Minister of his country, at the head of an apparently popular SNP administration. True, they were reliant on Green support, and sceptics still warned that, disillusioned with New Labour, Scots had voted for Salmond & Co's social policies rather than their Nationalism, but, even so, the SNP was in power.

The Nationalists could now look forward to the Independence Referendum of 18 September 2014 as (in Alex Salmond's words) the 'opportunity of a lifetime'. That British Prime Minister David Cameron had felt compelled to hold the vote at all was a mark of how the times and the mood had changed, a mark of the political traction the Nationalists had gained. The result of the referendum, Cameron claimed, would 'settle' the independence question 'for a generation' – but if a week is a long time in politics, a generation seems no time at all.

The long run-in to the referendum generated a great deal of political passion. In 2012 alone, there were no fewer than 13 mass demonstrations (pro-'Yes') on Calton Hill and in Princes Street Gardens, Edinburgh, with other large gatherings in Glasgow's George Square and up and down the country. Big-gun celebrities were deployed to exchange rhetorical volleys: Sean Connery vs Ewan McGregor, Alex Ferguson vs Frankie Boyle. Charges of misconduct were traded too, with claims of sinister strategic leakings from Whitehall to the London press on the one hand and the organised online baiting of prominent No-supporters by so-called 'cybernats' on the other.

Colourful, exciting stuff – but the aftermath was anticlimactic. Both sides were left with a sense of unfinished business. The 'No' side might have won, but it couldn't help being conscious that its campaign had been cackhanded; the sense that younger voters hadn't really been reached at all didn't augur well. The 'Yes' campaigners, on the other hand, had to deal with defeat after apparently dominating the debate before polling day – and with an almost instantaneous slump in price of the oil on which the Independence impulse had so depended.

GAY SCOTLAND

The idea of homosexuality as a distinct identity is a surprisingly recent one, though some men were certainly branded as effeminate in the pre-modern past. There had, notoriously, been whisperings about James VI/I, who indeed in one letter addressed his 'favourite' George Villiers, Duke of Buckingham, as his 'sweet child and wife' – which seems hard to interpret platonically. It's a great deal harder to say where 18th-century Libertinism fits in. In 1732, the 'Beggar's Benison' – Anstruther's answer to Sir Francis Dashwood's English 'Hellfire Club' – brought together young Scottish aristos in some seriously homosocial bonding. So successful was the Beggar's Benison (an archaic word for 'blessing') that a chapter was opened in Edinburgh in 1766.

In 1809, Edinburgh's New Town was scandalised by the story that Miss Marianne Woods and Miss Jane Pirie – who ran a prestigious little private school at the top of Drumsheugh Gardens – showed 'inordinate affection' towards each other. Hearing the ladies' suit against their accuser, Judge Lord Meadowbank was far too sophisticated to be taken in by the suggestion that there could be anything so improbable as sexual relations between women – 'equally imaginary', he considered, 'with witchcraft, sorcery or carnal copulation with the devil'. Both women were ruined, despite their eventual victory after a decade's legal wrangling. Lilian Hellman's play about the affair, The Children's Hour, *was banned in Britain when it came out in 1943.*

In 1903, after a distinguished military career, General Hector MacDonald ('Fighting Mac'), a crofter's son from Rootfield, Dingwall, committed suicide after being accused of having sexual relations with Ceylonese boys. Whether the groundswell of public sympathy for his case was prompted by broad-mindedness or deep denial, huge crowds turned out for his supposedly 'secret' funeral in Edinburgh.

Homophobia remained entrenched in Scottish law long after homosexuality had been legalised in England (1967): it

*wasn't decriminalised in Scotland until 1980. Flash forward
20 years, however, and Scotland was rather quicker to repeal
Mrs Thatcher's Section 28 (of the Local Government Act,
1988; outlawing what it called the 'promotion of homosexuality'
by local authorities in everything from schoolbooks to plays
put on in council-owned theatres). England and Wales didn't
manage this until 2003. In 2004, the Gender Recognition Act
acknowledged transsexual people's gender realignments.*

*Gay civil partnerships were allowable across the United
Kingdom from 2004; Scotland's first gay weddings were held the
minute after Hogmanay at the very start of 2015. Joe Schofield
and Malcolm Brown tied the knot at Glasgow's Trades Hall;
Susan and Gerrie Douglas-Scott were wed privately (but with
the SNP's Nicola Sturgeon and Green Co-Convener and MSP
Patrick Harvie acting as witnesses). By 2016 a majority of the
leaders of Scotland's major political parties leaders identified
as gay or in same-sex relationships: Patrick Harvie; Ruth
Davidson, who had become Conservative leader in 2011, and
Labour's Kezia Dugdale, who was elected leader in 2015.*

Making History

It's impossible to say, this close to events, which aspects of
what's most recently been happening could be described as
'historical'. Who's to say that there won't one day be a monument to mark the spot in Edinburgh's St James Centre shopping mall where Labour leader Ed Miliband was forced to
abandon a public walkabout by 'Yes' campaigners accusing
him not just of lying but of being a 'serial murderer'? Or, for
that matter, the stretch of pavement on Aberdeen's Union
Terrace, overlooking the gardens, on which Sky TV's Kay
Burley made something like Scottish history by describing a
'Yes' campaigner as looking 'a bit of a knob'?

Perspective is important even at the same point in
time. Many of the events we now look back on as being

self-evidently important completely passed most people by when they took place. Take the 'historic' visit of Pope Benedict XVI to Scotland in 2010. While cheering crowds came out to welcome His Holiness on 16 September, and several hundred Protestant demonstrators turned out to register their disgust, much of Edinburgh continued all but oblivious on what, for them, was just another day. Workplaces and schools simply carried on with what they were doing, the momentous occasion marked for most by only a more-than-usually difficult rush-hour, or a brief slot on the early-evening news. (They may have taken more notice when, in 2013, Cardinal Keith Patrick O'Brien, leader of the Roman Catholic Church in Scotland, was forced to resign in disgrace after revelations of his inappropriate sexual conduct with young priests.)

Benedict was subsequently to become the first Pope to step down of his own accord in 700 years, which arguably makes his papacy particularly 'historic' in itself. Looked at another way, it was the only rational outcome in the modern age for a man who felt he could no longer do his job because he was sick – pretty much a non-event, in other words. Times change, and as they do they change us – and as we're changed, we change history.

The Cardinal's residence, where Benedict had his lunch that day, is in Greenhill Gardens, in one of the leafiest neighbourhoods of what's arguably the country's most salubrious city. Who'd have thought – even at the time of his visit – that after the General Election of 2015, that district, Edinburgh South, would boast Scotland's sole surviving Labour MP? Scots might have said 'No' to independence the year before, but they'd certainly said 'Yes' to the SNP, awarding them a landslide 56 out of 59 Scottish seats. For Labour there was the ignominy of tying with the Tories and the Liberal Democrats – just one seat each in Scotland for all the 'main' British parties.

Even now, though, it's hard to see independence as an inevitability. Who can possibly tell what the coming decades will bring? The economic ups and downs apart, what other factors will help shape our future? What wars? What environmental events? What technological developments?

It's not just that we change our attitudes – become Protestant after the Reformation; radical after the French Revolution; prudish in Victorian times; suspicious of Germany during World War I or II ... We change in what might seem our most intimate, essential sense of self. For centuries, women's subjection seemed no more than common sense, just as homosexuality, as an 'identity', did not exist. 'The world is so full of a number of things,' observed the great Scottish poet Robert Louis Stevenson. Factor in the chronological dimension, and it's full of a great many more. This book can't possibly hope to pin the whole thing down: it can at least remind us how complex, eventful and exciting Scottish history has been.

SELECT BIBLIOGRAPHY

Bambery, Chris, *A People's History of Scotland* (London: Verso, 2014)

Barrow, G.W.S., *Kingship and Unity: Scotland 1000–1306* (Edinburgh: Edinburgh University Press, 1989)

Bower, Walter, *Selections from Scotichronicon*, ed D.E.R. Watt (Edinburgh: Mercat Press, 1998)

Brown, Chris, *Scottish Battlefields: 300 Battlefields that Shaped Scottish History* (Stroud: Tempus, 2008)

Cameron, Ewan A., *Impaled Upon a Thistle: Scotland Since 1880, New Edinburgh History of Scotland* (Edinburgh: Edinburgh University Press, 2010)

Cowan, Edward J. (ed.), *Why Scottish History Still Matters* (Edinburgh: Saltire Society, 2012)

Crawford, Robert, *Scotland's Books: The Penguin History of Scottish Literature* (London: Penguin, 2007)

Cunliffe, Barry, *Britain Begins* (Oxford: OUP, 2012)

Dawson, Jane E.A., *Scotland Re-formed, New Edinburgh History of Scotland* (Edinburgh: Edinburgh University Press, 2007)

Devine, T.M., *Scotland's Empire: 1600–1815* (London: Penguin, 2004)

Devine, T.M., *The Scottish Nation: A Modern History* (London: Penguin, 2012)

Fleet, Christopher, Wilkes, Margaret, and Withers, Charles W.J., *Scotland: Mapping the Nation* (Edinburgh: Birlinn, 2011)

Gibson, Rosemary, *The Scottish Countryside: Its Changing Face, 1700-2000* (Edinburgh: John Donald, 2007)

Harvie, Christopher, *No Gods and Precious Few Heroes: Scotland 1900-2015* (Edinburgh: Edinburgh University Press, 2016)

Select Bibliography

Henderson, Lizanne and Cowan, Edward J., *Scottish Fairy Belief: A History* (East Linton: Tuckwell Press, 2001)

Herman, Arthur, *The Scottish Enlightenment: The Scots' Invention of the Modern World* (London: Fourth Estate, 2003)

Keay, John and Keay, Julia, *Collins Encyclopaedia of Scotland* (London: HarperCollins, 1994)

Lynch, Michael, *Oxford Companion to Scottish History* (Oxford: Oxford University Press, 2001)

Macmillan, Duncan, *Scottish Art, 1460-2000* (Edinburgh: Mainstream, 2000)

Meighan, Michael, *Scotland's Lost Industries* (Stroud: Amberley, 2012)

Noble, Robin, *Castles in the Mist: The Victorian Transformation of the Highlands* (Glasgow: Saraband, 2016)

Purvis, June, *Women's History: Britain, 1850-1945: An Introduction* (London: Routledge, 1997)

Richards, Eric, *The Highland Clearances* (Edinburgh: Birlinn, 2013)

Ritchie, Anna, *Scotland: An Oxford Archaeological Guide* (Oxford: Oxford University Press, 1998)

Smith, Robin, *The Making of Scotland: A Comprehensive Guide to the Growth of its Cities, Towns and Villages* (Edinburgh: Canongate, 2003)

Smout, T.C., *A History of the Scottish People, 1560–1830* (London: Fontana Press, 1998)

Wightman, Andy, *The Poor Had No Lawyers: Who Owns Scotland and How they Got It* (Edinburgh: Birlinn, 2010)

Woolf, Alex, *From Pictland to Alba 789–1070, New Edinburgh History of Scotland* (Edinburgh: Edinburgh University Press, 2007)

ACKNOWLEDGEMENTS

This book is the product of a great deal of reading. For 20 years, between 1993 and 2013, I contributed a review column, 'Books in Brief', to *The Scotsman* newspaper. Among what often seemed more arrestingly compelling titles on international politics, current affairs, cultural studies and you-name-it, came regular round-ups of the latest Scottish books. For better and for worse, all Scottish publishing life was there: from breezy little guides to whisky and haggis, to dusty monographs on landholding and kingship; from earnest histories of Scottish regiments, through meticulous records of forgotten railway lines and folk remedies, to recipe books; from musings on national identity to memoirs of island life. Whilst much of this reading was (between ourselves) done a bit grudgingly, in the spirit of eating my greens, in hindsight it looks like invaluable, if inadvertent, research. For keeping me conscientious – and for a great many other kindnesses along the way – I have to thank successive Books Editors, Catherine Lockerbie and David Robinson.

I can't, however, except in the indeterminate mass, thank the hundreds of authors who, had I but realised it, were contributing to my knowledge and appreciation of Scotland's life and times. At a few points, where I've made specific references, or where some particular book seems especially useful for further reading, I've given brief details in my text. Otherwise, I'm afraid, a vast sea of sources and influences go unacknowledged. I am grateful to Carcanet Press for their permission to include passages from the poems of Hugh MacDiarmid and Sorley MacLean. A number of individuals and institutions responded when I ran into trouble on particular points, including Christine Kelly of the University of Glasgow and the staff of the Montrose Museum & Art Gallery. Charlie Holmes, Archie Vickers, Peter, Francis and Antonia Kerrigan all helped to clarify particular questions or

Acknowledgements

to run down specific sites, and I owe them my thanks. As, of course, I do all my family for their support at home.

I wouldn't have thought of writing this book at all had it not been for Sara Hunt of Saraband. Not for the first time, she's turned out to know me better than I do myself. I wouldn't be a historian of any sort if it hadn't been for the help and encouragement of Tony Allan, long ago my editor at Time-Life Books, but a supportive friend ever since. I wouldn't have taken the broad and almost all-encompassing view of history I do if it hadn't been for the influence of Alison Hennegan over many years. Copyeditor Craig Hillsley made this book much better than it might otherwise have been. A deeply reassuring presence, Graham Whyte has had my back throughout the writing of this book. He's read the script at every stage, saving me from historical howlers, spotting typos, identifying omissions and pointing out new possibilities. His instincts, in my view, are invariably spot-on. It goes without saying that any errors or infelicities that remain are my own responsibility.

INDEX

Index

Index

Index

Index

Ethic 196, 223; *see also* Calvinism;
Episcopalianism; Lutheranism;
Orange Order; Presbyterianism;
sectarianism
Rae, John 206–7
railways 215–19, 247, 267, 291:
nationalisation of 314; steam 218
Ramsay, Allan 143, 231
Ramsay Garden, 248–50
Ratho Murder, the 127
recession 182–83, 281, 291–92,
294–95, 304, 330, 341, 343
'Red Clydeside' 274–76, 277
Reformation, the 55, 57, 58,
79–80, 85–89, 90–91, 125, 189;
see also Calvinism; Knox, John;
Lutheranism; Protestantism
refugees 301, 302, 332
Reid, Jimmy 341
rent strikes 242, 273–75, 276, 277
Ring of Brodgar 20
Robertson, William 147–48, 151
Rob Roy *see* MacGregor; Scott
Romans 24–29, 31, 61
Rosslyn Chapel, Midlothian 57–58
'Rough Wooing', the 78–79
Rùm 311
runes 34–35
run rig tenure 50, 155, 156
Ruthwell Cross 33
saints: St Andrew 54; St Columba
32–33, 149; St Margaret 40, 59,
60; St Mungo 55
Salmond, Alex 354, 356–57
Scone, Stone of 61, 326
'Scots Confession', the 81, 84
Scott, Sir Walter 92, 127, 132, 164,
170, 186–89, 191, 197, 198, 201,
220, 269: Abbotsford House 188;
Rob Roy 132, 187; *The Bride of
Lammermoor* 187; *The Heart of
Midlothian* 127, 187; *Waverley* 186
Scottish Colourists 282–83
Scottish Crannog Centre 24

Scottish Nationalist Party 2, 296,
326, 332, 339–30, 354, 356,
359–60
Scottish Renaissance 282–87
sectarianism 234–39, 237–39
Selkirk, Alexander 123
sheep 19, 27, 52, 141, 144, 156,
165, 180–81, 229, 242, 293: haggis
165 *see also* Clearances; tweed; wool
Sheridan, Tommy 348
Sheriffmuir, Battle of 130
Shetland 22, 38, 40, 75, 105, 167,
183, 310, 337: Gurness 22; Jarlshof
38; Mousa 23; Muckle Flugga 183;
Sullom Voe 337; Sumburgh 337;
Symbister 75
shipbuilding 204, 263, 291, 340–41
shortbread 8
Singh, Duleep 332–33
Skara Brae 5, 19, 21
slave trade 177–80
slavery 179–80, 207, 257
Smith, Adam 151–54, 158, 172, 177
Smollett, Tobias 141, 143, 149
Soutar, William 284, 285
Spanish Civil War 302–3, 304
Spark, Muriel 304: *The Prime of Miss
Jean Brodie* 304
standing stones: Callanish 19–20;
Ring of Brodgar 20
Stark, Johnnie 294–95
steam engine, invention of 158, 184
steam-powered ships 205, 219–20,
240
steam trains 218 *see also* railways
steel 204, 214, 245–46, 291, 314,
342, 343
St Kilda 293
Stevenson, Robert (lighthouse
designer) 183
Stevenson, Robert Louis 160, 178,
218, 361: *Jekyll and Hyde* 160;
Kidnapped 178
Stirling 26, 47, 49, 54, 61, 62, 64,

Index

ABOUT THE AUTHOR

Michael Kerrigan's many books include *The Ancients in their Own Words* (2009), *The Catholic Church: A Dark History* (2014), *Illuminated Manuscripts* (2014) and *Celtic Legends* (2016). He adapted John Galt's *The Ayrshire Legatees* for BBC Radio Scotland (2000) and has contributed to *Ancient Civilisations* (Duncan Baird Publishing, 2005), the *Times Encyclopedia of World Religion*, the *Reader's Digest Illustrated History of the World* (2005–8), the Time-Life *History of the World* and *Lost Civilisations* series, Grolier's *The World and Its Peoples* series, the Flame Tree *Reference Guide to Irish History* (2nd edition, 2015) and the Dorling Kindersley *History of Britain and Ireland* (2011). He is a regular reviewer for the *Times Literary Supplement* and has also written for a range of other journals, including the *Scotsman*, *Scotland on Sunday*, *Independent* and *Guardian*. He was born in Liverpool and has spent his adult life in Edinburgh, where he lives with his family.

ALSO IN THIS SERIES

A Handbook of Scotland's Coasts

The ultimate guidebook for those who want to discover more about the thousands of miles of Scotland's spectacular coastlines – from its stunning geology and diverse plant, marine and bird life to its islands, coastal history, culture and natural and built landmarks. It includes sections on coastal foraging and great days out, as well as a chapter written by Michael Kerrigan, author of this volume.

A Handbook of Scotland's Wild Harvests

This inspirational guide is packed with know-how on what, where, when and how you can find, harvest and use your bounty in sustainable ways – from the most useful and widespread of species to the less well-known, and from leaves and berries to saps, seeds, seaweeds, mosses and wood. Learn how to begin or extend a repertoire of wild foods as well as materials that can be used as dyes, remedies, and around the home. Edited by Fi Martynoga.

A Handbook of Scotland's Trees

A concise, comprehensive handbook from Reforesting Scotland experts, edited by Fi Martynoga, covering species commonly found in Scotland. From provenance, diseases and propagation to history and lore, this single source contains all the information you need to select the right trees for your site and grow them successfully. An invaluable reference for anyone with an interest in our trees and woodlands.